Faunt Le Roy Senour

Major General William T. Sherman and his campaign

Faunt Le Roy Senour

Major General William T. Sherman and his campaign

ISBN/EAN: 9783337810566

Printed in Europe, USA, Canada, Australia, Japan

Cover: Foto ©ninafisch / pixelio.de

More available books at **www.hansebooks.com**

MAJOR GENERAL

WILLIAM T. SHERMAN,

AND HIS

CAMPAIGNS.

By Rev. F. SENOUR,

AUTHOR OF "MORGAN AND HIS CAPTORS," "THE CHRISTIAN SOLDIER," ETC.

"I cannot say a word too highly in praise of General Sherman's services, from the beginning of the rebellion to the present day. Suffice it to say, the world's history gives no record of his superiors, and but few equals.

"U. S. GRANT, *Lieut. Gen'l.*"

CHICAGO:
HENRY M. SHERWOOD, PUBLISHER.
1865.

Entered according to Act of Congress, in the year 1865,

By Rev. F. SENOUR,

In the Clerk's Office of the District Court of the United States, for the Northern District of Illinois.

DEDICATION.

TO THE

BRAVE OFFICERS AND SOLDIERS

WHO FOLLOWED

THEIR NOBLE LEADER,

Major General William T. Sherman,

THROUGH

LONG MARCHES AND HARD-FOUGHT BATTLES,

AND WHO HAVE

CROWNED THEMSELVES WITH GLORY,

THIS WORK IS

MOST RESPECTFULLY DEDICATED,

BY

THE AUTHOR.

PREFACE.

'Never name your child after a living man," said a very wise man to the author of this volume. As we do not know what the future of any man will be, it may be unwise to honor him by giving his name to your child. For a similar reason, it may be injudicious to write the history of a living man.

Whatever the future history of General W. T. Sherman may be, the world witnesseth that he has carved out for himself a name and a place in history, and won a home in the hearts of his countrymen, that can never be blotted out. It is our hope and prayer to God, that no act of his in the future may tarnish his great name and heroic deeds.

It is because General Sherman has occupied so prominent a place in many of the most important and stirring scenes of the great war against the rebellion, that we have endeavored to cull the most important facts and incidents, and make as full and fair a record of them as can now be done, in order that as little as possible of valuable history may be lost to posterity.

It may be said that the time has not yet come to write a history of our generals and the war. We reply, that we desire only to put on record events still fresh in our memory, leaving to the Bancroft of the future the task of writing a true and philosophical history of the war. If we aid the future historian, we shall not feel that we have labored in vain.

We have endeavored to tell our story in plain Saxon, and with such perspicuity as will enable the simplest mind to read and understand. That we have exhausted the subjects introduced in this volume, is not pretended. We have omitted much that we would have been glad to have put on record. It would take a volume larger than this to record every event of any one of Sherman's great campaigns. The most that we could do was to unite the great outlines of his history.

In preparing this work, we have made free use of whatever material has fallen into our hands, separating, as best we could, the wheat from the chaff. That we have succeeded in making wise discriminations, must be left to the judgment and the leniency of the reader.

We had access to official reports and documents, which have greatly aided us. And here we wish to acknowledge our indebtedness to various letter writers, correspondents of public journals, and to all who have imparted oral information to us. Without this aid, we could not have written this book.

And now we place this work in the hands of our generous fellow-countrymen, trusting that it may be a source of pleasure and profit to those who read it, and serve a purpose in preserving great events, and honoring the brave soldiers and their great leader, whose deeds of glory are herein recorded—that it may keep alive the fires of patriotism in the hearts of our countrymen, and illustrate the wonderful providence of God in preserving our national life

CONTENTS.

CHAPTER I.
GENERAL SHERMAN'S EARLY HISTORY.
PAGE

Introductory Remarks—Parentage and Birth of Sherman—Death of his Father—Hon. Thomas Ewing and his Friendship—Appointed a Cadet at West Point—Graduated—His Rank—Enters the Service of the United States—In the Florida War—At Fort Moultrie—In California—Promotion—In the Commissary Department—Military Post of New Orleans—Resignation and Return to California—President of a Military Academy in Louisiana—Opposes Secession—Resignation as President—Incidents—A Remarkable Law Firm.. 15

CHAPTER II.
GENERAL SHERMAN AND THE BATTLE OF BULL RUN.

The Politicians' Battle—General Scott—Strength of the Army—The Divisions—An Imposing Scene—Confidence of the People—Generals McDowell and Tyler—Centreville and Manassas—Position of the Divisions of the Army—The Moonlight March to Battle—Plan of the Battle—The Irish Regiment—Part taken by Sherman's Brigade—The Retreat and Panic—Sherman at Fort Corcoran—Appointed a Brigadier — In Command of the Department of the Cumberland — Relieved — At Sedalia and Benton Barracks — At Paducah — Incidents.. 31

CHAPTER III.

GENERAL SHERMAN AND THE BATTLE OF PITTSBURG LANDING.

The Battle of Pittsburg Landing the Most Desperate and Decisive of the War — The Troops Engaged — Skirmishing — Battle Opens — Surprise of Union Troops — Sunday's Fight — The Union Troops Driven from their Camps — The Lexington and Tyler — The Part taken by them — Lew. Wallace's and Buell's Forces Arrive — Monday's Operations — Cavalry Charge by Grant — Pursuit by Sherman — Grant's Opinion of Sherman — The Part taken by Sherman and his Division — Extract from Halleck's Report — Sherman a Major General — The Opinions of Distinguished Generals — Incidents — Sherman's Letter to Professor Coppee.................. 52

CHAPTER IV.

SHERMAN AND THE SIEGE OF CORINTH.

March Towards Corinth — Skirmishing at Monterey and Purdy — Siege of Corinth Commences — Battle of Russell's House — Evacuation of Corinth — Occupation of the City by the Union Troops — Pursuit by General M. L. Smith to Tuscumbia Creek — Sherman's Congratulatory Order — Incidents — Takes Possession of Holly Springs — Appointed Military Commander of Memphis, Tennessee.................... 84

CHAPTER V.

SHERMAN AND THE CAMPAIGNS AGAINST VICKSBURG.

Preparations for the Vicksburg Campaign — Sherman's Command Sails for Vicksburg — Arrival at Johnston's Landing — First Assault upon Vicksburg — McClernand takes

Command—Sherman's Congratulatory Order to his Troops
—Capture of Arkansas Post—Steele's Bayou Expedition—
Feint on the North of Vicksburg—Fight at Fourteen Mile
Creek—Advance upon Jackson—Occupation of the City—
Battle of Big Black River—Takes Possession of Walnut
Hills—Second Assault upon Vicksburg—Surrender—Oc-
cupation—Pursuit after Johnston—Second Occupation of
Jackson—Recommended by General Grant for Promotion
as Brigadier General of Regular Army..........................107

CHAPTER VI.

SHERMAN'S GREAT MARCH TO CHATTANOOGA, AND THE BATTLES OF
MISSIONARY RIDGE AND LOOKOUT MOUNTAIN.

Brief Rest of Sherman's Command—Starts for Chattanooga—
Narrow Escape of Sherman—The Fight at Cane Creek—
Takes Command of the Army of the Tennessee—Arrives at
Chattanooga—Battle Before Chattanooga—First Day's Bat-
tle—Second Day—Battle of Lookout Mountain, Third
Day—Account of an Eye Witness of the Battle of Tunnel
Hill—Battle of Missionary Ridge—Incidents................135

CHAPTER VII.

SHERMAN AND THE SIEGE OF KNOXVILLE, AND THE EXPEDITION
THROUGH MISSISSIPPI.

Pursuit of the Enemy after the Battle of Missionary Ridge—
March to Knoxville to Relieve Burnside—Returns to Chattanooga—At Memphis—Letter of Sherman—Expedition
through Mississippi—Incident.................................153

CHAPTER VIII.

SHERMAN'S GREAT CAMPAIGN FROM CHATTANOOGA TO ATLANTA.

Sherman Appointed the Successor of Grant—Tour of Inspection and Plan of the Campaign—Commencement of the

Campaign—Strength of the Army—The Strength of the Enemy—Position of our Forces on the 6th of May—The Enemy Flanked out of their Position at Dalton—The Battle of Resaca—The Result—Incidents..................................167

CHAPTER IX.

SHERMAN'S GREAT CAMPAIGN FROM CHATTANOOGA TO ATLANTA.

The Pursuit of the Enemy—Their Wounded—Order of the Pursuit—An Ambuscade—Fighting and Skirmishing—An Account by an Eye-Witness—Capture of Rome, Kingston and Cassville—Guerrilla Operations—Movement across the Etowah—Skirmishing—Loss of Wagons—The Gallant Action of the 25th—Another Ambuscade—Sherman's Object—A Furious Assault—Occupation of Dallas—The Situation on June 1st—Sherman's Strategy—The Enemy Abandoned their Works—Sherman's Dispatch—What the Army had Accomplished—Character of Sherman—Incidents...194

CHAPTER X.

SHERMAN'S GREAT CAMPAIGN FROM CHATTANOOGA TO ATLANTA.

Operations of the Army from June 7th to the Capture of Atlanta—Sherman's Report—Efforts to Break the Enemy's Lines Between Kenesaw and Pine Mountains—Death of General Polk—McPherson's Operations—Two Direct Assaults—Kenesaw Abandoned—The Pursuit—Passage of the Chattahoochee—The Battle of the 20th—Johnston Relieved—Attack on our Right—Positions of our Forces—Sudden Attack—Death of McPherson—Grand Movement of the Right Flank—Kilpatrick's Operations—Sherman's Flank Movement and the Capture of Atlanta—Bombardment of Atlanta—Sherman's Congratulatory Order..218

CHAPTER XI.

SHERMAN'S GREAT CAMPAIGN FROM CHATTANOOGA TO ATLANTA.

Additional Accounts of the Campaign—The Value of this Chapter—Campaign Reviewed by a Distinguished General..237

CHAPTER XII.

SHERMAN AND THE OCCUPATION OF ATLANTA.

Sherman a Military Genius—Opinions of his Campaign—The London Times and London Star—Measures for Holding Atlanta—Citizens Ordered from Atlanta—Sherman and Hood—Their Correspondence—An Atlanta Exile—Permanent Occupation Intended—Operations of Forrest and Others—Hood's Northern Movement—Attack and Repulse at Altoona—The Pursuit—Hood Crosses the Tennessee—Sherman's Plans—Battles of Franklin and Nashville—Sherman Returns to Atlanta—A Facetious Letter..............262

CHAPTER XIII.

SHERMAN'S GRAND MARCH FROM ATLANTA TO SAVANNAH.

Movement Towards Atlanta—Preparations for the March—The Army—Orders of Sherman and Slocum—Concentration of Forces—The "Gate City" Burned—Communications Cut Off—Under a Cloud—The Enemy Deceived—The Rebel Press—The General Lines of the March—Progress of the Army—Fight at Griswoldville—Encamped on Howell Cobb's Farm—Milledgeville Occupied—Incident—March to Millen and Savannah—Scouts Sent Out—Howard's Dispatch to the Navy—Fort McAllister Captured—Journal of the March—Investment and Capture of Savannah—Poetry—Sherman's Orders—Correspondence—British Consul at Savannah..296

B

CHAPTER XIV.

SHERMAN'S CAMPAIGN IN THE CAROLINAS.

The Consummation of the Great Plan—Movements of the Two Wings of the Army, Under Howard and Slocum—Transfer of the Forts and City to General Foster—Capture of Fort Fisher by Porter and Terry—Determination of Sherman—Strategy at the Salkehatchie—Wading Through Deep Water—Pursuit of the Enemy to Branchville—Destruction of the Railroad—Official Report of Sherman—Fall of Charleston—Horrors of the Evacuation—Incidents..........361

CHAPTER XV.

SHERMAN'S CAMPAIGN IN THE CAROLINAS.

In the Heart of North Carolina—Results of the Campaign—The Sentinels—Davis and an English Paper—Advance of Sherman and Retreat of the Enemy—Effect of the Capture of Richmond—Fall of Richmond, and Surrender of Lee's Army—Coöperation of Sherman—Memorandum or Agreement Between Sherman and Johnston—Special Order of Sherman—Disapproval of the Agreement by the Cabinet—Grant Sent to North Carolina—Result of his Mission—Explanation of Sherman's Course—Remarks...................406

CHAPTER XVI.

SHERMAN'S OFFICIAL REPORT AND FAREWELL ADDRESS.

The March by Way of Richmond to Washington—The Grand Military Review—Official Report and Farewell Address.....431

GEN. W. T. SHERMAN,

HIS LIFE AND CAMPAIGNS.

CHAPTER I.

GEN. SHERMAN'S EARLY HISTORY.

INTRODUCTORY REMARKS — PARENTAGE AND BIRTH OF SHERMAN — DEATH OF HIS FATHER — HON. THOMAS EWING AND HIS FRIENDSHIP — APPOINTED A CADET AT WEST POINT — GRADUATED — HIS RANK — ENTERS THE SERVICE OF THE UNITED STATES — IN THE FLORIDA WAR — AT FORT MOULTRIE — IN CALIFORNIA — PROMOTION — IN THE COMMISSARY DEPARTMENT — MILITARY POST OF NEW ORLEANS — RESIGNATION AND RETURN TO CALIFORNIA — PRESIDENT OF A MILITARY ACADEMY IN LOUISIANA — OPPOSES SECESSION — RESIGNATION AS PRESIDENT — INCIDENTS — A REMARKABLE LAW FIRM.

At the commencement of the civil war in our country, the want of well known and able military leaders, placed our Government in a most embarrassing situation. It was well known that the noble old military hero, General Winfield Scott, was too infirm to command our armies, and lead them on to victory after victory, until the flag of

Washington, which had been struck down by traitors, should again wave over every inch of the territory that rightly belonged to the Government.

One leader after another was selected, and each, in his turn, was hailed as a hero by the people, until bitter experience taught them to call no man a hero before he had proved himself worthy of that title, by heroic achievements on the field of conflict. As one general after another failed, the people became anxious, and prayed that God would raise up men who would lead our brave armies on to victory and glory. These prayers were answered. In Generals Grant, Sherman, Thomas, and Sheridan, the people recognize the men for whom they looked and prayed. While all these men have acted well and nobly their part, and have covered themselves with imperishable glory, none of them have done more to make a name in history, and to be remembered by a free and grateful posterity, than Major General WILLIAM TECUMSEH SHERMAN.

General Sherman is the son of Hon. Charles R. Sherman, once a Judge of the Supreme Court of the State of Ohio; and a brother of the Hon. John Sherman, United States Senator from the same State. He was born in Lancaster, Ohio, on the eighth day of February, A. D. 1820.

Judge Sherman died when William, his present distinguished son was only eight years of age. During the lifetime of the Judge, he was a warm friend of the Hon. Thomas Ewing, of Ohio. That honorable gentleman heartily reciprocated and appreciated his friendship. After his death, he took his son William to his home, and treated him as one of his family, and secured to him important educational advantages. Through his influence, young Sherman was undoubtedly, admitted into the Military Academy at West Point, as a cadet appointed from the State of Ohio. This important event took place in the year 1836, when he was about sixteen years of age. He pursued the curriculum of studies, prescribed and required by that institution, with credit and honor to himself, until the 30th of June, 1840, when he was graduated, ranking sixth, in a class of forty-two members.

The day after Sherman was graduated, at West Point, he entered the regular service of the United States, and was appointed to the office of Second Lieutenant of artillery, and was connected with the Third Regiment. His services, in this office, were of such a character as to secure for him, within a few months, promotion to the rank of First Lieutenant.

Lieutenant Sherman and his company were engaged in the Florida war with the Indians. He soon became well known as a strategist, and distinguished for prompt movements and rapid marching.

In the year 1841, Sherman was ordered to Fort Moultrie, in Charleston harbor, which fort has since become quite famous in the early history of the rebellion.

In the year 1846, Lieutenant Sherman was sent to California, where he was appointed to the position of an acting assistant adjutant general. He administered the affairs of his office with so much ability, that Congress, in March, 1851, appointed him a brevet captain in the regular army, to date from May 30th, 1848, "for meritorious service in California during the war with Mexico."

In the year 1850, Sherman was appointed a Commissary of Subsistence, with the rank of captain, and was connected with the department of the West, his headquarters being at St. Louis. Subsequently, he was ordered to the military post at New Orleans, where he had the opportunity of becoming acquainted with many Southern people, their political views and institutions. This knowledge has since been of great value to him and the Government.

In the year 1853, Sherman resigned his office in the United States army, and removed to California, where he was connected with the well known banking house of Lucas, Turner & Co., of San Francisco, for a period of about four years. While in that position, he acquired a good reputation as a business man. Here he had a connection with the State military organizations, and took an active part in suppressing the lawless mobs that once disgraced that city.

Sherman returned to the States, practiced law in Kansas, and afterwards was appointed President of the Military Academy of the State of Louisiana, where he trained not a few of the men whom he has since fought and conquered.

In the autumn of 1860, when the secession movement commenced in the Southern States, many and strong inducements were offered to him to unite his destiny with the cause of the South, but they were all in vain. On the 26th of January, 1861, the Convention of the State of Louisiana passed the ordinance of secession; whereupon, Sherman tendered to the State of Louisiana his resignation as President of the Military School, and at once proceeded North, to the city of St. Louis, Mo. In fact, Sherman personally had given notice of his intention to resign, in the event that Louisiana seceded.

The following is a true copy of his letter of resignation:

January 18th, 1860.

Gov. THOMAS O. MOORE,

 Baton Rouge, Louisiana.

Sir: As I occupy a quasi-military position under this State, I deem it proper to acquaint you, that I accepted such position, when Louisiana was a State in the Union; and when the motto of the Seminary was inserted in marble, over the main door, "By the liberality of the General Government of the United States." *The Union Esto Perpetua.*

"Recent events foreshadow a great change, and it becomes all men to choose. If Louisiana withdraws from the Federal Union, I prefer to maintain my allegiance to the old Constitution as long as a fragment of it survives; and my longer stay here would be wrong in every sense of the word. In that event, I beg you will send, or appoint some authorized agent to take charge of the arms and munitions of war here, belonging to the State, or direct me what disposition should be made of them.

"And furthermore, as President of Board of Supervisors, I beg you to take immediate steps to relieve me as Superintendent the moment the State determines to secede; for on no earthly account will I do any act, or think any thought, hostile to or in defiance of the old Government of the United States.

   "With Great Respect, &c.,

      "W. T. SHERMAN."

INCIDENTS.

When Sherman was a member of the Hon. Mr. Ewing's family, it is said that, with childlike simplicity, he would sometimes speak of a little daughter of that gentleman as "his sweetheart." "Coming events cast their shadows before." In the year 1850, Captain W. T. Sherman and Miss

Ellen E. Ewing were united in the bonds of matrimony.

In the beginning of the secession excitement, before the election of 1860, and when Sherman was President of the Military Academy, in Louisiana, a party of secessionists approached him, for the purpose of inducing him to unite with the South in the rebellion, when, it is said, the following conversation took place:

"Gentlemen," said Sherman, "while I am in the South, I shall do nothing, and say nothing, in opposition to the Southern interests; but I will never join in any movement that may lead to an armed resistance to the authority of the United States. I have fought under the 'Stars and Stripes' too long to be induced to raise my hand for its downfall."

"Mr. Sherman," replied one of the party, "we have no intention to go to war with the United States. We have so divided the North that if the Abolitionists should even elect the next President, we can so cripple his power that he can do nothing to resist a secession of the Gulf States, and the establishment of a separate Government."

"If you suppose, gentlemen," said Sherman, "that the North will allow any portion of this glorious Union to be severed from the remainder, you will find yourselves mistaken. I tell you it will lead to war, and a cruel war; but the Union must be kept intact."

'But our slaves?"

"When it is a question of preserving the unity of the country, slavery and all other abstract principles will have to succumb. Your very supporters in the North will turn against you, and will fly to arms to preserve the honor of their flag, and the integrity of the Union. Gentlemen, you have my answer."

As the party left the presence of Sherman, the following conversation occurred among themselves:

"I do not like to trust that man. I do not believe he is true to the cause of the South."

"I think you are mistaken," replied another one of the party. "He speaks plainly and fearlessly, which shows that he is not afraid of us. I would rather trust an outspoken man like that, than all the oily, sneaking fellows, whose remarks are fair to our face, yet who, for a few dollars, would betray our very wives to our enemies. When the time comes, and he sees we are likely to separate from the North in reality, he will readily join us. Besides," continued the speaker, "he is too good an officer for us to part with, if we can only retain him with us."

The following extract will be read with interest, as giving a part of the history of this remarkable man:

A REMARKABLE LAW FIRM, AND A QUARTETTE OF GENERALS.

[From the Leavenworth Conservative.]

Citizens of Leavenworth will remember that there stood, on Main street, between Delaware and Shawnee, in 1857–8–9, on the ground now occupied by handsome brick buildings, a shabby looking, tumbling, cottonwood shell. It was occupied, on the ground floor, by Hampton P. Denman, ex-Mayor, as a land agency office. The rooms above were reached by a crazy looking stairway on the outside, up which none ever went without dread of their falling. Dingy signs informed the curious that within was a "law shop," kept by Hugh Ewing, Thomas Ewing, Jr., W. T. Sherman, and Daniel McCook. These constituted the firm known here as Ewing, Sherman & McCook. All were comparatively young men. All were ambitious; the one who has gained the greatest fame, perhaps, the least so of the associated lawyers. The Ewings had the advantage of high culture, considerable natural abilities, cold, impressive temperaments, and a powerful family influence, to aid their aspirations. Hugh Ewing was but little known hereabouts, though acknowledged to be a brilliant and versatile genius by his friends. "Young Tom," as the other scion is familiarly called, has always been a prominent and influential man.

The third member of the firm fills, to-day, one of the proudest pages in the history of our land. His name and fame take rank with the greatest of earth. All conspire to do him honor. Aliens bow to his genius, and enemies show the extent of their fears of its power, by the virulence of their hate and its manifestations.

W. T. Sherman never mingled in our public affairs. He lived among us for several months, having some landed interests here. An outlying part of our city plat is marked on the maps as "Sherman's Addition." Prior to entering upon the practice of the law in this city, he lived for some time in the vicinity of Topeka, upon a farm of 160 acres, which we believe he still owns. His neighbors tell of his abrupt manner; reserved, yet forcible speech and character. Previous to his residing in Kansas, Sherman had lived in California, where, as a miner, banker, and lawyer, he made and lost a large fortune. A graduate of West Point, he had previously held a captain's commission in the Topographical Engineer Corps, and, in pursuance of duty, had made several important surveys and explorations, the reports of which had been duly published by the Government. They relate principally to routes for the Pacific Railroad.

The fourth member of the firm, Daniel McCook, was known and appreciated here by the fraternity as one of the best of "good fellows." He was young, active, ardent, an intense partisan and ambitious wight, who held the tolerable good opinion of his capacity—common to the "pin-feather" state of the *genus homo*. "Dan." practiced law before the lower courts, doing the justice and probate, and always having plenty of work in the United States District Court, which was often the scene of amusing sparring between him and the Judge—the able, but indecent Petit—whose judgments Dan. was in the habit of freely criticising.

All of the firm were "Buckeyes," the Ewings being the sons of the able and venerable Hon. Thomas Ewing, of that State. Sherman is connected with them by marriage. He is a brother of Senator Sherman. McCook belonged to the since famous "fighting" family of that name. His father was the well known Major McCook, who was killed in the Ohio Morgan raid. One brother was killed at the first Bull Run battle. Another was the Brigadier General McCook, murdered by guerrillas in Tennessee. Another brother or uncle, we know not which, is the famous Major General

c

McCook, of the armies of the Cumberland and Tennessee.

In politics, the firm were unequally proportioned—Thomas Ewing, Jr., being a conservative Republican, while his brother Hugh, Sherman, and McCook, were all Democrats, the latter being an active local politician, and, at one time, elected Probate Judge of this county. The city being then largely Democratic, and somewhat pro-slavery, the firm possessed considerable influence.

A good story is told of Sherman's experience as counsel, and of his dissolution of partnership to take the position held by him when the war broke out—that of the Military College of Louisiana.

While in the practice of the law here, Sherman was consulting partner, having an almost insurmountable objection to pleading in court. He is accorded the possession, as a lawyer, of a thorough knowledge of legal principles; a clear, logical perception of the points and equity involved in any case. He could present his views in the most direct manner, stripped of all verbiage, yet perfectly accurate in form. He was perfectly *au fait* in the authorities.

But to return to our story. Shortly after the reception of the offer from the Governor of Louisiana, in relation to the college, Sherman was compelled to appear before the Probate Judge—

Gardner, we believe. The other partners were busy, and Sherman, with his authorities and the case all mapped out, proceeded to court. He returned in a rage two hours after. Something had gone wrong. He had been pettifogged out of the case by a sharp petty attorney opposed to him, in a way which was disgusting to his intellect and his convictions. His *amour propre* was hurt, and he swore that he would have nothing more to do with the law in this State. That afternoon, the business was closed, partnership dissolved, and in a very short time Sherman was on his way to a more congenial clime and occupation. The war found him in Louisiana, and, in despite of his strong pro-slavery opinions, found him an intense and devoted patriot.

We met him here, and, though but slightly acquainted, have remembered ever since the impression he left on our mind. He sphered himself to our perception as the most remarkable intellectual embodiment of force it had been our fortune to encounter. Once since we met him, in our lines before Corinth, where he had command of the right wing of Halleck's magnificent army. The same impression was given then, combined with the idea of nervous vitality, angularity of character, and intense devotion to what he had in hand. Sherman is truly an idealist, even to fanaticism, though, in all probability, if told so, he would retort back an unbelieving sarcasm. He outlines himself to our memory as a man of middle stature, nervous, muscular frame, with a long, keen head, sharply defined from the forehead, and back of the ears. His eyes have an introverted look, but full of smouldering fire. His mouth is sharp and well cut; the lower part of the face powerful, though not heavy. His complexion fair, hair and beard of a sandy red, straight, short, and strong. His temperament is nervous-sanguine, and he is full of crochets and prejudices, which, however, never stand in the way of practical results. The idea, or rather object, which rules him, for the time, overrides everything else. Round the mouth, we remember a gleam of saturnine humor, and in the eyes a look of kindness, which would attract to him the caresses of children.

Such are the impressions left on our mind by the only military educated member of this legal quartette—all of whom have held commissions as generals in the army.

Hugh Ewing went early into the war, as Colonel of an Ohio regiment, to which State he had returned before the rebellion. He was soon promoted to a Brigadiership. He has served honorably through most of the campaigns in the central south. He has been wounded more than once.

Dan McCook's name has passed into history, as one of the most gallant young lives offered as a sacrifice to secure American nationality. He was, we think, the second captain mustered in from this State, in the veteran First Kansas, as early as the beginning of May, 1861. He was all through its famous Missouri campaign, under Lyon. His friends here remember the jubilant expression to which his ambition gave vent, when he first left for the field: "Here's for a colonel's epaulettes, or a soldier's grave." He knew not how prophetic was the utterance. He won the first, and more, and the latter is now his lasting inheritance of fame. After the regiment returned to Kansas, in the Fall of 1861, Captain Dan was placed on staff duty, we believe, with one of the Generals McCook, then in Kentucky. Soon after, he was prostrated with sickness. On recovering, he raised, and commanded the Fifty-Second Ohio. For a long time he was acting Brigadier, participating through all Rosecrans' famous campaigns in Tennessee. He was wounded, and after promotion as Brigadier, returned to Ohio sick, where he died.

"As man may, he fought his fight,
 Proved his truth by his endeavor;
Let him sleep in solemn night,
 Sleep forever, and forever."

The remaining member of the firm, General Thomas Ewing, Jr., is too well known to need particularizing by us. The war found him our Chief Justice. In the summer of 1862, he resigned, raised the Eleventh Regiment, became its colonel, and participated in all the engagements of the Army of the Frontier, during the following Fall and Winter. He was afterward promoted to a Brigadiership, and has since been in command of the Western Missouri and Kansas District. He has, for over a year, been in command of the District of Southeast Missouri, with St. Louis as headquarters, where he is popular. His undoubted administrative ability comes into play there. The defense of, and retreat from, Pilot Knob, during the late campaign, reflect great credit upon his skill and courage as a soldier.

Taking it all in all, the legal military firm, of which we have been giving these random notes, is one of the most remarkable proofs of the versatility and adaptability of the American character, that the war, fruitful as it has been in examples, has yet produced.

CHAPTER II.

GENERAL SHERMAN AND THE BATTLE OF BULL RUN.

THE POLITICIANS' BATTLE — GEN. SCOTT — STRENGTH OF THE ARMY — THE DIVISIONS — AN IMPOSING SCENE — CONFIDENCE OF THE PEOPLE — GENERALS MC DOWELL AND TYLER — CENTREVILLE AND MANASSAS — POSITION OF THE DIVISIONS OF THE ARMY — THE MOONLIGHT MARCH TO BATTLE — PLAN OF THE BATTLE — THE IRISH REGIMENT — PART TAKEN BY SHERMAN'S BRIGADE — THE RETREAT AND PANIC — SHERMAN AT FORT CORCORAN — APPOINTED A BRIGADIER — IN COMMAND OF THE DEPARTMENT OF THE CUMBERLAND — RELIEVED — AT SEDALIA AND BENTON BARRACKS — AT PADUCAH — INCIDENTS.

Before giving the history of the part taken by Colonel, now General Sherman, in the battle of Bull Run, it may be necessary to make a few preliminary statements, that we may have a clearer understanding of what that gallant officer did, in that most remarkable battle of the Rebellion.

That battle ought to be called the "politicians' battle." Politicians most clamorously urged the President and the Cabinet, and pressed General Scott to attack the enemy, then in a position of his own choosing. The incessant cry of these men, in which the political newspapers of the day joined, was "ON TO RICHMOND! ON TO RICHMOND!" Military science was derided. The wise policy, and military sagacity of General Scott, were ridiculed, and that old hero and true patriot, was even accused of being "unwilling" to invade his native State. Had he not moved on the enemy, and "on to Richmond," he would have been called a disloyal man. The pressure was too great to be resisted. It was resolved that the army should move. Accordingly, on the 17th day of July, 1861, our army of raw and undisciplined troops, marched forward to fight the "politicians' battle;" while they, the politicians, were very careful to keep themselves at a respectful distance from the smell of powder.

The army, about forty thousand strong, marched in five divisions. The first division was commanded by General Tyler, of the Connecticut militia; the second, by Colonel Hunter; the third, by Colonel Heintzelman, of the regular army; the fourth, by Colonel Runyon; and the fifth, by Colonel Miles. The whole army was commanded by Brigadier General Irwin McDowell. Each division was composed of three brigades. Colonel W. T. Sherman commanded the third brigade of the first division.

The march of this great army, was an imposing scene; such as had never before been witnessed by the men of this generation. The most unbounded enthusiasm prevailed throughout the country. But few of the people of the North dreamed of defeat and disaster. Here, and there, a man might be found who believed that our first great battle would not be a victory. They looked at the war, not from a human stand-point, or in the light of man's wisdom,—but in the light of God's providence, firmly believing that God, who governs the affairs of men, and nations, intended, by this war, to establish more firmly, the great principles which lie at the foundation of our beneficent government, and secure to every man who puts his foot upon our soil, the inestimable boon of Freedom. A protracted war seemed necessary, to produce this grand result.

The army marched on, driving back the enemy's pickets, until the main column entered Fairfax, and encamped for the night.

General McDowell ordered General Tyler to proceed to Centreville, and carefully observe all the approaches to that place. On the 18th, without orders from General McDowell, Tyler pushed on to Bull Run, at Blackburn's Ford, and commenced throwing shells at the enemy. An artillery duel followed, which resulted in the withdrawal of our batteries. Great fault has been found with this movement, as it might have resulted in bringing on a general engagement prematurely, and while the army was on the march. It, however, had the good effect to reveal the fact that the enemy were too strong on their right wing, to make the attack at that point.

On the evening of the 20th, the army was mostly at, or near, Centreville. The enemy was at Manassas, about seven miles south-west of Centreville. The road from Centreville to Manassas Junction, is on a ridge, which runs nearly a north and south course. The distance from Centreville to Bull Run, along this road, is about three miles. The Warrenton turnpike runs nearly east and west over this ridge, and through the village of Centreville, and crosses Bull Run, about four miles distant from this point. General Tyler's division was stationed on the north side of Warrenton turnpike, and on the eastern slope of the Centreville ridge. Two brigades were stationed on the north side of the same road, a mile and a half in advance, to the west of the ridge, and one brigade on the road from Centreville to Manassas, where it crosses Bull Run, at Blackburn's Ford. The second division, commanded by Colonel Hunter, was on the Warrenton turnpike, one mile east of Centreville. The third division, commanded by Colonel Heintzelman, was on the Old Braddock Road, south-east of the village about a mile and a half. The fifth division, under Colonel Miles, was on this same road, between the position of the third division, and Centreville. The fourth division, commanded by Colonel Runyon, was placed about seven miles in the rear of Centreville, for the purpose of guarding our communications by way of Vienna, and the Orange and Alexandria Railroad.

General McDowell having perfected his plans and arrangements to commence the battle, orders were given to march. The movement was delayed two hours or more, owing to the failure of the first division to get out of its camp, on the road. This delay had no little influence on the final result of the battle. About four o'clock in the morning, July 21st, the divisions commenced moving. It was a beautiful and bright moonlight night. The stillness that brooded over the grand old forests around, was unbroken, except by the muffled tread of soldiers, and the rumbling noise of artillery carriages. The divisions, separating like the rays of a fan, moved away to the parts of the field assigned to them. Colonel Richardson, with his brigade, moved to Blackburn's Ford, on the extreme left, for the purpose of presenting the appearance of an attack from that quarter, and guarding against a flank movement of the enemy, if it should be undertaken.

General Tyler moved with Sherman's and Schenck's brigades, and Ayres' and Carlisle's batteries, down the Warrenton turnpike, to the bridge, on Bull Run, for the purpose of protecting that point, and presenting the appearance of an attack on the front and centre of the enemy. In the meantime, Hunter, with his division, was moving to a ford, which was unguarded, about ten miles up Bull Run, for the purpose of crossing over the stream, and making a sudden attack on the enemy, turning his left wing, and driving him down the stream, which runs in a south-eastern direction. He was closely followed by the division of Heintzelman, who was to take a position at a ford, three miles up the stream, above the bridge. The road along which he was to march to the position assigned, was found to have no existence, except upon the map. He, therefore, followed along after Hunter's division, and reached the ford at Dudley Springs, at eleven o'clock, just as the last brigade, of Hunter's division, was entering the water, to cross over Bull Run. Just at this time, clouds of dust, from the direction of Manassas, indicated the immediate approach of a large force. The enemy, by some means, had discovered the movement of our army. From high points of observation large masses of troops could be seen moving rapidly towards the threatened point. The roar of artillery soon announced that Hunter was engaged with the enemy. The fire began with artillery, and was followed up with infantry. The leading brigade, commanded by the gallant Burnside, sustained this shock, for a short time, without support, and did it well. The battalion of regular infantry was sent to sustain it, and shortly afterwards the other corps of Porter's brigade, and a regiment detached from Heintzelman's division to the left, forced the enemy back. Our forces succeeded in driving the enemy back and down the stream, to a point nearly opposite, where Tyler's forces were stationed, and where the first gun of the battle was fired, on the morning of that eventful day, at 6 o'clock, and which warned the enemy that the hour of conflict was at hand. As soon as it was discovered that Hunter had thus driven the enemy's flank, General Tyler sent forward and across the run, the right wing of his column, composed of Sherman's and Key's brigades, to co-operate, and thus a grand force was brought to bear most effectually against the enemy. The famous Irish regiment led the van, followed by the Seventy-ninth, (Highlanders), and Thirteenth New York and Second Wisconsin.

* "It was a brave sight indeed—that rush of the Sixty-ninth into the death struggle! With such cheers as won the battles on the Peninsula, with a

---

* Correspondent of the N. Y. World.

quick step at first, and then a double quick, and at last a run, they dashed forward and along the edge of the extended forest. Coats and knapsacks were thrown to either side, that nothing might impede their work. As the line swept along, Meagher galloped towards the head, crying: "Come on, boys! You've got your chance at last!"

It was now noon, and the battle was raging with fierceness. The noise of the cannonading mingled with the sharp quick sound of musketry, was deafening. It was heard at Fairfax, Alexandria and Washington City.

We need not relate what followed, or remind the reader that we drove the enemy before us until about 3 o'clock in the afternoon, when he was reenforced by ten thousand fresh troops, from Winchester, under command of Gen. Johnston, which Gen. Patterson failed to hold in check.

We need not speak of the retreat, the rout, and the most disgraceful panic that followed. But, as we have given a brief sketch of the battle, up to the time Colonel Sherman entered it, we will now give a particular account of the part taken by that distinguished hero.

Sherman's brigade, on the day of the battle, was composed of the Thirteenth New York regiment, Colonel Quinby; Sixty-ninth New York, Colonel

Corcoran; Seventy-ninth New York, Colonel Cameron; Second Wisconsin, Lieutenant-Colonel Peck; and company E Third Artillery, under command of Captain R. B. Ayres, Fifth Artillery.

Sherman's brigade marched with the column of General Tyler, and took a position near the stone bridge at Bull Run. Here the brigade was deployed in line along the skirt of timber, and remained quietly in position, until after 10 o'clock A. M. The enemy had remained very quiet, but about that time a regiment was seen leaving its cover in front of Sherman's forces, and moved in double quick time, on the road towards Sudley Springs, which was evidence that the column of Colonels Hunter and Heintzelman was approaching. About the same time a large force of the enemy was seen in motion, below the stone bridge. Colonel Sherman directed Captain Ayres to take position with his battery near our right, and open fire on the enemy. The smooth bore guns did not reach the position, hence the fire from them ceased. Sherman then sent for the thirty-pounder rifled gun, attached to Capt. Carlisle's battery. In the mean time, the New York Sixty-ninth was shifted to the extreme right of the brigade. There this force remained till they heard the musketry fire across Bull Run. The firing was brisk, and showed that Hunter was driving before him the enemy, till about noon, when it became certain that he had come to a stand, and that our force on the other side of Bull Run was all engaged, artillery and infantry.

It was at this time that Sherman was ordered to cross over the Run, with his whole brigade, to assist Hunter. Early in the day, when reconnoitering the ground, Sherman saw a horseman descend from a bluff to a point, across the stream, and show himself in the open field. This he supposed was designed to show him the place at which he was expected to cross over, when the proper time should come. He sent forward a company as skirmishers, and followed with the entire brigade, the New York Sixty-ninth leading the way. They found no difficulty in crossing over, and met no opposition in ascending the steep bluff opposite, with the infantry, but it was impassable to the artillery. Sherman then sent word to Capt. Ayres to follow if possible, otherwise to use his discretion. The Captain did not cross, but did good service during the day. Sherman then advanced slowly and continuously, with the head of the column, to give time for the regiments, in succession, to close up their ranks. They first encountered a party of the enemy, retreating along a cluster of pines. Lieutenant-Colonel Haggerty of the Sixty-ninth regiment, without orders, rode over and endeavored to intercept their retreat. One of the enemy, in full view and within short range, shot Haggerty, and he fell dead from his horse. The Sixty-ninth opened fire on this party, which was returned. But Sherman, was determined to effect a junction with Hunter's division, and therefore, ordered this fire to cease. This force, then proceeded, with caution, toward the field, and soon saw our forces engaged. Colonel Sherman then ordered our colors to be displayed conspicuously, at the head of his column, for the purpose of attracting the attention of his friends—Hunter's forces. In a short time he succeeded in forming the desired junction, and formed his brigade in rear of Colonel Porter's. Here he learned that Colonel Hunter was disabled by a severe wound, and that General McDowell was on the field. Sherman promptly sought him out, and received his orders to join in the pursuit of the enemy, who were falling back to the left of the road, by which the army had approached from Sudley Springs. Placing Col. Quinby's regiment of rifles in front, in column by division, he directed the other regiments to follow in line of battle, in the order of the Wisconsin Second, New York Seventy-ninth, and New York Sixty-ninth.

Quinby's regiment advanced steadily down the hill and up the ridge, from which he opened fire upon the enemy, who had made another stand, on ground very favorable to him. The regiment continued advancing, as the enemy gave way, till the head of the column reached the point near which Rickett's battery was so severely cut up. The other regiments descended the hill in line of battle, under a severe cannonading, and the ground affording comparative shelter against the enemy's artillery, they changed directions by the right flank, and followed the road before mentioned. At the point where this road crossed the bridge, to the left, the ground was swept by a most severe fire of artillery, rifle, and musketry, and Sherman's brigade saw in succession, several regiments driven from it, among them the Zouaves, and a battalion of marines. Before reaching the crest of the hill, the roadway was worn deep enough to afford shelter, and here Sherman kept his regiments as long as possible; but, when the Wisconsin Second was abreast the enemy, by order of Major Wadsworth, of General McDowell's staff, he ordered that regiment to leave the roadway by the left flank, and attack the enemy. This regiment ascended to the brow of the hill steadily, received the severe fire of the enemy, returned it with spirit, and advanced, delivering its fire. It was uniformed in gray cloth, almost identical with that of the greater part of the secession army, and when it fled in confusion, and retreated toward the roads, there was a universal cry that they were fired upon by our own men. The regiment rallied again, passed the brow of the hill a second time, and was again repulsed in disorder. By this time the New York Seventy-ninth had closed up, and in like manner it was ordered to cross the brow of the hill, and drive the enemy from cover. It was impossible to get a good view of the ground. One battery of artillery poured an incessant fire upon our advancing column, and the ground was irregular, with small clusters of pines, affording shelter, of which the enemy took good advantage. The fire of rifles and musketry was very severe. The Seventy-ninth, headed by Colonel Cameron, charged across the hill, and for a time the contest was doubtful. They rallied several times under fire, but finally broke and gained the cover of the hill. This left the field open to the New York Sixty-ninth, the regiment headed by Colonel Corcoran. He led his regiment over the crest of the hill, and had a full, open view of the ground so severely contested. We have heretofore described the manner in which the regiment went into the fight. The roar of cannon, musketry, and rifles, was incessant. It was manifest, the enemy was here in great force, far superior to ours. The Sixty-ninth held the ground for some time, but finally fell back, in disorder.

Quinby's regiment occupied another ridge to the left of Sherman, overlooking the same field of action, and were engaged with the enemy. Here, about 3½ o'clock, P. M., began the scene of disorder and confusion that characterized the remainder of the day. Sherman's forces had kept their places, and seemed perfectly cool, having become accustomed to the shot and shell that fell comparatively harmless. But their loss had been very heavy. The intense fire of small-arms, at close range, had killed many, wounded more, and produced disorder in all the battalions. Colonel Cameron had been mortally wounded, carried to an ambulance, and reported dying. Many of the officers were reported dead or missing, and many of the wounded were making their way, with more or less assistance to the hospitals. On the ridge to the west, Sherman succeeded in partially re-forming the regiments, but it was manifest they would not stand; and he then directed Colonel Corcoran to move along the ridge to the rear, near the position where the brigade had first formed. General McDowell was there in person, and used all possible efforts to reassure the men. By the active exertions of Colonel Corcoran, an irregular square was formed against the enemy's cavalry, which was then seen issuing from the position from which our forces had been driven. At once the retreat commenced toward the Ford of Bull Run, by which they had approached the field of battle. The retreat was disorderly; in fact, it had been going on for an hour by the operations of the men themselves.

After putting in motion the irregular square, Sherman pushed forward to find Captain Ayres' battery, occupied chiefly at the point where Rickett's battery was destroyed. Lieutenant-Colonel Haggerty had been killed, Colonel Cameron mortally wounded, and Colonel Corcoran missing, after the cavalry charge near the hospital building. Sherman was left to do as best he could, in effecting the safe retreat of his men.

They retreated to Centreville, and there Sherman supposed the forces would rally, and make a stand. But, about 9 o'clock at night, he received from General Tyler, in person, the order to continue the retreat to the Potomac. The retreat was by night, and disorderly in the extreme. The men of different regiments mingled together, and some reached the river at Arlington, some at Long Bridge, and the greater part returned to their former camps, at or near Fort Corcoran and a few made no halt, until they reached New York. Sherman arrived at Fort Corcoran, the day after the battle, about noon, and found a miscellaneous crowd crossing over the aqueduct and ferries. He promptly commanded the guard to be increased, and all persons attempting to pass over to be stopped. This soon produced the desired effect. Men sought their proper companies and regiments, comparative order was restored, and all were posted to the best advantage.

Colonel Sherman expressed himself very strongly and indignantly with regard to the disgraceful conduct of the militia; especially in regard to some of the officers in his command. This gave rise to many disparaging reports concerning the skill and character of Sherman, as a commander. But, whoever will read, with care, the foregoing truthful account of the part taken by him in the battle of Bull Run, will not find the shadow of a reason to doubt that a high order of bravery and military skill characterized his movements. He will see nothing in his conduct, in that disastrous battle, to rob him of the laurels which have since crowned his brow.

After the disastrous battle of Bull Run, the army was re-organized. A number of general officers were appointed by the President, and confirmed by the Senate. It will be remembered that an extra session of Congress was then convened, at Washington. Colonel Sherman, at the urgent request of the Ohio delegation, was appointed a brigadier-general of volunteers. His name was the sixth on the lineal roll of Brigadier-Generals. At that time, he outranked General Grant. His commission was dated from the 17th of May, 1861.

Subsequent events have proven that the honorable title of brigadier has seldom, if ever, been conferred more worthily.

At this time, General Robert Anderson, of Fort Sumter memory, was in command of the Department of the Cumberland—which then embraced the States of Kentucky and Tennessee. His head-quarters were in the city of Louisville. General Sherman, a few days after the battle of Bull Run, was appointed second in command to General Anderson, in the Department of the Cumberland, with head-quarters in the field. For a short time these officers acted together, without jealousy or a spirit of rivalry; but the ill-health of General Anderson soon compelled him to relinquish all active service, and on the 8th of October, 1861, General Sherman became chief commander of this department.

For weeks previous to this time, large bodies of rebel soldiers had been collected in Tennessee, in camps of instruction, on the very borders of Kentucky. Suddenly, and while Sherman and Anderson were in command, the rebel General S. B. Buckner, at the head of a large army, invaded the State, with the evident intention of capturing the city of Louisville, and driving out the Union troops. Sherman had but two fragmentary regiments, of about seventeen hundred men, and a volunteer force of about one thousand Home Guards, to meet and hold in check Buckner's army of at least eight or ten thousand. This he did most successfully, until his little army was reënforced. It, however, never was sufficiently large to justify him in making an advance upon the enemy. When his force amounted to fifteen thousand, that of the enemy amounted to nearly fifty thousand. It is a matter of astonishment to all who know the true situation of affairs at that time, that his little army was not captured or driven out of the State. Kentucky owes a debt of gratitude to Generals Anderson and Sherman, and to the brave soldiers enlisted and commanded by Colonels Rousseau and Pope, under Sherman as their general. They kept the rebel host in check, saved the city of Louisville, and a large portion of the State, until, by the fall of Forts Henry and Donelson, the rebel army was driven from the State.

General Sherman sent dispatch after dispatch to the War Department, and to General McClellan, explaining his situation, asserting his utter inability to defend his post against the overwhelming hosts of the enemy, in case he should be attacked, and requesting immediate reënforcements. Little attention was paid to his requests. Sherman became discouraged, and finally asked to be relieved of his command. His request was granted, and on the

10th of November, 1861, his department was consolidated with that of Ohio.

At this time, General Halleck was in command of the Department of the West. General Sherman was ordered to report to him, and by him was assigned to a command in the western part of Missouri, with head-quarters at Sedalia.

Shortly afterwards he was transferred to Benton Barracks, near St. Louis, where he was placed in command of a camp of instruction.

We next hear of Sherman, in command of the base of operations and supplies at Paducah, at the mouth of the Tennessee river; from which place he sent supplies and reënforcements to General Grant, when he was engaged in capturing Forts Henry and Donelson. So faithfully did Sherman discharge the duties of this position, that General Grant acknowledged that to "General Sherman's promptness he was largely indebted for the success of his operations." Afterwards, Sherman was assigned, by the request of General Grant, to him as a division commander. We shall next meet Sherman on the bloody field of Shiloh.

INCIDENTS.

On one occasion Sherman said to the Adjutant General of the United States, that if the Government intended to open the Mississippi River to its mouth, it would require a force of at least two hundred thousand men, to accomplish the work.

This revived the name which Sherman had received for his manly attempt to restore order among the Bull Run fugitives, "Crazy Sherman," as some of his opponents called him. Time has proven that the "crazy man" was right in his judgment.

While Sherman's army was confronting General Buckner's forces, south of Elizabethtown, Kentucky, one of his brigadiers, the gallant Rousseau, suddenly approached one of his chaplains, the Rev. James H. Bristow, a true and noble man, and put his hand on his shoulder, looked him square in the face, and without turning away his eagle eyes, thus addressed him:

"Chaplain," said the general, "I think it possible that we may have a battle to-morrow, and I wish to ask you one question. Will you go with me into battle and stand by my side until I fall, or to the end of the fight?"

"What was your reply," said I to Mr. Bristow.

'To tell you the truth," said the chaplain, "I thought of an old song, which I used to sing, and which went somewhat after this fashion: '*The spirit is willing, but the flesh is weak.*'"

This man has since proven himself to be one of the best chaplains in the army.

While Sherman was in command at Benton Barracks, he was in the habit of visiting every part of the barracks, and keeping himself familiar with everything that was going on. He wore an old brown coat and stove-pipe hat, and was not generally recognized by the minor officials and soldiers. One day, while walking through the grounds, he met with a soldier who was beating a mule unmercifully.

"Stop pounding that mule!" Said the general.

"Git eout!" said the soldier in blissful ignorance of the person to whom he was speaking.

"I tell you stop!" reiterated the general.

"You mind your business, and I will mind mine," replied the soldier, continuing his flank movements upon the mule.

"I tell you again, to stop!" said the general. "Do you know who I am? I am General Sherman."

"That's played out!" said the soldier. "Every man who comes along here with an old brown coat and stove-pipe-hat on, claims to be General Sherman."

For once, at least, Sherman was compelled to acknowledge himself outflanked.

CHAPTER III.

GENERAL SHERMAN AND THE BATTLE OF PITTSBURG LANDING.

THE BATTLE OF PITTSBURG LANDING THE MOST DESPERATE AND DECISIVE OF THE WAR—THE TROOPS ENGAGED—SKIRMISHING—BATTLE OPENS—SURPRISE OF UNION TROOPS—SUNDAY'S FIGHT—THE UNION TROOPS DRIVEN FROM THEIR CAMPS—THE LEXINGTON AND TYLER—THE PART TAKEN BY THEM—LEW WALLACE'S AND BUELL'S FORCES ARRIVE—MONDAY'S OPERATIONS—CAVALRY CHARGE BY GRANT—PURSUIT BY SHERMAN—GRANT'S OPINION OF SHERMAN—THE PART TAKEN BY SHERMAN AND HIS DIVISION—EXTRACT FROM HALLECK'S REPORT—SHERMAN A MAJOR GENERAL—THE OPINIONS OF DISTINGUISHED GENERALS—INCIDENTS—GEN. SHERMAN'S LETTER TO PROFESSOR COPPEE.

The battle of Pittsburg Landing, or Shiloh, was one of the most desperate conflicts ever known in history, and the most severe and hardest fought battle of the rebellion, as well as, up to that time, the most decisive of the war. With overwhelming numbers opposing them, and surprised as they were by the enemy, it was only by the bravest and most stubborn fighting, that the Union troops gained this most splendid victory. And, although the tide seemed turned against them during the early part of the battle, everything seemed to favor them on the second day; and, after two days fighting they had regained all they had lost, and driven back and conquered the rebels.

The troops engaged in this battle, were the divisions of Prentiss, Sherman, and McClernand, who were in advance, and Hurlbut's and Smith's, the latter, under command of General W. H. L. Wallace. Hurlbut's and Wallace's divisions were stationed between the Tennessee River and the others. On the second day, these were joined by the divisions of Generals Lewis Wallace, Nelson, Crittenden, and McCook.

On the evening of the fourth of April, the enemy made a reconnoissance with two of their regiments, and, after a slight skirmish, retired, as their forces under Price and Van Dorn had not yet arrived. Although the generals commanding the rebel army had fixed upon the fifth of April for the day of attack, they resolved to wait one day longer, until their reënforcements should arrive. This gave General Buell time to reach Grant, and, without doubt, saved the country from a terrible disaster which must have been the result, had his reënforcements failed to arrive. Johnston, and Beauregard were aware that Buell was advancing from Nashville, to join Grant, and for this reason, at first resolved to attack him before Buell should arrive.

Just at break of day, on Sunday morning, the 6th of April, the pickets of Prentiss and Sherman were driven in by the enemy, and the rebels were almost instantly in our camp. They found the troops entirely unprepared for anything like an attack. The officers and men were scattered about, some still in their beds, some dressing, and some eating their breakfast,—and none in readiness for their early and unexpected visitors.

The five divisions stationed at this point, were hurriedly drawn up in line of battle, and, without a moment's preparation, met the enemy. Many of the regiments were new troops, their officers inexperienced, and many of them became panic-stricken. General Prentiss, and the greater part of his division, were at this time, taken prisoners. Sherman used all his energies to rally his men. Riding along the lines, encouraging them, and exposing his own life, he did much to save the division from utter destruction. Although our forces returned their fire most vigorously, our men were driven back from their camp. The enemy bringing up a fresh force, opened fire upon our left wing, under General McClernand. Along the whole line, for a distance of over four miles, this fire was returned with terrible effect, by both infantry and artillery.

General Hurlbut's division was then brought forward, and a most desperate conflict ensued. The rebels were first driven back, with great loss of life, but rallied, and in turn, drove our men back.

The rebel forces, commanded by able generals, were handled with a skill that drew admiration from all, and although repulsed; again and again, they continued sending fresh troops to the front, and again bent their energies to the work.

Late in the afternoon, the most desperate fighting that had occurred during the entire day, took place. The rebels undoubtedly thought that if they failed in defeating us on that day, that their chances for success would be doubtful, as a part of General Buell's army had arrived on the opposite side of the river. The rebels could see the reënforcements from the river bank, and to this place they directed their attention. The Union troops were, indeed, contending against fearful odds, their army numbering about thirty-eight thousand men, while that of the rebels exceeded sixty thousand.

Many of the panic-stricken, and the skulkers, were gathered near the river, and no appeals from their officers could rally them.

General Lewis Wallace's division, which was at Crump's Landing, was ordered up in the morning, but being led by a circuitous route, failed to reach the scene of action until night.

About five o'clock, P. M., the rebels occupied about two-thirds of the Union camps, and were constantly driving them towards the river. Toward evening, the gunboats Lexington and Taylor, which had lain idle spectators during the day's fearful contest, seeking in vain for an opportunity to bring their guns to bear upon the enemy, commenced raining shells upon the rebel hordes. The boats fired rapidly, and well; and with the incessant clash of guns, on land, and the crash and roar of shells from the boats, that Sabbath evening wore away.

The men lay on their arms during the night, in line of battle. Buell and Lew. Wallace would be there, and ready to assist them in the morning, for all through the night, Buell's men were marching up from Savannah, and were being ferried across, or were coming upon transports; and Wallace's division had arrived in the evening, and would be in readiness ere the morning dawned. A heavy thunder storm came up about midnight, drenching the two armies, but proving a most excellent dressing for the wounds of the many who were suffering on that bloody field.

At daylight, on the morning of the seventh of April, the two divisions of Nelson and Crittenden, advanced upon the enemy. Lew. Wallace's division commenced the battle by an artillery fire upon a battery of the enemy, causing them to retreat.

Nelson's troops were in the advance, and the fighting was most desperate, continually driving back the rebels. The fire soon became general along the whole line,—Crittenden following close to Nelson, and next to him, McCook. Generals Sherman's, McClernand's and Hurlbut's men, although terribly jaded from the previous day's fighting, came up, and gallantly added new laurels to those already won.

But the rebels resisted at every point; they felt that all depended upon a most desperate effort on their part, and their generals urged them on, thinking to flank us on the right, and thus gain the day. Success seemed theirs for a time, but our left, under Nelson, was dividing them, and by eleven o'clock, General Buell's forces had succeeded in flanking them, and capturing their batteries. The rebels again rallied, but some regiments from Wood's and Thomas' coming in just then, were sent to General Buell, who again drove the enemy back. About three o'clock in the afternoon, General Grant, at the head of five regiments of cavalry, ordered a charge across the field, himself commanding. The men followed with a shout, and the rebels fled in dismay, and did not make another stand. The retreating rebels were followed by Buell, and by half-past five, their whole army was retreating towards Corinth.

The main army, well nigh worn out with hard fighting, gladly welcomed the close of this victorious day. On the following morning, General Sherman started forward with the remainder of his division, in pursuit. He met the enemy's cavalry on the road to Corinth, where a sharp skirmish ensued, and he drove them from the field with the loss of several killed and wounded.

General Grant, in his official report of the battle of Pittsburg Landing, says: "I feel it a duty to a gallant and able officer, Brigadier General W. T. Sherman, to make special mention. He not only was with his command during the entire two days of the action, but displayed great judgment and skill in the management of his men; although severely wounded in the hand, on the first day, his place was never vacant. He was again wounded, and had three horses killed under him. General Prentiss was taken prisoner on the first day's battle, and Gen. W. H. L. Wallace was mortally wounded."

From General Sherman's report we learn, that on Friday, the 4th instant, the enemy's cavalry drove in his pickets, posted about a mile and a-half in advance of his centre, on the main Corinth road, capturing one lieutenant, and seven men; that he ordered a pursuit by the cavalry of his division, driving them back about five miles, and killing many. On Saturday, the enemy's cavalry was again very bold, coming well down to their front, yet it was thought that he designed nothing but a strong demonstration. On Sunday morning, early, the 6th instant, the enemy drove our advance guard back on the main body, when General Sherman ordered under arms, all his division, and sent word to General McClernand, asking him to support his left; to General Prentiss, giving him notice that the enemy was in our front, in force, and to General Hurlbut, asking him to support General Prentiss. At this time, seven A. M., Sherman's division was arranged as follows:

First Brigade, composed of the Sixth Iowa, Colonel J. A. McDowell; Fortieth Illinois, Colonel Hicks; Forty-sixth Ohio, Colonel Worthington; and the Norton Battery, Captain Behr, on the extreme left, guarding the bridge on the Purdy Road, over Owl Creek.

Second Brigade, composed of the Fifty-fifth Illinois, Colonel D. Stuart; Fifty-fourth Ohio, Colonel T. Kilby Smith; and the Seventy-first Ohio, Colonel Mason, on the extreme left, guarding the ford over Lick Creek.

Third Brigade, composed of the Seventy-seventh Ohio, Colonel Hildebrand; Fifty-third Ohio, Colonel Appler; and the Fifty-seventh Ohio, Colonel Mungen, on the left of the Corinth Road, its right resting on Shiloh meeting-house.

Fourth Brigade, composed of the Seventy-second Ohio, Colonel Buckland; Forty-eighth Ohio, Colonel Sullivan; and the Seventeenth Ohio, Colonel Cockerill, on the right of the Corinth Road, its left resting on Shiloh meeting-house.

Two batteries of artillery, Taylor's and Waterhouse's, were posted, the former at Shiloh, and the latter on a ridge to the left, with a front fire over open ground between Mungen's and Appler's regiments. The cavalry, eight companies of the Fourth Illinois, under Colonel Dickey, were posted in a large open field to the left and rear of Shiloh meeting-house, which Sherman regarded as 'the centre of his position. Shortly after seven A. M., with his entire staff, Sherman rode along a portion of our front, and when in the open field before Appler's regiment, the enemy's pickets opened a brisk fire on his party, killing his orderly, Thomas D. Hollister, of Company H, Second Illinois Cavalry. The fire came from the bushes which line a small stream that rose in the field in front of Appler's camp, and flows to the north along the whole front of the place where this division was located. This valley afforded the enemy cover, but our men were so posted as to have a good fire at him as he crossed the valley and ascended the rising ground on our side.

About eight A. M. the glistening bayonets of heavy masses of rebel infantry could be seen to our left front, in the woods beyond the small stream alluded to, and Sherman became satisfied for the first time that the enemy designed a determined attack on our whole camp. All the regiments in his division were then in line of battle, at their proper posts. Sherman rode to Colonel Appler, and ordered him to hold his ground at all hazards, as he held the left flank of our first line of battle, and he had a good battery on his right and strong support in his rear. General McClernand had promptly and energetically responded to Sherman's request, and had sent him three regiments, which were posted to protect Waterhouse's battery and the left flank of Sherman's line. The battle began by the enemy opening a battery in the woods to our front, and throwing shell into our camp.

Taylor's and Waterhouse's batteries promptly responded, and the heavy battalions of infantry could be seen passing obliquely to the left across the open field in Appler's front; also other columns advancing directly upon Sherman's division. The Union infantry and artillery opened fire along the whole line, and the battle became general. Other heavy masses of the enemy's forces kept passing across the field to their left, and directing their course on General Prentiss. Sherman saw at once that the enemy designed to pass his left flank, and fall upon Generals McClernand and Prentiss, whose

F

line of camps was almost parallel with the Tennessee River, and about two miles back from it. Very soon the sound of musketry and artillery announced that General Prentiss was engaged, and about nine A. M. he began to fall back. About this time Appler's regiment broke in disorder; Mungen's regiment followed, and the enemy pressed forward on Waterhouse's battery, thereby exposed. The three Illinois regiments in immediate support of this battery, stood for some time, but the enemy's advance was vigorous, and the fire so severe, that when Colonel Raith, of the Forty-third Illinois, received a severe wound, and fell from his horse, his regiment and the others manifested disorder, and the enemy got possession of three guns of this (Waterhouse's) battery. Although our left was thus turned, and the enemy was pressing our whole line, Sherman deemed Shiloh so important, that he remained by it, and renewed his orders to Colonels McDowell and Buckland to hold their ground; and these positions were held until ten o'clock A. M., when the enemy had got his artillery to the rear of our left flank, and some change became absolutely necessary. Two regiments of Hildebrand's brigade (Appler's and Mungen's) had already disappeared to the rear, and Hildebrand's own regiment was in disorder. Sherman, therefore, gave orders for Taylor's battery, still at Shiloh, to fall back as far as the Purdy and Hamburg Road, and for McDowell and Buckland to adopt that road as their new line. He rode across the angle and met Behr's battery at the cross roads, and ordered it immediately to come into battery, action right. Captain Behr gave the order, but was almost instantly shot from his horse, when drivers and gunners fled in dismay, carrying off the caissons, and abandoning five out of six guns without firing a shot. The enemy pressed on, gaining this battery, and the Union troops were again forced to choose a line of defense. Hildebrand's brigade had substantially disappeared from the field, though he himself bravely remained. McDowell's and Buckland's brigades maintained their organization, and were conducted by Sherman's aids so as to join on McClernand's right, thus abandoning the original camps and line of Sherman.

This was about ten o'clock A. M., at which time the enemy made a furious attack on General McClernand's whole front. He struggled most desperately, but finding him pressed, McDowell's brigade was moved directly against the left flank of the enemy, forcing him back some distance, and the men were directed to avail themselves of every cover—trees, fallen timber, and a wooded valley to our right. This position they held for four long hours, sometimes gaining and at other times losing ground, Generals McClernand and Sherman acting in perfect concert and struggling to maintain this line. While they were so hard pressed two Iowa regiments approached from the rear, but could not be brought up to the severe fire that was raging in our front. At four P. M. it was evident that Hurlbut's line had been driven back to the river, and knowing that General Wallace was coming with reënforcements from Crump's Landing, Sherman and McClernand, on consultation, selected a new line of defense, with its right wing covering a bridge by which General Wallace had to approach.

The Union troops fell back as well as they could, gathering, in addition to their own, such scattered forces as they could find, and formed the new line. During this change the enemy charged them, but were handsomely repulsed by an Illinois regiment.

The Fifth Ohio cavalry, which had come up, rendered good service in holding the enemy in check for some time, and Major Taylor also came up with a new battery, and got into position just in time to get a good flank fire upon the enemy's column as he pressed on General McClernand's right, checking his advance, when General McClernand's division made a fine charge on the enemy, and drove him back into the ravines to our front and right. Sherman had a clear field about two hundred yards wide in his immediate front, and contented himself with keeping the enemy's infantry at that distance during the day. In this position his army rested for the night. His command had become decidedly of a mixed character. Buckland's brigade was the only one that retained organization. Colonel Hildebrand was personally there, but his brigade was not. Colonel McDowell had been severely injured by a fall from his horse, and had gone to the river, and the three regiments of his brigade were not in line.

The Thirteenth Missouri, Colonel Crafts J. Wright, had reported to Sherman on the field, and fought well, retaining its regimental organization, and formed a part of his line during Sunday night and all day Monday. Other fragments of regiments and companies had also fallen into his division, and acted with it during the remainder of the battle.

Generals Grant and Buell visited Sherman in his bivouac that evening, and from them he learned the situation in the other parts of the field. General Wallace arrived from Crump's Landing shortly after dark, and formed his line to the right and rear of Sherman. It rained hard during the night, but our men were in good spirits, and lay on their arms, being satisfied with such bread and meat as could be gathered at the neighboring camps, and determined to redeem on Monday the losses of Sunday.

At daybreak of Monday Sherman received General Grant's orders to advance and recapture their original camps. He dispatched several members of his staff to bring up all the men they could find, and especially the brigade of Colonel Stuart, which had been separated from the division the day before; and at the appointed time the division, or what remained of it, with the Thirteenth Missouri and other fragments of regiments, moved forward, and occupied the ground on the extreme right of General McClernand's camp, where they attracted the fire of a rebel battery near Colonel McDowell's former headquarters. Here Sherman remained awaiting for the sound of General Buell's advance upon the main Corinth Road. About 10 o'clock A. M. the firing in this direction, and its steady approach, satisfied him; and General Wallace being on his right, flanked with his well-conducted division, Sherman led the head of his column to General McClernand's right, formed in line of battle facing south, with Buckland's brigade directly across the ridge, and Stuart's brigade on its right, in the woods, and thus advanced steadily and slowly, under a heavy fire of musketry and artillery. Taylor had just come up from the rear, where he had gone for ammunition, and brought up three guns, which Sherman ordered into position to advance by hand-firing. These guns belonged to Company A, Chicago Light Artillery, commanded by Lieutenant P. P. Wood, and did most excellent service. Under cover of their fire, the troops advanced until they reached the point where the Corinth Road crosses the line of General McClernand's camp; and here was seen the well-ordered and compact Kentucky forces of General Buell, whose soldierly movement alone gave confidence to our new and less disciplined forces, Willich's regiment advancing upon a point of water oaks and thicket, behind which the enemy was in great strength, and entered it in beautiful style. Then arose some of the most severe musketry firing ever heard, lasting twenty minutes, when this splendid regiment had to fall back. This green point of timber is about five hundred yards east of Shiloh meeting-house, and it was evident that there was to be the struggle. The enemy could also be seen forming his line to the south. General McClernand sending to Sherman for artillery, he detached to him the three guns of Wood's battery, with which he speedily drove them back; and seeing some others in the rear, Sherman sent one of his staff to bring them forward, when, by almost Providential decree, they proved to be two twenty-four pounder Howitzers, belonging to McAllister's battery, and served as well as guns ever could be. This was about two P. M. The enemy had one battery close by Shiloh, and another near the Hamburg Road, both pouring grape and cannister upon any column of troops that advanced upon the green point of water-oaks. Willich's regiment had been repulsed; but a whole brigade of McCook's division advanced, beautifully deployed, and entered this dreaded wood. Sherman ordered his Second brigade, then commanded by Colonel Kilby Smith (Colonel Stuart being wounded,) to form on its right, and his Fourth brigade, Colonel Buckland, on its right—all to advance with the Kentucky brigade before mentioned (Rousseau's brigade of McCook's division). He gave personal direction to the twenty-four pounder guns, whose well-directed fire silenced the enemy's guns to the left, and afterwards at the Shiloh meeting-house. Rousseau's brigade moved in splendid order steadily to the front, sweeping everything before it, and at four P. M. the Union troops stood upon the ground of their original front line, and the enemy was in full retreat. Sherman directed his several brigades to resume at once their original camp.

General McCook's splendid division from Kentucky drove back the enemy along the Corinth Road, which was the great centre of the field of battle, and where Beauregard commanded in person, supported by Bragg's, Polk's and Breckinridge's divisions. Johnston was killed by exposing himself in front of his troops at the time of their attack on Buckland's brigade on Sunday morning.

Sherman's division was made up of regiments perfectly new, all having received their muskets for the first time at Paducah. None of them had ever been under fire, and to expect the coolness and steadiness of older troops would be wrong. They knew not the value of combination and organization. When individual fear seized them, the first impulse was to get away. His third brigade broke much sooner than it should have done. Colonel Hildebrand, its commander, was as cool as man could be, and no one could have made stronger efforts to hold his men to their places than he did. He kept his own regiment, with individual exceptions, in hand an hour after Appler's and Mungen's regiments had left their proper field of action. Colonel Buckland managed his brigade well. General Sherman commended him to General Grant as a cool, intelligent and judicious man, who needed only confidence and experience to make a good commander. His subordinates, Colonels Sullivan and Cockerill, behaved with great gallantry, the former receiving a severe wound on Sunday, and yet commanding and holding his regiment well in hand all day, and on Monday, until his right arm was broken by a shot. Cockerill held a larger proportion of his men than any colonel in Sherman's division, and was with him from first to last. Colonel J. H. McDowell, commanding the First brigade, held his ground on Sunday until ordered to fall back, which he did in line of battle, and when ordered he conducted the attack on the enemy's left in good style. In falling back to the next position he was thrown from his horse and injured, and his brigade was not in position on Monday morning. His subordinates, Colonels Hicks and Worthington, displayed great personal courage. Colonel Hicks led his regiment in the attack on Sunday, and received a severe wound. Lieutenant-Colonel Walcutt, of the Ohio Forty-sixth, was severely wounded on Sunday. Sherman's Second brigade, Colonel Stuart, was detached nearly two miles from headquarters. He had to fight his own battle on Sunday against superior numbers, as the enemy interposed between him and General Prentiss early in the day. Colonel Stuart was wounded severely, and yet reported for duty on Monday morning. He was compelled to leave during the day, when the command devolved on Colonel Kilby Smith, who was always in the thickest of the fight, and led the brigade handsomely

Lieutenant-Colonel Kyle, of the Seventy-first, was mortally wounded on Sunday.

Several times during the battle cartridges gave out, but General Grant had thoughtfully kept a supply coming from the rear. General Sherman commended the Fortieth Illinois and Thirteenth Missouri for steadfastly holding their ground under heavy fire, although their cartridge-boxes were empty. The following is the number of killed, wounded and missing in Sherman's division:

	KILLED		WOUNDED		MISSING	
	Off's.	Men.	Off's.	Men.	Off's.	Men.
Sixth Iowa,	2	49	3	117	...	39
Fortieth Illinois,	1	42	7	148	...	2
Forty-sixth Ohio,	2	32	3	147	...	52
Fifty-fifth Illinois,	1	45	8	183	...	41
Fifty-fourth Ohio,	2	22	5	128	...	32
Seventy-first Ohio,	1	12	...	52	1	45
Seventy-seventh Ohio,	1	48	7	107	3	53
Fifty-seventh Ohio,	2	7	...	82	...	33
Fifty-third Ohio,	...	7	...	30	...	5
Seventy-second Ohio,	2	13	5	85	...	49
Forty-eighth Ohio,	1	13	3	70	1	45
Seventieth Ohio,	...	9	1	53	1	39
Taylor's Battery,	...	...	...	...	...	...
Behr's Battery,	1	...	...	...	...	...
Barrett's Battery,	...	1	...	5	...	...
Waterhouse's Battery,	...	1	3	14	...	...
Orderly Holliday,	...	1	...	...	...	...
	16	302	45	1230	6	435

RECAPITULATION.

Officers—	Killed,	16
	Wounded,	45
	Missing,	6
Soldiers—	Killed,	302
	Wounded,	1230
	Missing,	435
	Aggregate loss in the Division,	2034

The enemy captured seven guns belonging to Sherman's division on Sunday, but on Monday the division recovered seven, not the identical guns lost, but enough in number to balance the account.

At the time of recovering their camps, the men were so fatigued, that they could not follow the retreating masses of the enemy; but on the next day, Sherman followed them up for six miles.

Captain Hannon, chief of staff, though in feeble health, was very active in rallying broken troops, encouraging the steadfast, and aiding to form the lines of defense and attack. Major Sanger's intelligence, quick perception and rapid execution, were of very great value to the commander-in-chief, especially in bringing into line the batteries that coöperated so efficiently in their movements. Captains McCoy and Dayton, aids-de-camp, were with Sherman all the time, carrying orders, and acted with coolness, spirit and courage. To Surgeon Hartshorn and Doctor L'Hommedieu, hundreds of wounded men were indebted for the kind and excellent treatment received on the field of battle, and in the various temporary hospitals created along the line of our operations. They worked day and night, and did not rest till all the wounded of our troops, as well as those of the enemy, were in safe and comfortable shelter. Major Taylor, chief of artillery, showed much good sense and judgment, in managing the batteries on which so much depended. The cavalry of Sherman's command kept to the rear, and took little part in the action, but it would have been madness to have exposed horses to the musketry fire under which they were compelled to remain, from Sunday at eight A. M. till Monday at four P. M.

Major-General Halleck, in a dispatch to Secretary Stanton, dated Pittsburg, Tenn., said:

"It is the unanimous opinion here that Brigadier-General W. T. Sherman saved the fortune of the 6th, and contributed largely to the glorious victory on the 7th. He was in the thickest of the fight on both days, having three horses killed under him, and being wounded twice. I respectfully request that he be made a Major-General of Volunteers, to date from the 6th instant."

General Nelson, a few days before his death, in conversation with several gentlemen, said: "During eight hours, the fate of the army on the field of Shiloh depended on the life of one man: if

General Sherman had fallen, the army would have been captured or destroyed."

General Boyle was speaking to a crowd of men at Willard's, in Washington, when Chief-Justice Ewing, of Kansas, entered the room and heard him say: "You do not know how to appreciate our military men. If Napoleon Bonaparte had commanded at Shiloh, he would have made General Sherman a field-marshal on the field of battle."

General Rousseau, who was also in the battle of the 7th, in a public speech, at an ovation given him in Louisville, on the 15th of June, says: "I wish to say a word of General Sherman. You do not know him, though you may think you do. He stayed with us while Buckner was most expected, but at last, in obedience to commands, he left our State. He gave us our first lessons in the field, in the face of the enemy; and of all the men I ever saw, he is the most untiring, vigilant and patient. No man that ever lived could surpass him. His enemies say that he was surprised at Shiloh. I tell you, no. He was not surprised, nor whipped; for he fights by the week. Devoid of ambition, incapable of envy, he is brave, gallant, and just. At Shiloh, his old legion met him just as the battle was ended, and at the sight of him, placing their hats upon their bayonets, gave him three cheers. It was a touching and fitting compliment to the gallant chieftain. I am thankful for this occasion to do justice to a brave, honest, and knightly gentleman."

In a letter to the War Department, dated July 26th, 1863, General Grant says: "General Sherman, at the battle of Shiloh, on the first day, held, with raw troops, the key-point of the landing. It is no disparagement to any other officer, to say that I do not believe there was another division commander on the field, who had the skill and experience to have done it. *To his individual efforts I am indebted for the success of that battle.*"

A cavalry officer at the battle of Shiloh relates many incidents illustrative of Sherman's character. He says: "Having occasion to report personally to General Sherman about noon of the first day at Shiloh, I found him dismounted, his arm in a sling, his hand bleeding, his horse dead, himself covered with dust, his face besmeared with powder and blood; he was giving directions at the moment to Major Taylor, his chief of artillery, who had just brought a battery into position. Mounted orderlies were coming and going in haste; staff-officers were making anxious inquiries; everybody but himself seemed excited. The battle was raging terrifically in every direction. Just then, there seemed to be universal commotion on our right, where it was observed that our men were giving back. 'I was looking for that,' said Sherman; 'but I am ready for them.' His quick, sharp eyes flashed, and his war-begrimed face beamed with satisfaction. The enemy's packed colums now made their appearance, and as quickly the guns which Sherman had so carefully placed in position, began to speak. The deadly effect on the enemy was apparent. While Sherman was still managing the artillery, Major Sanger, a staff officer, called his attention to the fact that the enemy's cavalry was charging towards the battery. 'Order these two companies of infantry,' was the quick reply, and the general coolly went on with his guns. The cavalry made a gallant charge, but their horses carried back empty saddles. The enemy was evidently foiled. Our men, gaining fresh courage, rallied again, and for the first time that day, the enemy was held stubbornly in check. A moment more, and he fell back on the piles of his dead and wounded."

With the following interesting letter, we close this chapter, which will serve the purpose of correcting erroneous and widely circulated reports concerning two of the generals engaged in the battle of Shiloh, and at the same time will give us additional insight into the character of Sherman:

HEAD-QUARTERS MILITARY DIVISION } OF THE MISSISSIPPI.

PROF. HENRY COPPEE, *Philadelphia:*

DEAR SIR: In the June number of the *United States Service Magazine* I find a brief sketch of Lieutenant-General U. S. Grant, in which I see you are likely to perpetuate an error, which General Grant may not deem of sufficient importance to correct. To General Buell's noble, able and gallant conduct, you attribute the fact that the disaster of April 6th, at Pittsburg Landing, was retrieved, and made the victory of the following day. As General Taylor is said, in his latter days, to have doubted whether he was at the battle of Buena Vista at all, on account of the many things having transpired there, according to the historians, which he did not see, so I begin to so doubt whether I was at the battle of Pittsburg Landing of April 6th and 7th, 1862. General Grant visited my division about ten A. M., when the battle raged fiercest. I was then on the right. After some general conversation, he remarked that I was doing right in stubbornly opposing the progress of the enemy; and in answer to my inquiry as to cartridges, he told me that he had anticipated their want, and given orders accordingly; he then said his presence was more needed over at the left. About two P. M. of the 6th, the enemy materially slackened his attack on me, and about four P. M., I deliberately made a line behind McArthur's drill field, placing batteries on chosen ground, repelling easily a cavalry attack, and watched the cautious approach of the enemy's infantry, that never dislodged me there. I selected that line in advance of a bridge across Snake Creek, by which we had all day been expecting the approach of Lew. Wallace's division from Crump's Landing. About five P. M., before the sun set, General Grant came again to me, and after hearing my report of matters, explained to me the situation of affairs on the left, which were not as favorable; still the enemy had failed to reach the landing of the boats. We agreed that the enemy had expended the *furore* of his attack, and we estimated our loss, and approximated our then strength, including Lewis Wallace's fresh division, expected each minute. He then ordered me to get all things ready, and at daylight the next day to assume the offensive. That was before General Buell had arrived, but he was known to be near at hand. General Buell's troops took no essential part in the first day's fight, and Grant's army, though collected together hastily, green as militia, some regiments arriving without cartridges even, and nearly all hearing the dread sound of battle for the first time, had successfully withstood and repelled the first day's terrific onset of a superior enemy, well commanded and well handled. I know I had orders from General Grant to assume the offensive before I knew General Buell was on the west side of the Tennessee. I think General Buell, Colonel Fry, and others of General Buell's staff, rode up to where I was about sunset, about the time General Grant was leaving me. General Buell asked me many questions, and got of me a small map, which I had made for my own use, and told me that by daylight he could have eighteen thousand fresh men, which I knew would settle the matter.

I understood Grant's forces were to advance on the right of the Corinth Road and Buell's on the left, and accordingly at daylight I advanced my division by the flank, the resistance being trivial, up to the very spot where the day before the battle had been most severe, and then waited till near noon for Buell's troops to get up abreast, when the entire line advanced and recovered all the ground we had ever held. I know that with the exception of one or two severe struggles, the fighting of April 7th was easy, as compared with that of April 6th.

I never was disposed, nor am I now, to question anything done by General Buell and his army, and know that, approaching our field of battle from the rear, he encountered that sickening crowd of laggards and fugitives that excited his contempt and that of his army, who never gave full credit to those in the front line, who did fight hard, and who had, at four P. M., checked the enemy, and were preparing the next day to assume the offensive. I remember the fact better from General Grant's anecdote of his Donelson battle, which he told me then for the first time—that, at a certain period of the battle, he saw that either was ready to give way if the other showed a bold front, and he determined to do that very thing, to advance on the enemy when, as he prognosticated, the enemy surrendered. At four P. M. of April 6th, he thought the appearance the same, and he judged, with Lew. Wallace's fresh division and such of our startled troops as had recovered their equilibrium, he would be justified in dropping the defensive and assuming the offensive in the morning. And I repeat, I received such orders before I knew General Buell's troops were at the river. I admit that I was glad that Buell was there, because I knew his troops were older than ours, and better systematized and drilled, and his arrival made that certain which before was uncertain. I have heard this question much discussed, and must say that the officers of Buell's army dwelt too much on the stampede of some of our raw troops, and gave us too little credit for the fact that for one whole day, weakened as we were by the absence of Buell's army, long expected; of Lew. Wallace's division, only four miles off, and of the fugitives from our ranks, we had beaten off our assailants for the time. At the same time our Army of the Tennessee have indulged in severe criticism at the slow approach of that army which knew the danger that threatened us from the concentrated armies of Johnston, Beauregard and Bragg that lay at Corinth. In a war like this, where opportunities of personal prowess are as plenty as blackberries to those who seek them at the front, all such criminations should be frowned down; and were it not for the military character of your journal I would not venture to offer a correction of a very popular error.

I will also avail myself of this occasion to correct another very common mistake in attributing to General Grant the selection of that battlefield. It was chosen by that veteran soldier, Major General Charles F. Smith, who ordered my division to disembark there, and strike for the Charleston Railroad. This order was subsequently modified by his ordering Hurlbut's division to disembark there, and mine higher up the Tennessee to the mouth of Yellow Creek, to strike the railroad at Burnsville. But floods prevented our reaching the railroad, when General Smith ordered me in person also to disembark at Pittsburg, and take post well out, so as to make plenty of room, with

Snake and Lick Creeks the flanks of a camp for the grand army of invasion.

It was General Smith who selected that field of battle, and it was well chosen. On any other we surely would have been overwhelmed, as both Lick and Snake Creeks forced the enemy to confine his movements to a direct front attack, which new troops are better qualified to resist than where flanks are exposed to a real or chimerical danger. Even the divisions of that army were arranged in that camp by General Smith's orders, my division forming, as it were, the outlying picket, whilst McClernand's and Prentiss' were the real line of battle, with W. H. L. Wallace in support of the right wing, and Hurlbut of the left; Lew. Wallace's division being detached. All these subordinate dispositions were made by the order of General Smith, before General Grant succeeded him to the command of all the forces up the Tennessee—head-quarters, Savannah. If there was any error in putting that army on the west side of the Tennessee, exposed to the superior force of the enemy also assembling at Corinth, the mistake was not General Grant's—but there was no mistake. It was necessary that a combat, fierce and bitter, to test the manhood of the two armies, should come off, and that was as good a place as any. It was not then a question of military skill and strategy, but of courage and pluck, and I am convinced that every life lost to us that day was necessary; for otherwise at Corinth, at Memphis, at Vicksburg, we would have found harder resistance, had we not shown our enemies that, rude and untutored as we then were, we could fight as well as they.

Excuse so long a letter, which is very unusual from me, but of course my life is liable to cease at any moment, and I happen to be a witness to certain truths which are now beginning to pass out of memory, and form what is called history.

I also take great pleasure in adding that nearly all the new troops that at Shiloh drew from me official censure have more than redeemed their good name; among them that very regiment which first broke, the Fifty-third Ohio, Colonel Appler. Under another leader, Colonel Jones, it has shared every campaign and expedition of mine since, is with me now, and can march and bivouac and fight as well as the best regiment in this or any army. Its reputation now is equal to any from the State of Ohio.

   I am, with respect,
    Yours, truly,
     W. T. SHERMAN,
      Major General.

CHAPTER IV.

SHERMAN AND THE SIEGE OF CORINTH.

MARCH TOWARD CORINTH—SKIRMISHING AT MONTEREY AND PURDY—SIEGE OF CORINTH COMMENCES—BATTLE OF RUSSELL'S HOUSE — EVACUATION OF CORINTH — OCCUPATION OF THE CITY BY THE UNION TROOPS — PURSUIT BY GENERAL M. L. SMITH TO TUSCUMBIA CREEK—SHERMAN'S CONGRATULATORY ORDER—INCIDENTS — TAKES POSSESSION OF HOLLY SPRINGS — APPOINTED THE MILITARY COMMANDER OF MEMPHIS, TENNESSEE.

After the battle of Pittsburg Landing, cavalry skirmishes occurred at intervals, along the outposts of the Union army, but nothing of importance transpired, until the movement was made toward Corinth, on the 17th of April, 1862. All along the line of march, from Pittsburg Landing to Corinth, the advance of our army was signalized by reconnoissances and skirmishes. On the 27th of April, a cavalry skirmish took place near Monterey, ten miles from Corinth, at which time several rebel prisoners were taken. Two days after, skirmishing occurred again, resulting in the capture of more prisoners, and of the rebel camps. On the

30th day of April, Purdy, on the Jackson and Corinth Railroad, which place had been abandoned a few days previous, was occupied by the Union army, they succeeding in cutting off all railroad communications between Corinth and Northwestern Tennessee.

The siege of Corinth, may be said to have commenced on the 30th of April. The Union commanders were continually sending out reconnoissances, and on the 8th of May, we find their cavalry within a mile and a half of Corinth. The rebels made several dashes on the Union lines, causing some of the forces on the left to retire.

On the 11th of May, it was decided by the general officers, that an advance of the whole army should take place, and they accordingly pressed forward to Corinth, where all felt that a terrible battle would soon occur. The Union troops met with resistance as they proceeded on their march, and on the 17th of May, the Fifth Division under General Sherman, encountered the rebels near Russell's house, causing them to fall back, while the Unionists took possession of the position.

We learn from General Sherman's official report that in compliance with the purpose of Major-General Halleck, he made all possible inquiry as to the topography of the ground in his front, with its water courses, fields, and roads, and on the

H

17th made disposition to drive the enemy from his position at Russell's house.

He requested General Hurlbut to put in motion two regiments and a battery of artillery, at three o'clock P. M., on the road which passes the front of his line, and runs to Russell's house. He ordered General Denver to take a right-hand road with two regiments of his brigade and one battery of light artillery, namely, the Seventieth and Seventy-second Ohio, and Barrett's battery, and gave him a guide so to conduct his march as to arrive on the left of the enemy's position by the time he was engaged in front; and ordered General Morgan L. Smith's brigade, with Benton's battery, to follow the main road, drive back a brigade of the enemy's forces that held a position at Russell's with their skirmishers and pickets, down to the causeway and bridge across a small stream, about eight hundred yards from Russell's house, supposed to be a branch of Bridge Creek.

All these forces were put in motion at three P. M., General Denver's forces taking the right-hand road, and General Smith's the direct main road. On reaching the causeway, General Smith deployed his skirmishers forward, and sent out his advance-guard. The column advanced, and the skirmishers became engaged at once. The firing was brisk, but the enemy's pickets were driven steadily back, till they reached the position of their brigade at Russell's house, where their resistance was obstinate.

The ground was unfavorable to artillery till the skirmishers had cleared the hill beyond the causeway, when Major Taylor, chief of artillery, advanced first one of Benton's guns, and very soon after, the remaining three guns of the battery. These, upon reaching the hill-top, commenced firing at Russell's house and outhouses, in which the enemy had taken shelter, when their whole force retreated, and the position occupied three hundred yards in advance, where the roads meet. This was the limit to which Sherman had ordered the brigade to go, and there it halted. The head of General Denver's column reached its position as the enemy was beginning to retreat.

General Morgan L. Smith conducted the advance of his brigade handsomely, and the chief work and loss fell upon his two leading regiments, the Eighth Missouri, and Fifty-fifth Illinois. To General Smith was due the full credit of conducting the advance, and of carrying the position at Russell's. He held the ground till about daylight next morning, when, by order of General Sherman, he left a strong picket there, and placed his brigade back a short distance in easy support, where it remained until relieved by another brigade.

From Russell's could distinctly be heard the drums beating in Corinth. The house is nearly a mile and a quarter from the enemy's outer intrenchments.

There was no loss sustained by Generals Hurlbut's or Denver's commands in their flank movements on Russell's; but the loss in General Morgan L. Smith's was pretty heavy—ten killed and thirty-one wounded. The confederates left twelve dead on the ground. They removed their wounded, of which many traces were on the ground and in the house. Among their dead were one captain, and two lieutenants.

General Sherman's division was again brought in action on the 27th of May. The rebels, although outnumbering our forces, retreated, and it was thought the contest was for the purpose of detaining the advance of the Union army. On the 28th, a portion of the troops advanced to within gunshot of the rebel works, causing the rebels to retreat, with considerable loss. On the 30th of May, the Union army marched into Corinth, the enemy having withdrawn the last of their forces about midnight the night previous. A portion of our army followed the retreating rebels.

General Sherman, in his official report of the occupation of Corinth, says that after driving the enemy away from Russell's house, they found the place one of great natural strength, and proceeded to fortify it. Lines were laid off by the engineer, Captain Kossak, and a very excellent parapet was constructed by the men in a style that elicited the approval of General Halleck. Men worked day and night, and as soon as it was done, and the dense trees and undergrowth cleared away in front, to give range to our batteries, Sherman directed his pickets to drive the enemy further back behind a large open field to his front and right. This was handsomely executed by the regular detail of picket-guard, under the direction of the field officer of the day, Lieutenant-Colonel Loudon, of the Seventieth Ohio.

They remained in that intrenched camp until the night of the 27th, when Sherman received from Halleck an order by telegraph, "to send a force the next day to drive the rebels from the house in our front on the Corinth Road; to drive in their pickets as far as possible, and to make strong demonstrations on Corinth itself," authorizing him to call on any adjacent divisions for assistance. He asked General McClernand for one brigade and General Hurlbut for another, to coöperate with two brigades of his own division. Colonel John A. Logan's brigade, of General Judah's division of McClernand's reserve corps, and General Veatch's brigade, of Hurlbut's division, were placed subject to Sherman's orders, and took part with his division in the operations of the two following days.

The house referred to by General Halleck was a double log building, standing on a high ridge on the upper or southern end of the large field before referred to as the one to which our pickets had advanced. The enemy had taken out the chinks and removed the roof, making it an excellent block-house from which, with perfect security, he could fire among our pickets. The large field was perfectly overlooked by this house, as well as by the ridge along its southern line of defense, which was covered by a dense grove of heavy oaks and underbrush. The main Corinth Road runs along the eastern fence, whilst the field itself, about three hundred yards wide by about five hundred yards long, extended to the right into the low land of Philip's Creek, so densely wooded as to be impassable to troops or artillery. On the eastern side of the field the woods were more open. The enemy could be seen at all times in and about the house and the ridge beyond, and our pickets could not show themselves on our side of the field without attracting a shot.

The problem was to clear the house and ridge of the enemy with as little loss as possible. To accomplish this, Sherman ordered General J. W. Denver, with his brigade (Third), and the Morton battery of four guns, to march in perfect silence from our lines at eight A. M., keeping well under cover as he approached the field; General Morgan L. Smith's brigade (First), with Barrett's and Waterhouse's batteries, to move along the main road, keeping his force well masked in the woods to the left; Brigadier General Veatch's brigade to move from Hurlbut's lines through the woods on the left of and connecting with General M. L. Smith's and General John A. Logan's brigades, to move down to Bowie Hill Cut, on the Mobile and Ohio Railroad, and thence forward to the left, so as to connect with General Denver's brigade, on the extreme right; all to march at eight A. M., with skirmishers well to the front; all to keep well concealed, and, at a signal, to rush quickly on to the ridge, thus avoiding, as much as possible, the danger of crossing the open field exposed to the fire of a concealed enemy. It was impossible beforehand to ascertain the force of the enemy, and nothing is more embarrassing than to make dispositions against a concealed foe occupying, as this was, a strong natural position.

The preliminary arrangements having thus been made, two twenty-four pound Parrot rifle guns, of Silversparre's battery, under the immediate supervision of Major Taylor, chief of artillery, were moved silently through the forest to a point behind the hills, from the top of which could be seen the house and ground to be contested. The guns were unlimbered, loaded with shell, and moved by hand to the crest. At the proper time Sherman gave the order to Major Taylor to commence firing and demolish the house, or render it decidedly uncomfortable to its occupants. About a dozen shells, well directed, soon accomplished this; then designating a single shot of the twenty-four pound Parrot gun of Silversparre as a signal for the brigades to advance, he waited till all were in position, and ordered the signal, when the troops dashed forward in fine style, crossed the field, drove the enemy across the ridge and field beyond into another dense and seemingly impenetrable forest. The enemy was evidently surprised, and only killed two of our men, and wounded nine. After he had reached the ridge, he opened on us with a two-gun battery on the right and another from the front and left, doing but little harm, but killing three of General Veatch's men. With the artillery, the rebel guns were soon silenced, and by ten A. M. the Union troops were masters of the position. Generals Grant and Thomas were present, and witnessed the movement, which was admirably executed, all the officers and men keeping their places like true soldiers.

Immediately throwing forward a line of skirmishers in front of each brigade, we found the enemy reënforcing his front skirmishers; but the woods were so dense as to completely mask his operations. An irregular piece of cleared land lay immediately in front of General Denver's position, and extended obliquely to the left, in front of and across Morgan Smith's and Veatch's brigades, which were posted on the right and left of the main Corinth Road, leading directly south. For some time it was doubtful whether the artillery fire had come from the enemy's fixed or field batteries, and Sherman intended to move forward at great hazard to ascertain the fact, when, about three P. M., our troops were startled by the rattle of musketry along their whole picket line, followed by the cheers and yells of an attacking column.

The artillery, and Mann's battery of Veatch's brigade, had been judiciously posted by Major Taylor, and before the yell of the enemy had died away arose their reply in the cannon's mouth. The firing was very good, rapid, well directed, and the shells burst in the right place. Our pickets were at first driven in a little, but soon recovered their ground and held it, and the enemy retreated in utter confusion. On further examination of the ground, with its connection on the left with General Hurlbut, and right resting on Bowie Hill Cut, it was determined to intrench. The lines were laid out after dark, and the work substantially finished by morning.

All this time the Federal forces were within one thousand three hundred yards of the enemy's main intrenchments, which were absolutely concealed by the dense foliage of the oak forest, and without a real battle, which at that time was to be avoided, we could not push out our skirmishers more than two hundred yards to the front. For our security, Sherman was obliged to destroy two farm-houses, both of which had been loop-holed and occupied by the enemy. By nine A. M. of the 29th, the works of the Unionists were substantially done, and their artillery in position, and at four P. M. the siege-train was brought forward, and Colonel McDowell's brigade, (second,) of Sherman's division, had come from their former lines at Russell's, and had relieved General John A. Logan's brigade.

This officer during two days held the critical ground on the right, extending down to the railroad. All the time he had in his front a large force of the enemy, but so dense was the foliage, that he could not reckon their strength, save from what he could see on the railroad track.

Sherman had then his whole division in a slightly curved line, facing south, his right resting on the

Mobile and Ohio Railroad, near a deep cut, known as Bowie Hill Cut, and left resting on the main Corinth Road, at the crest of the ridge, there connecting with General Hurlbut, who, in turn, on his left, connected with General Davies, and so on down the whole line to its extremity. So near was the enemy that the sound of his drums, and sometimes of voices in command, could be heard, and the railroad cars arriving and departing at Corinth were easily distinguished. The arrivals and departures were so frequent, especially on the night of the 29th, that the suspicions of General Sherman were aroused.

Before daybreak he instructed the brigade commanders and field officers of the day, to feel forward as far as possible, but all reported the enemy's pickets still in force in the dense woods to the front. But about six A. M., a curious explosion, sounding like a volley of large siege-guns, followed by others singly, and in twos or threes, arrested the attention of the Union commanders, and soon after a large smoke arose from the direction of Corinth, when Sherman telegraphed to Halleck to ascertain the cause. He answered that he could not explain it, but ordered Sherman to advance his division and feel the enemy, if still in his front. He immediately put in motion two regiments of each brigade, by different roads, and soon after, followed with the whole division, infantry, artillery, and cavalry.

Somewhat to his surprise, the enemy's chief redoubt was found within thirteen hundred yards of his line of intrenchments, but completely masked by the thick forest and undergrowth. Instead of having as was supposed, a continuous line of intrenchments encircling Corinth, his defences consisted of separate redoubts, connected in part by a parapet and ditch, and in part by shallow rifle-pits, the trees being felled so as to give a good field of fire to and beyond the main road.

General M. L. Smith's brigade moved rapidly down the main road, entering the first redoubt of the enemy at seven A. M. It was completely evacuated, and he pushed on into Corinth, and beyond to College Hill, there awaiting the orders of Sherman. General Denver entered the enemy's lines at the same time, seven A. M., at a point midway between the wagon and railroads, and proceeded on to Corinth, about three miles from the camp, and Colonel McDowell kept further to the right, near the Mobile and Ohio Railroad. By eight A. M. Sherman's division was at Corinth, and beyond.

On the whole ridge extending from our camp into Corinth, and to the right and left, could be seen the remains of the abandoned camps of the enemy, flour and provisions scattered about, and everything indicating a speedy and confused retreat.

In the town itself many houses were still burning, and the ruins of warehouses and buildings, containing commissary and other confederate stores, were still smouldering; but there still remained piles of cannon balls, shells and shot, sugar, molasses, beans, rice and other property, which the enemy had failed to carry off or destroy. Major Fisher, of the Ohio Fifty-fourth, was left in Corinth with a provost guard, to prevent pillage and protect the public stores still left.

From the best information picked up from the few citizens who remained in Corinth, it appeared that the enemy had for some days been removing their sick, and valuable stores, and had sent away on railroad cars a part of their effective force on the night of the 28th. But, of course, even the vast amount of their rolling stock could not carry away an army of a hundred thousand men.

The enemy was, therefore, compelled to march away, commencing on the night of the 29th—the columns filling all the roads leading south and west all night—the rear guard firing the train which led to the explosions and conflagration, which gave the first notice that Corinth was to be evacuated. The enemy did not relieve his pickets that morning, and many of them were captured who did not have the slightest intimation of their purpose.

I

Finding Corinth evacuated by the enemy, Sherman ordered General M. L. Smith to pursue on the Ripley Road, by which it appeared they had taken the bulk of their artillery.

Captain Hammond, Sherman's chief of staff, was with General Smith's brigade, and pushed the pursuit up to the bridges and narrow causeway by which the bottom of Tuscumbia Creek is passed. The enemy opened with canister on the small party of cavalry, and burned every bridge, leaving the woods full of straggling soldiers. Many of these were gathered up and sent to the rear, but the main army had escaped across Tuscumbia Creek, and further pursuit by a small party would have been absurd, and Sherman kept his division at College Hill, until he received General Thomas' orders to return and resume their camps of the day before, which they did, slowly and quietly, in the cool of the evening.

The evacuation of Corinth at the time, and in the manner in which it was done, was a clear backdown from the high and arrogant tone heretofore assumed by the rebels. The ground was of their own choice. The fortifications, though poor and indifferent, were all they supposed necessary to our defeat, as they had two months to make them, with an immense force to work at their disposal.

Sherman's division had constructed seven distinct intrenched camps since they left Shiloh, the men working cheerfully and well all the time, night and day. Hardly had they finished one camp before they were called on to move forward and build another. Their intrenchments here and at Russell's, each built substantially in one night, were stronger works than the much boasted forts of the enemy at Corinth.

Our line of march was along a strongly marked ridge, followed by the Purdy and Corinth Road, and after leaving the "Locusts" the pickets were continually fighting. There was hardly an hour, night or day, for two weeks, without the exchange of hostile shots. We slowly and surely gained ground with a steadiness that presaged the inevitable result.

CONGRATULATORY ORDER OF GENERAL SHERMAN.

HEAD-QUARTERS FIFTH DIVISION ARMY OF TENNESSEE,
CAMP BEFORE CORINTH, May 31, 1862.

ORDER No. 30.

The General commanding Fifth division, right wing, takes this occasion to express to the officers and men of his command his great satisfaction with them for the courage, steadiness and great industry displayed by them during the past month.

Since leaving our memorable camp at Shiloh, we have occupied and strongly intrenched seven distinct camps in a manner to excite the admiration and high commendation of General Halleck.

The division has occupied the right flank of the grana army, thereby being more exposed and calling for more hard work and larger details than from any other single division—and the Commanding General reports that his officers and men have promptly and cheerfully performed their duty, and have sprung to the musket or spade, according to the occasion, and have just reason to claim a large share in the honors that are due the whole army for the glorious victory terminating at Corinth yesterday, and it affords him great pleasure to bear full testimony to the qualities of his command that have achieved this victory—a victory none the less decisive because attended with comparatively little loss of life.

But a few days ago a large and powerful rebel army lay at Corinth, with outposts extending to our very camp at Shiloh. They held two railroads extending north and south, east and west across the whole extent of their country, with a vast number of locomotives and cars to bring to them speedily and certainly their reënforcements and supplies. They called to their aid all their armies from every quarter, abandoning the sea coast and the great river Mississippi, that they might overwhelm us with numbers in the place of their own choosing. They had chosen leaders—men of high reputation and courage, and they dared us to leave the cover of our iron-clad gunboats to come to fight them in their trenches, and still more dangerous swamps and ambuscades of their southern forests. Their whole country, from Richmond to Memphis, and Nashville to Mobile, rung with their taunts and boastings, as to how they would immolate the Yankees if they dared leave the Tennessee River. They boldly and defiantly challenged us to meet them at Corinth. We accepted the challenge, and came slowly, and without concealment, to the very ground of their selection; and they have fled away. We yesterday marched, unopposed, through the burning embers of their destroyed camps and property, and pursued them to their swamps, until burning bridges plainly confessed that they had fled and not marched away for better ground. It is a victory as brilliant and important as any recorded in history, and every officer and soldier who lent his aid has just reason to be proud of his part.

No amount of sophistry or words from the leaders of the rebellion can succeed in giving the evacuation of Corinth, under the circumstances, any other title than that of a signal defeat, more humiliating to them and their cause than if we had entered the place over the dead and mangled bodies of their soldiers. We are not here to kill and slay, but to vindicate the honor and just authority of that government which has been bequeathed to us by our honored fathers, and to whom we would be recreant if we permitted their work to pass to our children, marred and spoiled by ambitious rebels.

The general commanding, while thus claiming for his division their just share in this glorious result, must, at the same time, remind them that much yet remains to be done, and that all must still continue the same vigilance and patience, industry and obedience, till the enemy lays down his arms and publicly acknowledges, for their supposed grievances, that they must obey the laws of their country, and not attempt its overthrow by threats, by cruelty, and by war. They must be made to feel and acknowledge the power of a just and mighty nation. This result can only be accomplished by a cheerful and ready obedience to the orders and authority of our leaders, in whom we now have just reason to feel the most implicit confidence. That the Fifth division of the right wing will do this, and that in due time we will go to our families and friends at home, is the earnest prayer and wish of your immediate commander.

W. T SHERMAN, *Major General.*
J. H. HAMMOND, *A. A. G., Chief of Staff.*

INCIDENTS CONNECTED WITH THE SIEGE OF CORINTH.

When the Federal lines advanced on the 28th of April, a battery was planted on an eminence commanding a considerable portion of the country, but completely shrouded by a dense thicket. Scouts were sent out to discover the exact position of the rebels, and were but a short distance in advance, to give a signal as to the direction to fire, if any were discovered.

One of the rebel commanders, unaware of their presence, called around him a rebel brigade, and commenced addressing them in something like the following strain:

"SONS OF THE SOUTH—We are here to defend our homes, our wives and daughters, against the horde of vandals who have come here to possess the first and violate the last. Here, upon this sacred soil, we have assembled to drive back the Northern invaders—drive them into the Tennessee. Will you follow me? If we cannot hold this place, we can defend no spot of our Confederacy. Shall we strike the invaders back, and strike to death the men who would desecrate our homes? Is there a man so base among those who hear me as to retreat from the contemptible foe before us? I will never blanch before their fire, nor ———"

At this interesting period the signal was given, and six shells fell in the vicinity of the gallant officer and his men, who suddenly forgot their fiery resolves, and fled in confusion to their breastworks.

THE EAGLE OF CORINTH.

"The finest thing I ever saw," said Mr. Howe, "was a live American eagle, carried by the Eighth

Wisconsin in the place of a flag. It would fly over the enemy during the hottest of the fight, then would return and seat himself upon his pole, clap his pinions, shake his head and start again. Many and hearty were the cheers that arose from our lines as the old fellow would sail around, first to the right, then to the left, and always return to his post, regardless of the storm of leaden hail that was around him. Something seemed to tell us that the battle was to result in our favor, and when the order was given to charge, every man went at them with fixed bayonets, and the enemy scattered in all directions, leaving us in possession of the battle-field."*

The incident just narrated awoke the harp of the poet, who thus sang:

>Did you hear of the fight at Corinth,
>   How we whipped out Price and Van Dorn!
>Ah! that day we earned our rations—
>(Our cause was God's and the Nation's,
>   Or we'd have come out forlorn!)
>A long and a terrible day!
>And, at last, when night grew gray,
>By the hundred there they lay,
>(Heavy sleepers, you'd say)
>   That wouldn't wake on the morn.

---

* Letter from Chester D. Howe, Company E, Twelfth Illinois Volunteers.

Our staff was bare of a flag,
We didn't carry a rag
  In those brave marching days—
Ah! no; but a finer thing!
With never a cord or string,
An eagle, of ruffled wing,
  And an eye of awful gaze!

The grape it rattled like hail,
The minies were dropping like rain,
  The first of a thunder shower—
    The wads were blowing like chaff,
(There was pounding, like floor and flail,
  All the front of our line!)
So we stood it, hour after hour—
But our eagle he felt fine!
'Twould have made you cheer and laugh
To see, through that iron gale,
  How the old fellow'd swoop and sail
Above the racket and roar—
To right and to left he'd soar,
  But ever came back, without fail,
    And perched on his standard staff.

All that day, I tell you true,
  They had pressed us steady and fair,
*   *   *   *   *   *   *
But our cross-fire stunned them in flank,
They melted, rank after rank—
(O'er them, with terrible poise,
  Our bird did circle and wheel!)
    Their whole line began to waver—
Now for the bayonet, boys!
  On them with the cold steel!

Ah! well, you know how it ended—
  We did for them, there and then,
But their pluck, throughout, was splendid,
  They stood, to the last, like men;
Only a handful of them
  Found the way back again.
Red as blood, o'er the town,
  The angry sun went down,
    Firing flag-staff and vane—
And our eagle, as for him,
There, all ruffled and grim,
  He sat, o'erlooking the slain.   H. H. B.

On the 20th of June, Holly Springs, on the railroad from Jackson, Tenn., to New Orleans, was taken possession of by General Sherman's forces, who destroyed the bridge and several pieces of trestle work on the Mississippi Central Railroad, in order to prevent surprise by the rebels. Previous to the evacuation of the place, the enemy had removed their machinery for the repairing and making of arms to Atlanta, Ga.

Memphis, which surrendered soon after the evacuation of Corinth, was at once occupied by the Union troops. General Grant appointed Sherman to the command of that city, and on the 21st of July he took the post of military commander of Memphis. He ordered the most urgent measures to be adopted against all guerrillas, and soon put a stop to the contraband trade which was carried on in that city.

On the 28th of July, by orders from General Grant, he took possession of all unoccupied buildings, stores and manufactories within the city of Memphis, and collected the rents of such property for the United States Government.

CHAPTER V.

SHERMAN AND THE CAMPAIGNS AGAINST VICKSBURG.

PREPARATIONS FOR THE VICKSBURG CAMPAIGN — SHERMAN'S COMMAND SAILS FOR VICKSBURG — ARRIVAL AT JOHNSTON'S LANDING — FIRST ASSAULT UPON VICKSBURG — MCCLERNAND TAKES COMMAND — SHERMAN'S CONGRATULATORY ORDER TO HIS TROOPS — CAPTURE OF ARKANSAS POST — STEELE'S BAYOU EXPEDITION — FEINT ON THE NORTH OF VICKSBURG — FIGHT AT FOURTEEN MILE CREEK — ADVANCE UPON JACKSON — OCCUPATION OF THE CITY — BATTLE OF BIG BLACK RIVER — TAKES POSSESSION OF WALNUT HILLS — SECOND ASSAULT UPON VICKSBURG — SURRENDER — OCCUPATION — PURSUIT AFTER JOHNSTON — SECOND OCCUPATION OF JACKSON — RECOMMENDED BY GENERAL GRANT FOR PROMOTION AS BRIGADIER GENERAL OF REGULAR ARMY.

During the autumn of 1862, General Sherman, who had been placed in command of the Fifteenth Army Corps, consisting of four divisions, and known as the "Right Wing of the Army of the Tennessee," began to make preparations for the Vicksburg campaign.

On the 28th of November, the advance of the army was made by the Jackson and Grand Junction Railroad, and proceeded steadily on their march until the surrender of Holly Springs, December 20th, when Grant was compelled to fall back to preserve his line of communication. The plan was for Grant to threaten an attack by way of Jackson, while Sherman assaulted the defences of Walnut Hill, by way of the Yazoo River.

On the 20th of December, General Sherman embarked his forces at Memphis. The fleet consisted of one hundred and twenty-seven steamers, besides gun-boats. General Sherman and staff arrived on the "Forest Queen" at Friar's Point on the following day.

General Sherman was entirely unaware that Grant had retraced his steps from Oxford to Holly Springs, and as Grant had intended moving upon Jackson by the railroad, and thence to Vicksburg, a combination of the forces under Grant and Sherman was needed to secure success.

General Sherman proceeded with a part of his expedition, and landed a small force, under General M. L. Smith, at Milliken's Bend. They proceeded to Delhi and Dallas, on the Vicksburg and Texas Railroad, destroyed the depôts and part of the track, cutting off the retreat of the rebels from Vicksburg.

On the 26th of December, the troops under Sherman arrived at Johnston's Landing, near the mouth of the Yazoo River, and prepared for an assault upon the northern works that defended the city of Vicksburg.

From Johnston's Landing, Vicksburg is peculiarly situated, being a hill, with a line of hills surrounding it at a distance of several miles, and extending from Haines' Bluff, on the Yazoo River, to Warrentown, ten miles beyond the city, on the Mississippi River. The low country in the vicinity is swampy, filled with sloughs, bayous and lagoons. To approach Vicksburg with a large force by this route, even in times of peace, would be a matter of great difficulty, and with an enemy in front, it was almost an impossibility.

On the 27th of December, the troops formed in line of battle, and prepared to assault the enemy's works. By night they had succeeded in driving the rebels about a quarter of a mile from their former position.

On the following day the Union troops showed great bravery, but Grant's forces failing to arrive, as Sherman had confidently expected, entirely disarranged the plan of battle. Owing to the reënforcement of the enemy by the troops that had fled before Grant's advance, they were well prepared to resist Sherman's men, and the rebels refused to come from behind their works, employing the time during the night in throwing up earthworks in every direction. Sherman's small force had much

J

to contend against, the woods being filled with sharp-shooters, the position of the enemy being made doubly strong by nature and art, and the rebels outnumbering them.

On Monday, the 29th, our troops made several charges on the enemy's works, but all to no use, and the men fell back. General Blair's brigade, headed by himself, on foot, particularly distinguished itself, and of the eight hundred and twenty-five men engaged in this assault, six hundred and forty-two were killed, wounded and captured.

After the burial of the dead and removal of the wounded, Sherman gave orders for his troops to reëmbark.

On the 1st of January General McClernand arrived, and as he ranked General Sherman by over a month in the date of his commission, he assumed command, and ordered the troops to withdraw from the Yazoo River and return to the Mississippi River. The title of the army was changed by General McClernand, and General Sherman issued the following order:

> HEAD-QUARTERS, RIGHT WING ARMY OF TENNESSEE,
> STEAMER FOREST QUEEN,
> MILLIKEN'S BEND, January 4, 1863.

GENERAL ORDERS No. 5.

Pursuant to the terms of General Orders No. 1, made this day by General McClernand, the title of our army ceases to exist, and

constitutes in the future the Army of the Mississippi, composed
of two "army corps," one to be commanded by General G. W.
Morgan, and the other by myself. In relinquishing the command
of the Army of the Tennessee, and restricting my authority to
my own corps, I desire to express to all commanders, to soldiers
and officers recently operating before Vicksburg, my hearty
thanks for the zeal, alacrity and courage manifested by them on
all occasions. We failed in accomplishing one purpose of our
movement—the capture of Vicksburg—but we were part of a
whole. Ours was but a part of a combined movement, in which
others were to assist. We were on time; unforeseen contingencies
must have delayed the others. We have destroyed the Shreve-
port Road; we have attacked the defences of Vicksburg, and
pushed the attack as far as prudence would justify; and having
found it too strong for our single column, we have drawn off in
good order and good spirits, ready for any new move. A new
commander is now here to lead you. He is chosen by the President of the United States, who is charged by the Constitution to
maintain and defend it, and he has the undoubted right to select
his own agents. I know that all good officers and soldiers will
give him the same hearty support and cheerful obedience they
have hitherto given me. There are honors enough in reserve for
all, and work enough too. Let each do his appropriate part, and
our nation must in the end emerge from this dire conflict purified
and ennobled by the fires which now test its strength and purity.
All officers of the general staff now attached to my person will
hereafter report in person and by letter to Major General McClernand, commanding the Army of the Mississippi, on board the
steamer Tigress, at our rendezvous at Gaines' Landing, and at
Montgomery Point.

By order of   Major General W. T. SHERMAN.
J. H. HAMMOND, *A. A. G.*

    General Sherman had with Admiral Porter de-
vised a plan for the capture of Arkansas Post, on

the Arkansas River. Sherman was prevented from assuming the chief command of the military portion of this expedition — McClernand having arrived — but to Sherman was due the planning and carrying out of the attack.

The Thirteenth and Fifteenth corps left the Yazoo River, and passed up the Mississippi River to Montgomery Point, opposite the mouth of the White River. On the 9th of January, 1863, the iron-clads and transports moved up the White River, and after ascending that stream for fifteen miles, the fleet passed through a cut-off to the left, into the Arkansas River.

From General McClernand's and General Hovey's official reports we learn that the former assumed the command of the Thirteenth and Fifteenth army corps, on the 4th of January, 1863, after they had retired from Vicksburg. McClernand sailed with them, for the purpose of reducing Fort Hindman, which had been laboriously and skilfully enlarged and strengthened, since the commencement of the rebellion; it formed the key to Little Rock, the capital of the State of Arkansas, and the extensive and valuable country drained by the Arkansas River, from which hostile detachments were constantly sent to obstruct the navigation of the Mississippi River and thereby our communications.

The forces landed at Notril's farm, on the left bank of the river, three miles below the fort, at five o'clock, P. M., on the 9th of January, and the work of disembarking was busily continued until noon the next day, when it was completed.

On the 10th instant, the enemy abandoned a line of rifle-pits about half a mile above the levee, under stress of fire of one of the gunboats.

General McClernand communicated with General Sherman, and suggested to him the eligibility of the river-road, from which he might diverge at or near the levee, in making a detour for the purpose of investigating the upper side of the fort. His column was put in motion at eleven o'clock A. M., but diverging below that point, the head of it, consisting of General Hovey's brigade of General Steele's division, after meeting and dispersing a strong picket of the enemy, soon encountered a swamp, about a fourth of a mile wide. Passing this swamp with much difficulty, the brigade rested upon an open space called "Little Prairie." Several small squads of the enemy's cavalry hovered in their advance and were captured. About two o'clock the column was ordered to return to the landing, where it arrived just before dark, and bivouacked for the night.

Hardly had the camp-fires been lighted, when orders were received to move immediately by another route and by a night-march to their original destination. Over marshy ground, thickly covered with wood, without a guide and with the only direction, "to take a north-westerly course," they set out. Fortunately the North Star was in full view, and by its aid they were enabled to reach the point indicated, after a fatiguing march of more than eight miles. It was after two o'clock in the morning when they reached the deserted camps of the enemy.

By half past ten o'clock A. M., the two corps were in position, and were ready to commence the attack. General Steele's division formed the extreme right of the line of battle, and General Stuart's, and General A. J. Smith's divisions were formed on its left.

Port Arkansas, a small village, the county seat of Arkansas county, is situated on elevated ground above the reach of floods, and defining for some miles, the left bank of the river.

Fort Hindman, a square, full-bastioned fort, is erected within this village, upon the bank of the river, at the head of a bend resembling a horse-shoe.

At one o'clock P. M., the gun-boats opened fire, immediately followed by artillery. By half past one o'clock Hovey's and Thayer's brigades, and Giles A. Smith's and T. K. Smith's brigades of General Sherman's corps, had crossed in double quick time, a narrow space of cleared ground, in their front, and gained position in a belt of woods extending irregularly some three hundred yards, quite to the enemy's rifle-pits; checked here, for a time, by a sudden and severe fire of musketry and artillery from the cover of the enemy's works, they boldly resumed and continued their advance, supported by Blair's brigade, as a reserve, until they had approached within short musket-range of the enemy's line, and found shelter in some ravines lined by underbrush and fallen timber.

In executing this movement General Hovey was wounded by a shell, but continued upon the field in the gallant discharge of duty.

At half past four o'clock, after three hours and a half hard fighting, the Union forces entered and took possession of all the enemy's defences, General Churchill having surrendered the post, its armament, garrison, and all its stores to General McClernand.

During the early part of 1863, Sherman took a very important part in one of the expeditions sent out by General Grant for the purpose of drawing off the enemy's attention from the main operations.

On the 16th of March, 1863, General Grant ordered General Stuart to prepare the infantry of his division — the Second division of the Fifteenth

Army Corps—to move at daylight the next morning. Leaving everything, except ammunition, arms, and rations, they embarked and proceeded up the Mississippi to Eagle Bend. Admiral Porter and General Grant had made a personal reconnoissance of a proposed route to the Yazoo above Haines' Bluff, a few days previous, and General Sherman was ordered to take charge of the opening of the route. General Sherman left at once with the pioneer corps of Stuart's division and the Eighth Missouri. General Grant received dispatches in the evening from Admiral Porter, announcing that his gunboats were meeting with great success, and requested that the land force be sent at once, and General Stuart was ordered to immediately proceed with his division. The distance by land from the Mississippi, along the Muddy Bayou, is about one mile. And the infantry were ordered to cross by this route to Steele's Bayou, it being impossible to take anything but small steamers through the bayou. On reaching Eagle Bend, it was ascertained that two long bridges were necessary to the movement of troops, and the building of these occupied a day and a half. When completed, the division marched across Steele's Bayou, and a part of the First brigade embarked on the Silver Wave, and started up through the wilderness of forest and water.

Three streams, Steele's Bayou, Deer Creek, and the Sunflower, traverse the country north of the Yazoo, for fifty miles, between the Mississippi and the line of railway from Memphis to Jackson, emptying into the Yazoo. Their course is very tortuous, like the streams in the wild marshes.

The fleet going up the Yazoo River seven miles, thence up Steele's Bayou twelve miles, came to Muddy Bayou, which runs across from the Mississippi into Steele's. The troops came over on floating bridges, and embarked at this point, and from here were transported up Steele's and Black Bayou about twenty miles to Hill's plantation, and marched thence twenty-one miles on a levee north along Deer Creek, nearly to Rolling Fork. It was proposed to proceed on that creek a distance of seven miles, until the Sunflower was reached. Once upon that stream, they could reach the Yazoo, between Haines' Bluff and Yazoo City, and would be in a position to operate against the enemy at various points with great effect.

After a reconnoissance far enough to learn that gunboats could pass from the Yazoo into Steele's Bayou, Admiral Porter moved up the Bay, and General Sherman with a division of his army corps formed the land force. This was on the 15th, and before night on the 16th, the advance of the gunboats and land force were at Muddy Bayou. They arrived at Eagle Bend on the 17th. The 18th, and until noon of the following day, the men were employed in building the two bridges before referred to, and the troops were speedily transported to the place of rendezvous. They passed up the Black Bayou into Deer Creek, without any obstruction from the enemy until the 20th, when the rebels commenced annoying them with sharpshooters, and by felling trees in the creeks. They could proceed no further that night, and in the morning, they found considerable obstruction in the river, and an enemy, some 600 strong, with a field battery of rifles, disputing his passage. They were kept busy the greater part of the day, making but half a mile progress.

The Admiral sent a dispatch back to General Sherman, stating the condition of affairs, and a force was immediately sent to the relief of the gunboats. They made a forced march, skirmishing a part of the way, and arrived on the evening of the 22d, a distance of twenty-one miles, over a terrible road. The enemy had been largely reënforced during the day, and now numbered some 5,000 men. The boats were surrounded with rebels, who had cut down trees before and behind them, were moving up artillery, and making every exertion to cut off retreat and capture our boats. For a mile and a half, the creek was full of obstructions.

Heavy batteries were on its bank, supported by a large force, and to advance was impossible; to retreat seemed almost hopeless. The second night was passed on board the ship without sleep. The infantry had marched twenty-one miles without rest, but they, with their energetic leader, kept a successful watch of the boats and their valuable artillery.

At seven o'clock on the morning of the 22nd, General Sherman received a dispatch from Admiral Porter, stating his perilous condition, and he at once marched with his Second brigade, and a part of the First. About midday the enemy commenced moving upon the Union troops, with the purpose of reaching the bank of the creek below the gunboats and below the infantry. General Sherman was some six miles distant. The rebels had advanced with about 4,000 men, and came down with the intention of turning his right and reaching the creek below. The gunboats opened fire upon them, which embarrassed their movements and considerably retarded them. They debouched through the wood and became engaged with the skirmishers. The fight was beginning to be in good earnest, but the enemy were gaining ground. The object was to pass our forces, and not a battle. As soon as General Sherman heard the first firing of the gunboats, he urged his men forward, and after an hour's hard fighting, the advance came upon a body of the enemy who had passed by the force which had been engaged. Our troops immediately opened fire upon them, and the enemy after fighting for a short time gave way. They were driven back some two miles, and the gunboats opened upon them thus hemmed in, and the day was ours. The enemy retreated, and the gunboats were saved. Further advance being deemed impracticable, the boats at once commenced moving backward, and made several miles that evening.

The rebels next endeavored to pass around our lines in the afternoon and night, and bring their whole force still further below, but they found General Stuart's forces in their way, and abandoned the attempt to cut off the gunboats for that day. During the night and the afternoon of the next day, skirmishing ensued, and the troops who were now at Hill's plantation, waited for the rebels to appear; but they refused to give or receive battle, and our men embarked on transports and gunboats and returned to Miliken's Bend.

The following we copy from an account given by an eye-witness:

"Black Bayou, a narrow stream, heretofore, only navigated by dug-outs, was made the width of our steamers, with great labor of felling trees and sawing stumps below the surface. Every foot of our way was cut and torn through a dense forest, never before traversed by steamers. I never witnessed a more exciting and picturesque scene than the transportation, on the last day, of the Third brigade, by General Stuart. Crowded with men, the steamer, at the highest possible speed, pushed through overhanging trees, and short round curves. Sometimes wedged fast between trees, then sailing smoothly along, a huge cypress would reach out an arm and sweep the whole length of the boats, tearing guards and chimneys from the decks. The last trip through the Black Bayou was in a night pitchy dark and rainy.

"While the adventure was of uncertain success — when the result seemed almost accomplished, and when our gunboats were surrounded with an enemy confident of victory, and their extrication seemed almost an impossibility — officers and men worked with equal alacrity, whether in building bridges or making forced marches, both by day and night. The whole time was used in labor — constant and severe. It seems almost a miracle that the boats were saved. If Generals Sherman and Stuart, by their utmost exertions and labors, had forwarded their troops a single half day later, if the second forced march under General Sherman had been retarded a single hour, in all human probability the whole force would have been lost."

The advance upon Vicksburg by the Louisiana shore commenced shortly after this expedition.

In order to deceive the rebels as to the precise direction from which he proposed to attack Vicksburg, and to prevent reënforcements from being sent from Grand Gulf to that place, General Grant ordered some excellent feints to be made in all directions. One of these, made on the north, was conducted by General Sherman. His corps in moving from Milliken's Bend, had been set apart to bring up the rear—so that it was the last to start upon the southern march. General Sherman had made every preparation to move by April 26th, 1863, but receiving a letter from General Grant with orders to delay his march, he remained at Milliken's Bend, until the 29th.

On the 28th General Sherman received a letter in cypher, stating the time when General Grant proposed to attack Grand Gulf, and that could a feint be made on the enemy's batteries, near Haines' Bluff, on the Yazoo River, it would be most desirable, provided it could be done without the ill effect on the army and country of an appearance of a repulse. Accordingly General Sherman made the necessary orders, embarked the Second division on ten steam transports, and sailed for the Yazoo River.

On the morning of April 29th, he proceeded with this force to the mouth of the Yazoo River, where he found several vessels ready to coöperate with the feigned movement. The united forces at once proceeded up the river, and lay for the night of April 29th, at the mouth of the Chickasaw Bayou. At an early hour the next morning, the fleet passed up within easy range of the enemy's batteries. The gunboats immediately made an attack upon the works, and for four hours a brisk demonstration was kept up. At the expiration of this time the vessels were ordered out of range, and toward evening General Sherman disembarked his troops, in full view of the enemy, and made preparations as if to assault the works. The gunboats reöpened their fire upon the rebel defenses as soon as the landing was effected.

It could be distinctly seen that the enemy was deceived, as they were making every preparation to resist an attack. This was the fulfilment of the plan, and Sherman and his troops reëmbarked during the night. Similar movements were made the next day, and also reconnoissances of all the country on both sides of the Yazoo River.

Sherman received orders at this time to rejoin Grant at Grand Gulf, and ordered the two divisions which were at Milliken's Bend to march *via* Richmond, Louisiana, to a landing nearly opposite Grand Gulf, while he kept up the feint along the Yazoo. He then went down the river with the remainder of his troops to Young's Point, when the whole corps, with the exception of one division left behind as a garrison, marched to Hard Times, four miles above Grand Gulf, on the Louisiana shore, where it arrived the 6th of May, after having marched sixty-three miles. The troops were immediately taken across the Mississippi, and on the 8th commenced their march into the interior.

The Fifteenth Army Corps moved forward on the Edward's Station Road, and crossed the Fourteen Mile Creek at Dillon's plantation. Considerable skirmishing occurred while crossing the creek, but the rebels gave way, and the Union army moved on.

On the 12th of May, General Grant ordered them to move towards Raymond, and on the 14th, the Fifteenth and Seventeenth Corps advanced upon Jackson — the march being made during a heavy storm of rain. The roads were in a bad condition, but notwithstanding this, the troops marched in excellent order, nearly fourteen miles, and engaged the enemy about noon near Jackson.

When the movement was discovered by Johnston, who commanded the rebel forces at Jackson, he determined to delay the advance as long as possible, and meet them outside of the city, that he might have an opportunity to remove the property of the rebel government, then at Jackson. His forces being small in numbers, he ordered a feigned resistance to be made against the advance of the Fifteenth Army Corps by the turnpike road, with artillery and a small portion of infantry, while with the greater part of his army, he marched out on the Clinton Road, and about two miles and a half from the city engaged the Seventeenth Corps.

The skirmishers of the Fifteenth Corps drove the rebels into their rifle-pits, which had been thrown up just outside of the city. General Sherman, by a reconnoissance to his right, soon discovered the weakness of the enemy, and this flank movement caused an evacuation of the rebel position on that part of their line.

In the meantime the Seventeenth Corps engaged the main portion of the enemy's force from Jackson, and after a spirited contest, for more than two hours, defeated them, the rebels retreating northward along the Canton Road.

After the army had taken possession of Jackson, May 14th, General Grant learned that Johnston had ordered Pemberton peremptorily to move out of Vicksburg and attack General Grant's forces in the rear. He at once ordered General Blair's division, of the Fifteenth Army Corps, to move with the Thirteenth Corps toward Bolton, with a view of marching upon Edwards' Station. The remainder of the Fifteenth Corps was left at Jackson to destroy everything that could be used by the enemy in a hostile manner. On the following morning General Grant ordered General Sherman to bring forward his entire command at once, and to move with all possible speed until he came up with the main forces at Bolton. The battle of Champion Hills, or Baker's Creek, was fought on the 16th by Hovey's division of McClernand's corps, and Logan's and Quinby's divisions (the latter commanded by Brigadier General M. M. Crocker), of McPherson's corps.

Orders were now sent back to General Sherman to turn his corps toward Bridgeport, on the Black River, some miles north of the railroad, and to General Blair to join him at that place. By crossing the river at that point, General Sherman would be on the flank of the enemy if they made a stand at the railroad crossing of the river. On the evening of the 17th he reached Bridgeport, and by the following morning had crossed the river upon pontoon bridges, and was ready to march upon Vicksburg. The rebels having set fire to the railroad bridge, Generals McClernand and McPherson crossed their troops on the morning of the 18th on floating bridges made the previous night, General Sherman having the only pontoon train with him.

From General Grant's official report, we learn that the march was commenced by Sherman at an early hour, by the Bridgeport and Vicksburg Road, turning to the right when within three miles and a half of Vicksburg, to get possession of Walnut Hills and the Yazoo River. This was successfully accomplished before the night of the 18th. McPherson crossed Black River above the Jackson Road, and came into the same road with Sherman, but to his rear. He arrived after nightfall with his advance to where Sherman turned to the right. McClernand moved by the Jackson and Vicksburg Road to Mount Albans, and then turned to the left to get into Baldwin's Ferry Road. By this disposition the three army corps covered all the ground their strength would admit of, and by the morning of the 19th the investment of Vicksburg was made as complete as could be by the forces at his (Grant's) command.

During the day there was continuous skirmishing, and the commanding general was not without hopes of carrying the enemy's works. Relying upon the demoralization of the enemy, in consequence of repeated defeats outside of Vicksburg, General Grant ordered a general assault at two P. M.

The Fifteenth Army Corps, having arrived in front of the enemy's works in time on the 18th to get a good position, were enabled to make a vigorous assault. The Thirteenth and Seventeenth Corps succeeded no further than to gain advanced positions, covered from the fire of the enemy. The two days following were spent in perfecting communications with our supplies.

On the 21st, orders were issued for a general assault upon the whole line, to commence at 10 A. M. on the 22d. All the corps commanders set their time by that of the commanding general, that there should be no difference between them in movement of assault. Promptly at the hour designated the three army corps then in front of the enemy's works commenced the assault. General Grant took a commanding position near McPherson's front, and from which he could see all the advancing columns from his corps, and a portion of each of Sherman's and McClernand's. A portion of the commands of each succeeded in planting their flags on the outer slopes of the enemy's bastions, and maintained them there until night. Each corps had many more men than could possibly be used in the assault, over such ground as intervened between them and the enemy. More men could only avail in case of breaking through the enemy's lines, or in repelling a sortie. The assault was gallant in the extreme on the part of all the troops, but the enemy's position was too strong, both naturally and artificially, to be taken in that way.

The assault of this day proved the quality of the soldiers of this army. Without entire success, and with heavy loss, there was no murmuring or complaining, no falling back, nor other evidence of demoralization.

From the 22d of May until the 25th of June no attempt upon the city of any serious nature was made, with the exception of the attack of the gunboat Cincinnati, for the purpose of silencing one of the land batteries.

The progress of the mining operations was such that a fort on the right of the Jackson Road was blown up on the 25th of June.

After the failure of the 22d, General Grant determined upon a regular siege. The troops, now being fully awake to the necessities of this, worked diligently and cheerfully. The work progressed rapidly and satisfactorily until the 3d of July, when all was about ready for a final assault.

On the afternoon of the 3d of July a letter was received from Lieutenant General Pemberton, commanding the Confederate forces at Vicksburg, proposing an armistice, and the appointment of commissioners to arrange terms for the capitulation·

of the place. The correspondence resulted in the surrender of the city and garrison of Vicksburg at 10 o'clock A. M., July 4th, 1863.

The rebel General Johnston crossed the Big Black River with a portion of his force, and every thing indicated that he would make an attack about the 25th of June. The position of the Union army in front of Vicksburg having been made as strong against a sortie from the enemy as his works were against an assault, General Sherman was placed in command of all troops designated to look after Johnston.

About two weeks before the surrender of Vicksburg, Johnston threatened the rear of the besieging army with a large rebel force. Grant at once sent the following message to General Sherman: "You must whip Johnston fifteen miles from here." But Johnston drew back upon Jackson, and Sherman was notified to be ready to march against the latter place on the 6th of July. Grant, in his official report, says: "I placed Major General Sherman in command of all the troops designated to look after Johnston. Johnston, however, not attacking, I determined to attack him the moment Vicksburg was in our possession, and accordingly notified Sherman that I would again make an assault on Vicksburg at daylight of the 6th, and for him to have up supplies of all descriptions ready to move upon receipt of orders, if the assault should prove a success. His preparations were immediately made, and when the place surrendered on the 4th, two days earlier than I had fixed for the attack, Sherman was found ready, and moved at once with a force increased by the remainder of both the Thirteenth and Fifteenth Army Corps, and is at present (July 6th) investing Jackson, where Johnston has made a stand."

General Sherman was now intrusted with the greater part of Grant's army, and his movements were made so quickly that General Grant telegraphed to Washington, July 12th: "General Sherman has Jackson invested from Pearl River on the north to the same river on the south. This has cut off many hundred cars from the Confederacy. Sherman says he has force enough, and feels no apprehension about the result."

On the 11th of July, General Sherman sent out a company of cavalry on a foraging expedition, and during the trip they ascertained that the extensive library belonging to Jeff. Davis was secreted in a house near by. The cavalry at once proceeded to the house and found thousands of volumes of books and several bushels of private and political papers belonging to the rebel President, written by persons North and South who had been engaged in the plot of inciting the rebellion. They also found many valuable gold-headed walking canes, one of them presented to Davis by Franklin Pierce.

On the 12th of July, General Sherman sent a battalion of cavalry on an expedition east of Jackson, about fifteen miles, in order to destroy the railroad bridges, culverts, rolling stock, or anything else that would be of use to the rebels.

On the following day the rebels made a sudden and heavy sortie from their works, and advanced their infantry and artillery against the right of the line, with the intention of breaking it. The advance was made under cover of a dense fog, but they found Sherman prepared, and were met with a determined resistance. General Johnston, on the night of the 16th of July, hastily evacuated the city and retreated toward the east. Sherman at once dispatched expeditions in all directions for the purpose of destroying railroads, bridges, water-tanks, and other valuable property belonging to the enemy.

Under date of July 23d, 1863, General Grant says:

"I would respectfully, but urgently, recommend Major General W. T. Sherman, now commanding the Fifteenth Army Corps, to the position of Brigadier General in the Regular Army.

"To General Sherman I am greatly indebted

for his promptness in forwarding to me, during the siege of Fort Donelson, reënforcements and supplies from Paducah. At the battle of Shiloh, on the first day he held with raw troops the key-point to the landing. To his individual efforts I am indebted for the success of that battle. Twice hit, and several (I think three) horses shot under him on that day, he maintained his position with raw troops. It is no disparagement to any other officer to say that I do not believe there was another division commander on the field who had the skill and experience to have done it. His services as division commander in the advance on Corinth, I will venture to say, were appreciated by the new General-in-chief beyond those of any other division commander.

"General Sherman's arrangement as commander of troops in the attack on Chickasaw Bluffs, last December, was admirable; seeing the ground from the opposite side from the attack, I saw the impossibility of making it successful. The conception of the attack on Arkansas Post was General Sherman's. His part of the execution, no one denies, was as good as it possibly could have been. His demonstration at Haines' Bluff, in April, to hold the enemy about Vicksburg, while the army was securing a foothold east of the Mississippi; his rapid marches to join the army afterwards; his management at Jackson, Miss., in the first attack; his almost unequaled march from Jackson to Bridgeport, and passage of Black River; his securing Walnut Hills on the 18th of May, and thus opening communications with our supplies, all attest his great merit as a soldier. The siege of Vicksburg and last capture of Jackson and dispersion of Johnston's army, entitle General Sherman to more credit than usually falls to the lot of one man to earn. The promotion of such men as Sherman always adds strength to our arms."

CHAPTER VI.

SHERMAN'S GREAT MARCH TO CHATTANOOGA, AND THE BATTLES OF MISSIONARY RIDGE AND LOOKOUT MOUNTAIN.

BRIEF REST OF SHERMAN'S COMMAND — STARTS FOR CHATTANOOGA — NARROW ESCAPE OF SHERMAN — THE FIGHT AT CANE CREEK — TAKES COMMAND OF THE ARMY OF THE TENNESSEE — ARRIVES AT CHATTANOOGA — BATTLE BEFORE CHATTANOOGA — FIRST DAY'S BATTLE — SECOND DAY — BATTLE OF LOOKOUT MOUNTAIN, THIRD DAY — ACCOUNT OF AN EYE WITNESS OF THE BATTLE OF TUNNEL HILL — BATTLE OF MISSIONARY RIDGE — INCIDENTS.

After the occupation of Jackson by the Union army, Sherman and his men enjoyed a brief rest. The Fifteenth Corps during the month of September was in camp along the Big Black River, guarding the region east of Vicksburg. Sherman received a telegram from Grant on the 22d of September to immediately send a division to reënforce Rosecrans, who had just lost an important and severe battle with Bragg near Chattanooga. At four o'clock P. M. of the same day Osterhaus' division was on the road. On the 23d Sherman was summoned to follow with the remainder of his corps, and his troops, which were always in readiness, started instantly. He was on his way to Memphis on the 27th, followed by a fleet of boats transporting his two divisions. On account of the low water in the Mississippi, and the scarcity of fuel, the voyage was very slow, but with his usual energy, Sherman supplied the lack of fuel by frequently landing and gathering fence-rails, and hauling wood in wagons from the interior to the boats. They reached Memphis on the 2d, 3d and 4th of October, and Osterhaus' division was at that time in front of Corinth.

Sherman received orders from General Halleck at Memphis to transport his corps and all other available troops in his vicinity to Athens, Ala., to repair the railroad, and to depend on himself for supplies of all kinds. Although the men were immediately ordered to work day and night on the railroad, Sherman saw that his troops could move faster by road under escort, and accordingly moved his entire Fourth division by land.

The enemy were considerably alarmed by this eastward movement, and a body of rebel cavalry and infantry had concentrated at Salem and Tuscumbia, with the intention of thwarting it, and, if possible, put a stop to Sherman joining Rosecrans. A body of cavalry and infantry four thousand strong, besides a number of pieces of artillery, under Colonel Chalmers, made their appearance upon the railroad, several miles beyond Colliersville, on the morning of October 11th. As soon as the regular passenger train, which the enemy had allowed to pass, although in his power, had run by, the track was torn up in several places and the ties stacked upon the road and fired. General Sherman and staff, accompanied by his bodyguard, a battalion of the Thirteenth infantry (his own regiment), started the same day on a special train, and upon approaching the fires, the troops on board prepared for an attack, though they did not disembark. On approaching Colliersville, which was defended by a few troops in a stockade, the train was fired upon, as was expected, wounding several persons. It was soon discovered that Chalmers was investing the place, and General Sherman ordered his regulars to charge directly upon the enemy, in order to cover the transit of the United States troops to the train, causing the rebels to flee in all directions in a perfect panic. The Union troops then succeeded in taking refuge within the stockade, and acted entirely on the defensive.

Before General Sherman's arrival, the little garrison had engaged the enemy in a severe conflict, and at the time of his appearance they had been overwhelmed and driven within the fortifications of the place. Fighting continued but a short time after the timely arrival of Sherman, though while it did the General took an active part among the men, and had much to do with keeping up their spirits. The troops reached Corinth on the night of the 12th, and Sherman immediately sent General Blair to Iuka with the First division, sending the troops as fast as they came up to Bear Creek, a few miles east of Iuka.

Sherman, foreseeing the difficulty in crossing the Tennessee, had written to Admiral Porter at Cairo to send up gun-boats as soon as the water would permit, and to General Allen at St. Louis to dispatch a ferry-boat to Eastport, which requests were promptly complied with. He continued, in accordance with orders, to work at the railroad, protecting his working parties from the enemy's attacks. He dispatched Blair with two divisions at the same time, to rout the enemy from Tuscumbia, where they were encamped, five thousand strong, under Stephen Lee. They succeeded in driving the rebels from their position, after a severe fight at Cane Creek; and occupied Tuscumbia on the 27th of October.

In the mean time General Grant had been placed in command of the three great armies of the Ohio, the Cumberland and the Tennessee, and he at once put Sherman in command of the latter, Grant's former department. Sherman heard of this at Iuka, and recognized his new command. He sent Ewing, on the day of the fight at Cane Creek, with a division to cross the Tennessee, and move as rapidly as possible to Eastport, which he did. A messenger from General Grant came down the Tennessee over the Muscle Shoals the same day, with an order to "drop all work on the railroad east of Bear Creek," and push on to Bridgeport, which message exactly suited Sherman. This was at once executed, and the march resumed, all the columns bearing toward Eastport, the only practicable plan of crossing the Tennessee. Sherman himself crossed on the 1st of November, passed to the head of the column, leaving General Blair in charge of the rear, and marched to Rogersville and the Elk River. But he found the river impassable, and as there was no time for ferrying or building a bridge, there seemed no alternative but the long march to Fayetteville, and then to Bridgeport. This march accomplished, the route for each sub-command was prescribed, and General Sherman hurried in person to Bridgeport, and telegraphed to General Grant the position of his various divisions.

On the 15th of November the head of General Sherman's column arrived at Chattanooga, where they formed a junction with the forces under General Thomas, on the right of the main army.

General Grant received him very cordially, and at once ordered him to cross the Tennessee with his troops, effect a lodgment on the terminus of Missionary Ridge, and with a part of his command to make a demonstration against Lookout Mountain. Although his men were nearly exhausted with an almost superhuman march, Sherman says: "I saw enough of the condition of men and animals in Chattanooga to inspire me with renewed energy." He at once directed Ewing's division to make the intended demonstration, and returned himself to Bridgeport, rowing a boat down the Tennessee from Kelly's, and upon arriving instantly started his other divisions in the order they had arrived. The roads were in a most wretched condition, and it was only by the most incessant labor day and night that he succeeded in getting three divisions concealed behind the hills opposite the mouth of the Chickamauga, on the 23d of November. His Fourth division was left behind at Hooker's camp, on account of the breaking of Brown's Ferry Bridge, and it acted against Lookout Mountain. He moved a small force silently along the river the same night, capturing every guard of the enemy's picket of twenty men, except one. Eight thousand men were on the east bank of the Tennessee by daylight of November 24th, and had succeeded in throwing up a secure rifle trench. A pontoon bridge thirteen hundred and fifty feet long was begun immediately, and at one o'clock was completed, and the three divisions marched across, and up from the river, skillfully arranged for deployment to the right on meeting the enemy. Nature seemed to favor them, for a light drizzling rain and low hanging clouds completely covered these movements, so that at half past three P. M., the desired position on Missionary Ridge was gained. They pushed quickly up the hill, surprised the enemy, and held the hill in their possession. The enemy showed his chagrin at finding himself flanked and outmanœuvered so completely by the Union troops by brisk artillery and musketry firing; but our artillery, dragged up the steep ascent, in a sharp engagement quickly silenced him. The second spur of the ridge still beyond, was now seen to be the chief objective point. The present position was strongly intrenched at once, and at midnight orders were received to attack the enemy at dawn. The plan of the battle was for Hooker to hold the enemy at Lookout Mountain, and if possible carry it, and Sherman was to vigorously assault Missionary Ridge, which was their vital point, and the enemy would concentrate his forces to defend it. This would leave his centre weak, and Thomas would rush upon it, and penetrate it. To many who looked up at the frowning and precipitous heights which almost towered into the clouds, above Chattanooga, with rebel works covered thick with artillery, the idea of carrying them seemed but little short of madness, although the plan was simple and plausible, and proved in the end successful. The rebels — so secure did they feel — had sent out Longstreet's entire corps to Knoxville, where it closely besieged the forces under Burnside. "By half-past three P. M., of the 24th," says Grant, "the whole of the northern extremity of Missionary Ridge, to near the tunnel, was in Sherman's possession. During the night he fortified the position thus secured, making it equal, if not superior, in strength to that held by the enemy."

From a correspondent of the New York *Herald*, Mr. W. F. G. Shanks, an eye-witness, we have the following:

"Tuesday morning, November 24th, was gloomy, threatening rain, and until quite late our forces remained inactive. The day was chosen for operations on the flanks, and for that purpose Hooker and Sherman began to move quite early.

"Learning that General Sherman's position was not over two miles and a half distant, from where he was stationed, General Howard sent one of his staff on the dangerous mission of finding General Sherman, alone. The skirmishers were then thrown forward until the line became dangerously extended, and none of General Sherman's troops were found. The staff-officer departed on his mission of danger; but by keeping close to the river, succeeded in crossing and recrossing the gap without being captured. General Howard, on receiving his report, ordered his division to push further to the left, and started out to seek General Sherman. I pursued the same route and soon found General Sherman's troops, and was standing on the unfinished pontoon bridge which General Sherman was building, when General Howard came up. The last boat of the bridge was being placed in the centre of the stream as General Howard arrived, and introduced himself across the slight gulf between the two. Sherman, on the north end of the bridge, dressed loosely, with a worn overcoat thrown around him, was directing the completion of the bridge; and as soon as the boat was put in, sprang over and shook the hand of the princely Howard. It was exactly at noon.

"I found on inquiry, that General Sherman had at an early hour thrown a portion of one of his divisions across the river, under the protection of a battery, and subsequently the other divisions, the greater portion being crossed by the steamer Dunbar, which, captured two months ago at Chattanooga, had been repaired, and was now serving good and loyal purposes. Immediately on arriving he had thrown up strong rifle-pits in two lines, covering the approach to the bridge, and adding much strength to a naturally strong position. The troops of his corps, at the hour of noon, held these works and were waiting for a division of the Fourteenth Corps, to cross the river and take up position in the works. This division had been sent to General Sherman in place of Osterhaus, who was acting with General Hooker, and was now being used by Sherman as a reserve.

"This division crossed the river, and went into line within the works about an hour after the meeting between Howard and Sherman. At the same moment General Sherman gave his orders to prepare for an attack. By this hour, one o'clock P. M., the drizzly rain, which had been threatening us, began to fall, and the object of the assault was soon hid from view. General Sherman stood on a prominent hill to the left of the pontoon bridge, and having succeeded, with the aid of two orderlies, and in despite of the rain, in lighting a cigar, stood puffing away at one end, chewing at the other, and observing all that could be seen in the country before him. Around him were gathered at this time Generals Frank Blair, Morgan L. Smith, Ewing, John W. Corse, and Howard. The troops of the several divisions were encamped

just in front of him, while on the left and rear
Davis' artillery was thundering over the bridge.

"In a very quiet tone Sherman gave his orders
to form for an assault, remarking that the enemy
was reported heavy in his front. The formation,
as ordered, was *echelon* on the left, General Morgan
L. Smith's division being the left, John E. Smith's
the centre, and Ewing's the right. The left was to
keep well toward Chickamauga Creek; 'and,'
added Sherman, 'I want you to keep up the formation, four hundred yards distance, until you get
to the foot of the hill.'

"'And shall we keep it after that?' asked Gen.
Ewing.

"'You may go up the hill,' answered Sherman,
'if you like, and can.'

"General Davis having got into position, and the
troops having been arranged as ordered, General
Sherman gave the orders to move to the assault.
They were couched in very common terms; but
which ought to be preserved? "I see Davis is up.
I guess you may as well go on and take the hill."
In a few moments the three columns were moving.

* * * * * * * *

But it was not destined that Tuesday should
witness a conflict for these hills. General Sherman
had anticipated skirmishing before reaching the
foot of the mountain, it having been reported by

citizens that the enemy held the position in strong force. But the foot of the hill was reached, after a short delay, without any serious skirmishing, only a few shells from Tunnel Hill passed over our heads, and exploded among the colored pioneers, who followed in our rear, doing no damage, but causing the negroes to lose all respect for orders to 'close up.'

"The enemy made no opposition to the occupation of the extreme end of the ridge. General Sherman was in possession of this at about four o'clock P. M. It then appeared that the hills occupied were separated from Mission Ridge by a narrow valley, through which the railroad runs.

"The hills occupied by Sherman were three in number, and semi-circular in shape, bending around and north of the end of Mission Ridge. The end of the ridge is generally and very properly called Tunnel Hill. It overlooks and commands the hills of which General Sherman found himself in peaceable possession; and, on examination, he found that the labor still remained to be done. A close inspection of the ground and the enemy's position determined Sherman to occupy the semi-circular ridge with his centre and right, and throw his left still further to the left, and in the region of Myer's Mill. The division moved promptly to this position, and took possession of the valley from the foot of the hills to Chickamauga River, securing at the time about one hundred rebels engaged in building rafts of fallen timber, with which to destroy our pontoon bridges.

"General Sherman ordered the erection of defenses on the ridge he had occupied, and finding he did not propose to push further during the little of daylight left him, I left his corps and proceeded to join that of General Hooker.

"Daylight on Wednesday morning revealed the signal flags waving over Lookout, and the artillery of Sherman opening from his position on Fort Buckner. I had seen General Rawlins, of Grant's staff, dash away a few minutes before towards Fort Wood, and knowing that he had gone to fire the signal for the assault, I hurried off to see Sherman's fight."

In the morning's dim light, before dawn, Sherman had made the entire tour of his position, and his quick eye perceived that a deep valley lay between him and the precipitous sides of the next hill in the series, which was only partially cleared, and of which the crest was narrow and wooded. The enemy held the further point of the hill, with a strong breastwork of logs and fresh earth, crowded with men, and carrying two guns. He appeared in greater force on a still higher hill beyond the enemy, and had a fair fire on the intermediate hill in dispute. From Sherman's position the gorge between these two latter hills, through which passes the railroad tunnel, could not be seen, but it formed the natural *place d' armes*, where the enemy covered his forces to resist our turning his right flank, and thus endangering his communications with the Chickamauga Depot.

The advance was led by General Corse. "And," says Sherman, "the sun had hardly risen before his bugle sounded the 'Forward.'" Briskly down into the valley and up the steep sides of the hill in front moved Corse's men, and succeeded in carrying a sort of secondary crest on the enemy's hill, which, however, was swept with a murderous fire from the breastworks in front. A bloody and desperate conflict now raged for more than an hour, the line of Union troops now swaying up very near to the breastwork, as though it would entirely engulf it, and then dashed back, receding to its first conquest. Sherman's left on the outer spur of the ridge, and his right abreast of the tunnel, were hotly engaged, and drew the enemy's fire in part from the assaulting party on the hill-crest. The fight raged most furiously about ten o'clock A. M., and General Corse was severely wounded. Two brigades were sent up as reënforcements, but, owing to the crowded condition of the crest, they were obliged to fall away to the west of the hill. The heavy masses of the enemy in the gorge could now be seen moving out on their right and rear, under cover of the thick undergrowth. The two brigades which came up the hill last were so suddenly overwhelmed that they fell back in some confusion to the lower edge of the field, where they formed again in good order. The attacking column was still stubbornly held by General Corse, Colonel Loomis and General M. L. Smith. Of these General Grant says: "The assaulting column advanced to the very rifle-pits of the enemy, and held their position firmly and without wavering." The enemy showed some signs of pursuit when the two supporting brigades fell back, but by the well-directed fire of one brigade on the wooden crest, he was caught in flank, and hastily sought his cover behind the hill.

This incessant and desperate attack of Sherman, which proved so triumphantly successful, was directed against the enemy's most northern and vital point, and was vigorously continued all day. Sherman not only threatened the right flank of the enemy, but also his rear and stores at Chickamauga. "At three P. M. column after column of the enemy was streaming towards me," writes Sherman; "gun after gun poured its concentric shot on us from every hill and spur that gave a view of any part of the ground." He waited long and anxiously for the centre to open its part of the contest, in the meanwhile holding stubbornly to his bloody ridge under murderous fire. Grant knowing the importance of this key-point, sent a division to Sherman's support, but it was sent back by him, with word that "he had all the force necessary." "Discovering that the enemy," says Grant, "in his desperation to defeat or resist the progress, was weakening his centre on Missionary Ridge, determined me to order the advance at once." The order was given, and gallantly executed. The rebel forces against which Sherman was contending, to their dismay, now found Thomas on their left flank, and their centre broken in. They turned, but all too late, for the white line of Thomas' musketry swept up from ridge to ridge, and Bragg's army fell back, defeated, into the valleys of Georgia.

The storming of Missionary Ridge is thus described by an eye witness: *

"And still the Union troops passed on, scaling unwaveringly the sides of Missionary Ridge. The blood of their comrades renders their footsteps slippery; the toil of the ascent almost takes away their breath; the rebel musketry and artillery mow down their thinned ranks—but still they press on! Not once do they even seem to waver. The color

---

* Correspondence of the Cincinnati Gazette.

bearers press ahead, and plant their flags far in advance of the troops; and at last, oh, moment of supremest triumph, they reach the crest, and rush like an avalanche upon the astonished foe. Whole regiments throw down their arms and surrender, the rebel artillerists are bayoneted by their guns, and the cannons which had a moment before been thundering on the Union ranks are now turned about, pouring death and terror into the midst of the mass of miserable fugitives who are rushing down the eastern slope of the ridge."

INCIDENTS CONNECTED WITH THE BATTLE OF MISSIONARY RIDGE.

Our troops met one loyal welcome on the height. How the Tennessean that gave it managed to get there nobody knows, but there he was, grasping a colonel's hand, and saying, while the tears ran down his face, "God be thanked! I knew the Yankees would fight!"

A little German in Wood's division is pierced like the lid of a pepper-box, but he is neither dead nor wounded. "See here," he says, rushing up to a comrade, "a pullet hit te preach of mine gun, a pullet in mine pocket-book, a pullet in mine coat-tail—they shoots me tree, five time, and I gives them ——; yet!"*

---
* Mr. B. F. Taylor's correspondence to the Chicago Journal.

We glean the following from a private letter from an officer:

"The charge of the army on Missionary Ridge astounded Bragg. Breckinridge's head-quarters were on the ridge, in full view of our troops. A lady who lives there related the following: 'Before you all came up here, I asked General Bragg, 'What are you going to do with me, general?' He says to me, 'Lord! madam, *the Yankees will never dare to come up here.*' 'And,' she added, with a blubber, 'it was not fifteen minutes until you were all around here.'"

CHAPTER VII.

SHERMAN AND THE SIEGE OF KNOXVILLE, AND THE EXPEDITION THROUGH MISSISSIPPI.

PURSUIT OF THE ENEMY AFTER THE BATTLE OF MISSIONARY RIDGE — MARCH TO KNOXVILLE TO RELIEVE BURNSIDE — RETURNS TO CHATTANOOGA — AT MEMPHIS — LETTER OF SHERMAN — EXPEDITION THROUGH MISSISSIPPI — INCIDENT.

The greater part of the struggle was over, but other work yet remained to be done. The same night that witnessed our success found Sherman pursuing the flying columns of the enemy. Having sent out his skirmishers and finding that the enemy had given way, he sent a division after him to the dépôt, and at four o'clock A. M., followed with a part of Major-General Howard's Eleventh Corps.

While at the dépôt, General Sherman, with other officers, assisted in putting out a portion of the fire around the railroad platform, as the rebels before leaving had set fire to the dépôt. As the column moved forward, they came upon wagons, guns, caissons, forage, stores, pontoons, and all the ruins of a defeated army, and an abandoned camp.

They met with but little opposition until nearly dark on the 26th, when as they emerged out of some low swampy land, the enemy opened fire upon them with musketry and artillery from a low hill. A sharp fight ensued, lasting nearly an hour, when they drove the enemy from the field. Their killed and wounded were left in our hands.

The next day all three armies passed on to Graysville, Thomas and Hooker sharing with Sherman the marching and fighting. Sherman in the meantime detached Howard to move against the railroad between Dalton and Cleveland and destroy it, which was soon done and the communication thereby cut between Bragg and Longstreet. He continued his march to Ringgold, where he found Grant. The enemy had been driven from Tennessee, and Sherman was now ordered to move leisurely back to Chattanooga. He destroyed the railroad on the next day from half-way between Graysville and Ringgold to the State line, and with General Grant's consent, instead of returning to Chattanooga, he sent back all his artillery, wagons, and impediments, and made a circuit by the north as far as Hiawassee, resulting in the destruction of more railroad and the capture of more stores.

"This," says Sherman, "was to have been the limit of our journey. Officers and men had brought no baggage or provisions, and the weather was bitter cold." But Grant had received an urgent appeal from General Burnside for relief, stating that his supplies could not last longer than the 3d of December, and nothing but the utmost energy would save Knoxville and its gallant commander. Grant had already ordered General Granger thither, but he had not as yet started, and the commanding general determined, notwithstanding the fact that two divisions of Sherman's forces had marched from Memphis and gone into battle immediately on their arrival at Chattanooga, to send him with his command. And General Sherman accordingly received command of all the troops designed for relieving Knoxville, including Granger's.

"Seven days before," writes Sherman, "we had left our camps on the other side of the Tennessee, with two days rations, without a change of clothing, stripped for the fight, with but a single blanket or coat per man, from myself to the private included. Of course, we then had no provisions, save what we gathered by the road, and were ill supplied for such a march. But we learned that twelve thousand of our fellow soldiers were beleaguered in the mountain town of Knoxville, eighty-four miles distant, that they needed relief, and must have it in three days. This was enough; and it had to be done."

Howard planked and repaired the railroad bridge that night, and at daybreak the army passed the Hiawassee and marched to Athens, fifteen miles. On the 2d of December the Union forces hurried towards London, twenty-six miles distant, the cavalry pushing ahead to save the pontoon-bridge across the Tennessee, held by Vaughn's brigade of the enemy. They moved with their usual rapidity, and succeeded in capturing every picket, but found Vaughn strongly posted in earth-works with artillery in position. They were obliged to wait till night, when Howard's infantry came up. The enemy retreated during the night, destroying the pontoons, running three locomotives and forty-eight cars into the Tennessee, and leaving for our army to capture a large quantity of provisions, four guns, and other property.

But one day of the three alloted Sherman's forces to reach Knoxville remained, and the bridge was gone. Sherman therefore sent word the same night to Colonel Long, commanding the cavalry brigade, that Burnside must know before the next night of his approach — ordered him to select his best material, to start at once for Knoxville, ford the Little Tennessee, and "at whatever cost of life or horse-flesh," to push into Knoxville. The road was the worst that could be imagined, and the distance to be traveled forty miles. They were on the road before dawn, and at daylight the Fifteenth Corps was turned from Philadelphia to Morgantown, but even here they found the Little Tennessee too deep for fording. General Wilson skillfully extemporized a bridge,—"working partly with crib-work and partly with square trestles made of the houses of the late town of Morgantown," and the bridge was ready and the troops passing by dark of December 4th. The welcome message came the next morning from Burnside, dated December 4th, that Long's cavalry had reached Knoxville on the night before, and all was well. The bridge had given away just before the reception of this news, causing delay, but it was soon mended, and the forced march continued, until the night of the 5th. Arriving at Marysville, a staff officer of General Burnside rode up and announced that Longstreet had raised the siege the night before. Sherman sent forward Granger's two divisions to Knoxville, and ordered the remainder of his army to halt and rest; for their work was accomplished.

From Marysville General Sherman rode to Knoxville, where he met General Burnside, and while there, received the following letter:

KNOXVILLE, December 7th, 1863.

To MAJOR-GENERAL SHERMAN:—

I desire to express to you and your command my most hearty thanks and gratitude for your promptness in coming to our relief during the siege of Knoxville, and am satisfied your approach served to raise the siege.

A. E. BURNSIDE, Major-General.

Knoxville being saved, it seemed best for Sherman's army, with the exception of Granger's two divisions, to support the suspended movement against Bragg, and they leisurely retraced their steps to Chattanooga. After an easy march of four days, we find them again at Chattanooga. The three months' campaign just ended was a most arduous one, Sherman's losses amounting to over two thousand men. In Sherman's official report, he states that the men under his command had marched for long periods, without regular rations or supplies of any kind, through mud and over rocks, sometimes barefooted, without a murmur. After a march of four hundred miles, without a moment's rest, and no sleep for three nights, they crossed the Tennessee River, fought their part in the battle of Chattanooga, pursued the enemy out of Tennessee, then turned and marched more than one hundred miles north, and compelled Longstreet to raise the siege of Knoxville, which had caused so much anxiety all over the country.

Soon after, while at Memphis, on his way to Vicksburg, General Sherman was honored with a magnificent dinner, at which time he paid General Grant a high compliment for his coolness and bravery.

He arrived at Vicksburg shortly after, and while there wrote an able and lengthy letter on the proper treatment of disloyal people in conquered territory, some extracts from which we subjoin:

"The war which now prevails in our land is essentially a war of races. The Southern people entered into a clear compact of government, but still maintained a species of separate interests, history, and prejudices. These latter became stronger and stronger, till they have led to a war which has devolved fruits of the bitterest kind.

"We of the North are, beyond all question, right in our lawful cause, but we are not bound to ignore the fact that the people of the South have prejudices, which form a part of their nature, and which they cannot throw off without an effort of reason or the slower process of natural change. Now, the question arises, should we treat as absolute enemies all in the South who differ from us in opinion or prejudice—kill or banish them? or should we give them time to think and gradually change their conduct, so as to conform to the new order of things which is slowly and gradually creeping into their country?

"When men take arms to resist our rightful authority, we are compelled to use force, because all reason and argument cease when arms are resorted to. When the provisions, forage, horses, mules, wagons, &c., are used by our enemy, it is clearly our duty and right to take them, because otherwise they might be used against us.

"In like manner, all houses left vacant by an inimical people are clearly our right, or such as are needed as storehouses, hospitals and quarters. But a question arises as to dwellings used by women, children and non-combatants. So long as non-combatants remain in their houses and keep to their accustomed business, their opinions and prejudices can in no wise influence the war, and, therefore, should not be noticed. But if any one comes out into the public streets and creates disorder, he or she should be punished, restrained, or banished, either to the rear or front, as the officer in command adjudges. If the people, or any of them, keep up a correspondence with parties in hostility, they are spies, and can be punished with death, or minor punishment.

"These are well-established principles of war, and the people of the South, having appealed to war, are barred from appealing to our Constitution, which they have practically and publicly defied. They have appealed to war, and must abide *its* rules and laws. The United States, as a belligerent party claiming right in the soil as the ultimate sovereign, have a right to change the population, and it may be, and is, both politic and just we should do so in certain districts. When the inhabitants persist too long in hostility, it may be both politic and right we should banish them and appropriate their lands to a more loyal and useful population. No man will deny that the United States would be benefitted by dispossessing a single prejudiced, hard-headed and disloyal planter, and substituting in his place a dozen or more patient, industrious, good families, even if they be of foreign birth. I think it does good to present this view of the case to many Southern gentlemen, who grew rich and wealthy, not by virtue alone of their industry and skill, but by reason of the protection and impetus to prosperity given by our hitherto moderate and magnanimous Government. It is all idle nonsense for these Southern planters to say that they made the South, that they own it, and that they can do as they please — even to break up our Government and to shut up the natural avenues of trade, intercourse and commerce.

* * * * * * * *

"Whilst I assert for our Government the highest military prerogatives, I am willing to bear in patience that political nonsense of slave rights, State rights, freedom of conscience, freedom of press, and such other trash, as have deluded the Southern people into war, anarchy, bloodshed, and the foulest crimes that have disgraced any time or any people.

"I would advise the commanding officers at Huntsville, and such other towns as are occupied by our troops, to assemble the inhabitants and explain to them these plain, self-evident propositions, and tell them that it is for them *now* to say whether they and their children shall inherit the beautiful land which by the accident of nature has fallen to their share. The Government of the United States has in North Alabama any and all rights which they choose to enforce in war—to take their lives, their homes, their lands, their everything; because they cannot deny that war does exist there; and war is simply power, unrestrained by Constitution or compact. If they want eternal war, well and good: we will accept the issue and dispossess them and put our friends in possession. I know thousands and millions of good people who, at simple notice, would come to North Alabama and accept the elegant houses and plantations now there. If the people of Huntsville think different, let them persist in war three years longer, and then they will not be consulted. Three years ago, by a little reflection and patience, they could have a hundred years of peace and prosperity, but they preferred war. Very well. Last year they could have saved their slaves, but now it is too late: all the powers of earth cannot restore to them their slaves, any more than their dead grandfathers. Next year their lands will be taken — for in war we can take them, and *rightfully* too — and in another year they may beg in vain for their lives. A people who will persevere in war beyond a certain limit, ought to know the consequences. Many, many people, with less pertinacity than the South, have been wiped out of national existence."

Before leaving Memphis for Vicksburg, Sherman ordered General W. S. Smith, with eight thousand cavalry to start from Memphis on the 1st of February, with instructions to move down to Meridian, destroy the enemy's railroads, and meet him at that point. They failed however to commence their movement at the proper time, and did not start until the 11th of February.

General Sherman, with a force of about twenty thousand infantry and twelve hundred cavalry, and a wagon train carrying twenty days rations — pushed boldly from Vicksburg on the 3d of February, holding no line of communication, but cutting himself loose from all, in a strict movable column. He anticipated some resistance and looked for fighting — but the rebels retreated before him, somewhat delaying him by skirmishing, destroying roads and bridges, and placing various impediments in the way.

The line of Sherman's march was easterly, first crossing the Big Black River, and then to Champion Hills, Clinton, and Jackson. McPherson's and Hurlbut's Corps, hitherto on different roads, met them at Jackson, and Sherman took command of the three divisions. The march was now continued, and at Line Creek they met the enemy, in a slight encounter, and overcoming them, still pressed on, and with but little opposition arrived at Quitman which was captured, and soon after the village of Enterprise shared the same fate. The rebels seemed paralyzed by the boldness and rapidity of his movements, and could offer no serious resistance to his march through the country. Sherman's column arrived at the Big Clumkey River on the 13th of February, and after crossing pushed forward to Meridian. He had now traversed the State of Mississippi from Vicksburg, which was at the extreme west of the State, to Meridian, which was at the east. He had traveled about one hundred miles, penetrated the very centre of the Confederacy, and the centre also of the negro, corn, and cotton region. He had captured an immense amount of stores, and had destroyed thousands of dollars worth of property belonging to the rebel Government, including railroads and mills.

General Sherman now halted his army, and waited for General Smith's cavalry column, which should have left Memphis on February 1st. He had met the rebels on his way, and was driven back defeated and disgraced. Sherman needed Smith's eight thousand cavalry to prosecute his onward movement, and without them he did not care to proceed further. After waiting a short time, destroying all within his reach, he returned to Vicksburg by the same route he had pursued in his advance. In all probability, had Smith joined him at the proper time, Sherman would have pushed through Alabama, and either struck at Mobile or Montgomery; but the failure of the cavalry to join him changed his plans entirely; but he damaged the enemy in many ways and to a great extent.

INCIDENT.

After the troops returned to Chattanooga, one of Sherman's men was challenged by a sentinel, and replied that he "belonged to the Fifteenth Corps."

"Where's your badge?" inquired the sentinel.

"What badge?" asked the man.

"The badge of your corps. We wear a crescent to designate us." The querist belonged to the Eleventh Corps.

"Badge?" he quickly replied. "Forty rounds of ammunition in our cartridge boxes; sixty rounds in our pockets; a march from Chattanooga; a battle and pursuit; another march to Knoxville; and victory everywhere. That is badge enough for us."

It is needless to add that he passed the sentinel without further questions.

CHAPTER VIII.

SHERMAN'S GREAT CAMPAIGN FROM CHATTANOOGA TO ATLANTA.

SHERMAN APPOINTED THE SUCCESSOR OF GRANT — TOUR OF INSPECTION AND PLAN OF THE CAMPAIGN — COMMENCEMENT OF THE CAMPAIGN — STRENGTH OF THE ARMY — THE STRENGTH OF THE ENEMY — POSITION OF OUR FORCES ON THE SIXTH OF MAY — THE ENEMY FLANKED OUT OF THEIR POSITION AT DALTON — THE BATTLE OF RESACA — THE RESULT — INCIDENTS.

After General Grant had been commissioned lieutenant-general and commander-in-chief of the Armies of the United States, General Sherman was appointed his successor of the Grand Division of the Mississippi. This appointment was made on the 12th day of March, A. D. 1864; but Sherman did not receive notice of it until the 14th, two days afterwards. The States of Kentucky, Tennessee, Mississippi, Alabama and Georgia, and all the troops in these several States, were included in this military division.

As soon as Sherman had made some very important improvements in the means of transportation, and felt perfectly secure in regard to a sufficiency of supplies, he immediately set out on a tour of inspection. He visited Athens, Decatur, Huntsville, Chattanooga, Knoxville, and other military points of his new command. In this preliminary tour of observation, he had interviews with Major General McPherson, commander of the Army of the Tennessee, at Huntsville; with Major General Thomas, commanding the Army of the Cumberland, at Chattanooga; and with Major General Schofield, commanding the Army of the Ohio, at Knoxville. In the interviews which Sherman had with the lieutenant-general, and the various subordinate army commanders, a general programme of the campaign was arranged.

On the 27th of April, all the troops organized under Sherman's command moved towards Chattanooga, and on that day he was there in person.

On the 1st of May, the effective strength of the several armies combined for offensive purposes was about as follows: The Army of the Cumberland, under command of Major General Thomas, contained an infantry force of 54,568 men; artillery, 2,337 men; cavalry, 3,828; total, 60,733, and 130 guns. The Army of the Tennessee, under command of Major General McPherson, contained 22,437 infantry, 1,404 artillery, and 624 cavalry; total, 24,465, and 96 guns. The Army of the Ohio, under command of Major General Schofield, contained 11,183 infantry, 679 artillery, and 1,679 cavalry; total, 13,541, and 28 guns. The grand aggregate number of troops was 98,739, and 254 guns.

We learn, from General Sherman's report, that these numbers were maintained during the campaign. The men constantly returning to the army, whose furloughs had expired, together with those from various hospitals, about compensated for the loss in battle and from sickness.

Sherman estimated the enemy, General Johnston's force, under Generals Hardee, Hood and Polk, at about 50,000 troops. General Hood has since reported the number 70,000.

On the morning of the 6th of May, the forces under Sherman were placed as follows: The Army of the Cumberland was at and near Ringgold; that of the Tennessee at Gordon's Mills, on the Chickamauga; and that of the Ohio near Red Clay, on the Georgia line, north of Dalton.

At this time the enemy occupied a strong position at Dalton, on the railroad, about forty miles south of Chattanooga, which could not be successfully assaulted in front, as it was covered by an inaccessible ridge, between which and Dalton is the famous pass of Buzzard Roost, well obstructed by abattis and flooded by the water from Mill Creek. Sherman resolved to compel the evacuation of that place by flank movements. In this he was perfectly successful, and compelled the enemy to evacuate Dalton, and fall back to Resaca, a place on the railroad, about fifteen miles south of Dalton.

THE BATTLE OF RESACA.

This battle was fought on Saturday and Sunday, May the 14th and 15th. Previous to this time there had been several sharp fights and some severe skirmishing. On the 9th, as the right wing of our army was passing through Snake Creek Gap, it had a sharp encounter with the enemy, while the left and centre of the army were engaged in skirmishing. Slight skirmishing took place on the 11th, and on the 13th General Kilpatrick was wounded in the foot, while making a cavalry reconnoissance before Resaca. But on the 14th and 15th of the month our army had the first battle of the campaign. Although the result was not every thing that was hoped for, yet General Sherman and the country may well be proud of it.

The following account of this battle, given in the language of an eye witness, will be read with great interest:

RESACA, GEORGIA, May 14th, 1864.

Our line as formed last night, was in the form of a semi-circle, to the north-west of Sugar Valley, while the Ostanaula River completes the circle on the south-east. Sugar Valley is a fertile little plain of about ten square miles in size, much broken by hills, which at this season of the year are covered by a dense undergrowth of small trees and vines, rendering them very difficult to penetrate. It was in this valley, between the projected Rome and Dalton Railroad and the river that encircles Resaca and Tilton, that the enemy made a stand after being closely pressed on his retreat from Dalton. From our centre to the river, the distance this morning was about seven miles. Our line extended completely around the valley, McPherson's right resting on the river near the junction with Oothkalaga Creek or Calhoun, while the left strikes the river north of Tilton near the junction of the river with Swamp Creek that takes its rise in the hill of Sugar Valley. Lick and Camp Creeks also burst out from the hills in the valley, and empty their waters in the Ostanaula River, which is very broad and deep, but can be forded when the water is low, at six points. The above is as intelligible a description as can be given without the aid of a map; and now

THE OPENING OF THE BATTLE.

As I have already said, our lines were formed in a half circle extending from the river on the left to a point on the river near Calhoun. The corps occupied positions in the line as follows, extending from right to left: first, McPherson; second, Hooker; third, Palmer; fourth, Schofield; fifth, Howard.

Skirmishing commenced early in the morning, and many prisoners were brought in as the result, although the attack made by us was but faintly responded to. Skirmishing continued, with occasional truces, lasting from ten to thirty minutes, all the morning. Meantime our general officers were not idle. Generals Sherman and Thomas with their indefatigable corps commanders, rode along the line with their staffs, personally superintending the parking of ambulances and ammunition trains, and assigning batteries to positions where they could be of the most service in the event of a general engagement.

CHANGE IN THE LINE.

At nine o'clock, General Schofield was ordered to withdraw his corps from the part of the line between Palmer and Hooker, and take a new position on the left of Newton's division of the Fourth Corps. Palmer closed up the gap between his left and Newton, and Judah's and Cox's division of Schofield's Corps came up in the place assigned to them. Hovey's brigade of the Second Corps was left in reserve and did not participate in the battle of to-day. By some mistake in the giving or reception of the order, General Cox's division failed to get up in time, and Judah and the force on his right advanced upon the enemy, thus leaving a gap of half a mile between Judah's left and Stabley's right, which was promptly filled by cavalry. Considerable confusion followed the announcement of the existence of this gap, and staff officers in vain rode for hours in search of Cox's division through the thick underbrush in which our line was formed. It was lost: and staff officers reported that General Schofield could obtain no intelligence from it.

JUDAH'S ATTACK AND REPULSE.

General Judah just before noon received an order from General Schofield to open the attack, and though his left flank was liable at any moment to be turned, he informed General Schofield of the fact, and at once moved forward upon the enemy's skirmishers. The boys moved rapidly through the vines and shrubbery, through the valley, drove the enemy before them, and with a cheer crossed the deep gorge near which the enemy had thrown up strong breastworks commanding the valley. The enemy opened a destructive fire from their artillery, which the brave division stood for some time, vainly striving by superhuman efforts to carry the breastworks. It was repulsed after a gallant effort, and retired into the valley in disorder. We had not yet got up on the left, and no artillery support was at hand. Nevertheless General Judah resolved not to retire without one more effort. Collecting together the fragments of his broken but not discouraged regiments, a new line was hastily formed and the whole division were just in the act of advancing in a charge which all felt would have put it in possession of the enemy's line of works when the division was

RELIEVED BY GENERAL NEWTON'S DIVISION

of the Eleventh Corps. In the meantime the gap in the line was filled, Cox took his position, and for an hour the incessant roll of the musketry, as volley after volley was poured into the ranks of the enemy, and as vigorously returned, told that the conflict was a desperate one. Artillery fire was delivered into the enemy's ranks rapidly and with excellent effect. Their artillery did not much injury, as Palmer had silenced eight guns with his regiments, who under cover acted as sharpshooters and picked off the cannoniers as often as they advanced to work their pieces. No better evidence can be given of the desperate nature of the conflict, than the loss in McLean's brigade, which went into the fight with 1,388 men, and lost 595 in the short time it was engaged. General Newton's division pressed the enemy strongly, and inflicted serious injury upon him. About two o'clock the firing in the centre in front of Newton subsided into a slight skirmish fire.

GENERAL COX'S DIVISION.

The division of General Cox, which finally turned up on Judah's left, fought with great pluck and obstinacy, driving the skirmishers back upon their main line and the line into their breastworks, from which they poured into the ranks incessant fire of shell and ball. Across valleys, up hills, through gorges and ravines they were driven, until they gained their first line of rifle pits. Cox soon dislodged them and sent them back howling to their more formidable breast-works. At this moment Cox found that he was out of ammunition, and by the stupid blunder on the part of somebody, the trains were too far in the rear from which to replenish his cartridge boxes. Yet he was determined not to be foiled, and gathering together all his strength, he advanced his line. A cheer went up from his boys and resounded through the hills as his serried line advanced upon the enemy's works, which they carried at the point of the bayonet in splendid style; but not without the loss of many brave men.

WHAT PALMER'S FOURTEENTH CORPS ACCOMPLISHED.

The heaviest fighting of the day was on the centre. Palmer's corps, on the right of Newton's division, had heavy skirmishing along the whole line, lasting from half-past twelve until one o'clock, when Carlin's brigade, of Johnston's division, advanced down a slope of a hill, and drove the enemy into their breastworks on the south side of a hill rising out of the valley on the south. An assault on the breastworks was not ordered. The brigade at once sought cover in a ditch formed by a dried up stream, and until night covered them, acted as sharp-shooters, and did good execution in silencing batteries engaged in enfilading Judah and Newton. Mitchell's brigade, of Davis' division, got into a similar position, and picked off every rebel whose head protruded above the breastworks.

Turchin's brigade, of Baird's division, joined Judah on the left of Palmer's corps, and fought desperately, but were compelled to fall back with Judah's division. The loss in the corps, outside of Turchin's brigade, was light.

WOOD'S DIVISION, FOURTH CORPS.

The Fourth Corps, under command of Major General Howard, the "one-armed veteran," as he is styled in the corps, played a very conspicuous part in the tragedy of war enacted to-day. All the corps, with the exception of Beatty's fighting brigade, for which room could not be found, as the circle was gradually compressed as we advanced, was engaged, and covered itself with imperishable glory. Wood's division was ordered into position on the right of General Stanley just before noon, and was soon hotly engaged with Hazen's and Willich's brigades, driving the enemy. For some time a destructive infantry and artillery fire was kept up, and ere long his main line advanced in overwhelming strength upon the enemy, who fled, at his approach, to his rifle-pits, from which the energetic Wood soon dislodged him, and compelled him to seek shelter under cover of their breastworks, but nothing in comparison with those in the Twenty-third Corps, which, to-day, bore the brunt of the battle.

After three o'clock the resistance offered by the enemy on the centre, through which he had vainly striven to force a passage, grew more lax, and very little firing other than skirmishing was heard.

THE ENEMY MASSING ON OUR LEFT.

Foiled at every point in his efforts to break our walls of iron that environed him, Johnston, early in the afternoon, commenced massing heavily on our left, where Stanley, with as brave a division as ever marched to the music of the Union, had been skirmishing and awaiting the developments of the enemy's attempt to break the centre. Generals Sherman and Thomas were not slow to detect the enemy's design, and

PREPARATIONS TO RESIST IT

were at once commenced. Joe Hooker's gallant Potomac veterans were selected at once, and immediately retired from the line and commenced moving to the left of Stanley, whose flank was covered by McCook's cavalry, in front of which Johnston was massing his columns for the desperate effort. Hooker arrived none too soon.

A MOMENT OF THRILLING INTEREST.

At seven o'clock, when quiet reigned along the whole line, with an occasional interruption from a sharp-shooter's rifle, the expected attack came. Down upon Stanley's exposed flank came the enemy in overwhelming numbers. For a few minutes the line nobly resisted the terrific attack; but as it was renewed with ten-fold fury by the enemy, who fought with a desperation equal to anything ever performed by our own soldiery, the line wavered, and the regiments on the left were giving back in confusion and disorder, when, above the roar of the artillery and musketry that seemed to make the old hills tremble and quake, a cheer was heard, and into the deadly breach, over the dead bodies of the fallen, came on the double-quick, Robinson's brigade, who advanced to the assault with desperate determination to drive back the solid columns of the enemy, and save the army from disaster. Nobly they met the enemy, and when the shock came, reeling like drunken men, the line of the enemy was broken and sent back, smarting under the shock. The contest was of short duration, but, while it lasted, the roar of artillery and the roll of musketry told that this was one of the most critical moments of the day—a period when the heart of the listener seemed to stand still in suspense. The Fourth Corps will never forget Hooker and the noble brigade which, at a moment when the fate of the army, and perhaps of the nation, hung upon a slender thread, which the enemy would have severed, came up and turned the tide of battle. A nation's thanks are due Joe Hooker, and may it never forget Robinson's brigade, whose gallantry to-night is on every tongue.

SUNDAY, May 15th.

During last night quiet reigned along the whole line, the enemy being very quiet, and rarely firing a shot. The falling of trees and the sound of axmen, however, convinced our commanders that the rebels were erecting stronger fortifications upon the innumerable hills that rise out of the valley. At half-past seven in the morning our skirmishers opened fire upon the rebel line, which was as vigorously returned on the left and left-centre. The enemy, however, did not seem disposed to attack with their main line, after the fearful slaughter and repulse that Hooker administered to them last night. It was not until nine or ten o'clock in the morning that the Twentieth Corps arrived from the right, and got into position on Stanley's left. The Twenty-third Corps was immediately withdrawn from the right of the line and thrown in on the left. As our line was nearly fourteen miles long, these necessary changes occupied nearly the entire morning, so that mid-day arrived ere we were ready to make the

ASSAULT ON THE ENEMY'S WORKS.

Hooker threw forward Butterfield's division against the enemy's strongest position, supported by Williams' and Geary's divisions, and the battle opened vigorously on both sides. Hooker fought for three or four hours, and made steady headway, carrying line after line of rifle-pits, until Butterfield's division encountered a lunette of formidable size. Several attempts were made to carry it, and capture its four guns, which were pouring a destructive fire into our lines, but the attempt was futile. The troops fought with great desperation, but as often as they advanced upon the lunette the terrific volleys of musketry from the enemy in the fortification hurled them back in confusion. At last Butterfield charged forward and took a position under the protecting works of the fort, so close to the guns within that they could be touched with the men's hands. In the effort to gain this unexposed position, the contest was a bloody one, Geary's division supporting Butterfield. Wood's brigade, which was participating in the first battle, fought with marked determination, and contributed much to secure the position.

HOOKER CARRIES THE LUNETTE BY STRATEGY.

After vain efforts to capture the lunette from which the enemy poured into our ranks grape, canister and shrapnel, Hooker's forces gave up the unequal contest, and during the balance of the day lay under the breastworks, protected from the enemy's fire, and picking off every rebel who showed himself above the works. Darkness found him in this position, and he at once matured plans for capturing the works by strategy, under cover of darkness. The pioneers were brought up; the ends dug out of the works, and the guns drawn out by the aid of ropes, under a destructive fire from the occupants of the works,

P

who were driven out or captured, as our troops swarmed in through the opening in overwhelming numbers. The guns were four twelve pound brass pieces; and a number of battle flags, including those of the Thirty-eighth and Thirty-fifth Alabama, were captured, with over 200 prisoners. Prisoners report General Walthall (rebel) killed, and General Tucker wounded.

THE LOSSES IN HOOKER'S CORPS

were very heavy, especially in the repeated charges upon the enemy's works. Butterfield lost about 500; Geary 100, and Williams' division about 150, making Hooker's loss about 750 in the battle of the afternoon. The Twenty-third Corps, which was moved around from the right, as a support for Hooker, lost slightly.

GLORIOUS VICTORY BY HOVEY'S INDIANA DIVISION.

About two o'clock the enemy, learning from prisoners taken from us, that Hovey's Indiana division of "raw recruits" held a position in the line, and smarting under their successive repulses on other portions of the line, hurled a heavy force upon Hovey, convinced that the recruits would run. Not so, however. The rebels held a stronger position in a gorge of the hills, and out of their breastworks they swarmed in large numbers and made a furious attack upon the division, which nobly repulsed them after a short and bloody contest of fifteen minutes. The assault was renewed, when the "raw Hoosiers" charged upon them on the double-quick, under a heavy fire of grape, and literally mowed them down. They did not assault the Indianians the third time. To-night the encomiums of the whole corps are being showered upon Hovey's division, who have written a glorious introductory chapter in their history.

A DESPERATE NIGHT BATTLE.

About ten P. M. Hooker's command commenced throwing up breastworks to strengthen their position, and to cover their movements, it was found necessary to advance their skirmish line. In doing so the skirmishers ran against the rebel line. Immediately after a heavy artillery and musketry fire opened from both contestants, which lasted until two o'clock in the morning. The night battle was desperate and losses on both sides heavy, probably three hundred killed and wounded. At two the rebels were repulsed along the whole line; a deafening cheer rang out on the night air, and all was still save the piteous moans of the dying, who lay upon the bloody field, awaiting with anxiety the early dawn, when they were gathered into the hospitals and every care bestowed upon them by our hard working surgeons.

MONDAY, May 16th.

The morning was very bright and the whole valley was filled with smoke and fog. At daylight not a gun was heard. Newton immediately advanced to feel the enemy, and discovered that they had disappeared.

THE RETREAT ACROSS THE OSTANAULA.

Immediately upon being informed of the evacuation of the valley, General Howard informed General Sherman, and our lines advanced. It was discovered that the enemy had made good his retreat, carrying off all his artillery, but destroying his wagon trains by fire lest they should fall into our hands. I have just made a tour of the field on the left, and find it covered with rebel dead and wounded, all of whom were left in our hands for burial and treatment. Prisoners at the hour I write, 9 A. M., are being brought in by hundreds. The victory is complete so far, but would have been more so had

M'PHERSON'S CORPS

been able to cross the river and take a position in the rebel rear. McPherson made several attempts to throw down the pontoons and cross his corps, but the enemy poured such a raking fire into his pontoons that the work had to be abandoned. I have no particulars of what was accomplished by McPherson's command, but I learn that the Fifteenth Corps under Logan lost 48 killed and 448 wounded.

OUR TOTAL LOSSES

are estimated at from 4,000 to 5,000, of whom fully 2,000 are so slightly wounded in the hands and feet that they will be fit for duty in two or three weeks. The killed will amount to about 800, among whom are many brave officers, who have left behind them brilliant records.

THE PRISONERS IN OUR HANDS.

We have taken nearly four thousand prisoners and deserters, including many colonels, lieutenant-colonels, majors, and line and staff officers. Many of them were willing prisoners, who remained in the rebel works and surrendered when we advanced in pursuit.

THE PURSUIT OF JOHNSTON.

On the evacuation of the valley, the enemy crossed all his cars and locomotives and burned five spans of the railway bridge, which can be repaired however, in one or two days. At nine this (Monday) morning, Hooker's corps threw down pontoons and crossed near Resaca, while Schofield is crossing on the left near Pelton. The cavalry under Stoneman and McCook, commenced the pursuit early in the morning, and at the present writing they are engaging the enemy with artillery. Brisk firing can be heard, and the rebel rear guard are evidently meeting with a warm parting salute from our cavalry, which this season is in excellent trim, and superior to that of former seasons. McCook, Stoneman, and Kilpatrick are dashing officers, who never refuse a fight, and invariably whip their antagonists, when the forces engaged are at all equal.

The following partial account of the battle of Resaca will give to the reader some interesting particulars not mentioned so fully in the statement already made:

"While the fight was progressing on Saturday and Sunday at Sugar Creek, McPherson was engaged in shelling Resaca, to interrupt the passage of the rebel army, which, late in the day, was observed to be moving in long and unbroken trains. The houses, stores, dépôt buildings and telegraph office were riddled by the exploding shells and round shot, and the place rendered very uncomfortable. The inhabitants, like most of the people from Dalton and Tilton, took the train with their household effects, provisions, &c., and went South.

The few who remained stated that a massacre and destruction of the place was expected, from the statement of the rebel officers and men. The order for the army to fall back was captured from a rebel courier on his way from Johnston's head-quarters, and the whole programme thus revealed to us.

"On the 14th heavy fighting began on the left, where the rebel corps of Hood and Polk pressed hotly upon the lines of Generals Howard and Schofield. Late in the afternoon Hooker's Twentieth Corps began shifting its position towards the left in support of that wing of the army. General Williams' division took the lead in this movement, and by six P. M. reached the main road leading from Dalton to Resaca. Here a portion of Stanley's division, of the Fourth Corps, was being heavily engaged, and was evidently on the point of being repulsed. General Williams immediately formed his command in line of battle along a series of heights running in a direction perpendicular to the lines of General Stanley. The troops were concealed by the dense timber, and were so posted as to overlook the narrow, open valley along which the enemy, with defiant yells, hotly pursued Stanley's routed regiments. The Fifth Indiana battery, which had been put in position in an open field opposite Colonel Robinson's brigade, on the left of General Williams' line, presented a tempting prize, apparently within easy grasp of the enemy. On he came, making directly for the battery, the feeble supports of which immediately gave way. The batterymen stood manfully by their guns, though the loss of them seemed inevitable. The deep-throated cannon vomited a terrific fire upon the advancing foe, but without checking him. The enemy had approached within one hundred yards of the battery when General Williams ordered Colonel Robinson to throw his brigade forward into the valley, and to assault and take the heights beyond it, which had now fallen into rebel possession. With tremendous cheers the Third brigade sprang from its covert in the woods, and swinging upon the right flank as a pivot, came up in rear of the battery, and opened a sweeping fire upon the enemy. Colonel Robinson ordered the One Hundred and First Illinois, which was upon the left of his line, to move immediately upon the wooded hill upon the left of the battery, which it did with almost as much precision and regularity of movement as might have been expected upon a review. It was a sublime movement throughout, and challenged the admiration of General Hooker, who declared that the regiments moved as if on parade. The enemy, completely disconcerted, retired in disorder to his intrenchments in the depths of the tangled forest. Darkness had now fallen, and though many prisoners were taken, it was extremely hazardous to pursue the enemy.

"On the 15th it was resolved to assault and, if possible, carry the fortified heights covering the right of the enemy's line. In this undertaking, the Fourth, Twentieth and Twenty-third Corps were to coöperate. The principal portion of the work, as the sequel proves, was reserved for General Hooker's command. At noon Butterfield's division began firing into the dense, tangled forest which covered and masked the enemy's position. General Geary's followed, then General Williams' in reserve. Butterfield's men pressed forward vigorously to the assault, though retarded by the thick, tangled character of the woods. The Second and Third divisions swept bravely on up the slope, and, spite of obstinate resistance and fearful losses, carried the enemy's first line. The assault of the second was at once attempted, but it was too strongly fortified and stoutly defended to be carried. The first line, however, was held firmly, in spite of all the enemy's desperate efforts to dislodge our troops.

"General Williams' division was now ordered to advance and take its position on the left of General Butterfield. The division at once moved forward in line of battle, and, without serious opposition, arrived at the prescribed point within half an hour. The troops remained quietly in their position until four o'clock P. M., when the enemy, seeing himself completely hemmed in, with the Ostanaula River in his rear, and his last line of works, covering Resaca, almost within our grasp, resolved to dislodge General Williams, and, if possible, turn the left flank of our army. Upon this scheme rested Johnston's forlorn hope, since a portion of McPherson's command had already succeeded in crossing the Ostanaula at Calhoun Ferry, and again threatened the rear of the rebel army. To Hood's rebel corps was assigned the desperate undertaking just mentioned. Massing Stuart's division four lines deep along our front, and supporting it with strong reserves, the rebel general pushed his columns forward to the assault. Colonel Robinson's brigade being upon the extreme left of the line, and having a wide, open field in its front, received the first onset of the enemy. As soon as the rebels emerged from the woods, the brave men of the First, Second and Third brigades opened a tremendous fire upon their advancing masses. The enemy checked, but not daunted, pressed steadily on, apparently determined to carry the position at every hazard. Colonel Robinson's brave men, with sweaty, powder-blackened faces, but unflinching hearts, redoubled their exertions, and poured upon the enemy a leaden storm, such as it seemed impossible to withstand. The enemy returned the fire with great energy, but at length hesitated, staggered and fell back. Then went up along the lines such pealing, heart-stirring cheers as only soldiers can give in the flush of victory. But the storm was not yet over. The enemy rallied again behind his woody covert, and once more advanced to the assault. Though he received a like greeting as before, his lines swept impetuously on, apparently goaded by a resolution stronger than death. The field became strewed with his wounded and dead, and his advancing lines grew thinner and thinner. There was no quailing in the Union ranks. Standing firm in their places, the brave defenders of human liberty seemed resolved not to yield. The enemy came on within fifty yards of their lines before he became convinced of the impossibility of driving General Williams' heroes from their positions. Then he turned and fled, leaving his killed and wounded, one battle-flag and hundreds of small arms lying upon the field. A number of the enemy who found it almost certain death to retreat in the face of our fire, surrendered as prisoners of war.

"Night now drew her sable curtain over the scene of carnage, as if to vail its horrors from the sight of men and angels. The fighting entirely ceased, and the stillness was broken only by the melancholy voice of the whip-poor-will, and by the piercing cries of the rebel wounded, who lay uncared for between the hostile lines. The brave men who had fought so well could not listen to these sounds of distress indifferently. They sallied forth, even far beyond the picket lines, and brought in and tenderly cared for the poor victims of a fiendish rebellion."

INCIDENTS OF THE BATTLE OF RESACA.

After storming a portion of the rebel works, by Butterfield's division, on the 15th, as heretofore described, and while our men were crouching about the fort, and protecting the captured guns, a man from the Seventieth Indiana regiment suddenly exposed himself to that close and terrible source of destruction, the rebel's line of masked breastworks, *"Shoot!"* and with an oath repeated *"shoot!"* The defiance was answered, and he fell dead with an oath on his lips and a bullet in his heart, and thus passed into eternity.

A Confederate soldier, who had been captured during the battle, and brought into the presence of General Sherman, without knowing that he was standing before Sherman, said: "The Confederates had a great horror of old Sherman's flank movements, that they could not find a position that he could not flank them out of it; they believed that he could outflank the devil, and that he must have come into the world by a flank movement."

General Dan. Sickles was present during the battle of the 14th and 15th, on a special mission to which he had been assigned by the President. He was in the saddle both days from morning till night, and was everywhere conspicuous where the fighting was the hardest. General Hooker, seeing how recklessly he exposed himself, said to him: "Dan, you must go back; we want to save that other leg of yours." Sickles did not take the advice, but remained on the field. As he rode along our lines, he was frequently applauded and cheered by our troops. "Who's that?" one would ask. Another would reply, "That is Dan Sickles, the man who saved the army at Chancellorsville." Sickles' staff volunteered their services, and were actively employed on Hooker's and Butterfield's staffs during the battle.

Q

CHAPTER IX.

SHERMAN'S GREAT CAMPAIGN FROM CHATTANOOGA TO ATLANTA.

THE PURSUIT OF THE ENEMY — THEIR WOUNDED — ORDER OF THE PURSUIT — AN AMBUSCADE — FIGHTING AND SKIRMISHING — AN ACCOUNT BY AN EYE-WITNESS — CAPTURE OF ROME, KINGSTON AND CASSVILLE — GUERRILLA OPERATIONS — MOVEMENT ACROSS THE ETOWAH — SKIRMISHING — LOSS OF WAGONS — THE GALLANT ACTION OF THE TWENTY-FIFTH INST. — ANOTHER AMBUSCADE — SHERMAN'S OBJECT — A FURIOUS ASSAULT — OCCUPATION OF DALLAS — THE SITUATION ON JUNE FIRST — SHERMAN'S STRATEGY — THE ENEMY ABANDONED THEIR WORKS — SHERMAN'S DISPATCH — WHAT THE ARMY HAD ACCOMPLISHED — CHARACTER OF SHERMAN — INCIDENTS.

On Monday, the day after the battle of Resaca, the army was in pursuit of the enemy. Our forces moved in three grand columns, sweeping the country for twenty miles. The wounded and dead of the enemy were scattered along the road and in the edges of the woods, where temporary hospitals had been established. They were taken to our hospitals, in the rear, where our surgeons did all they could to relieve their sufferings. The inhumanity of the men who have lifted their rebellious hands against the Government and the civilization of the age, to the dupes of their folly, is not to be envied, and will make a dark chapter in history. The kindness of our Government to the unfortunate and suffering, although not what it should have been in very many instances, will afford a most striking contrast.

As above stated, the army was in motion by noon of Monday. The general order of the march was as it had been previous to the affair at Resaca: the Army of the Tennessee was on the right; the Army of the Cumberland in the centre, and the Army of the Ohio on the left; of course we mean so much of the army as was then engaged in the pursuit. There are three good roads, in addition to the railroad, leading south from Resaca to the Etowah River. Several other roads cross there, by means of which, at several points between Resaca and the Etowah, the armies could be concentrated. The roads that run in a southern direction, and along which our forces moved, wind through valleys and are separated from each other by ranges of mountains. The difficulty of a rapid pursuit was great; the enemy had great advantages in the retreat. When about three miles south of the Ostanaula, General Sweeney's division of the Sixteenth Corps fell into an ambuscade. The troops moved into a large open field sheltered by the woods. It was not supposed that the enemy were in any considerable force on our front. The brigade commanded by Colonel Burke, of the Sixty-sixth Illinois regiment, was ordered forward to take a position on the left. They had proceeded but a short distance, when the enemy opened fire with artillery. Colonel Burke was mortally wounded and taken from the field. The whole force of General Dodge fell back until it met Osterhaus's division coming up on the double quick to their support.

The following morning, at five o'clock, the Seventeenth Corps marched, the Fifteenth Corps leading. Morgan L. Smith's division was in advance. In our front was Hardee's Corps, said to be commanded by Generals Morgan and Walker. About three o'clock, in the afternoon, the rebel cavalry drew up in line, in our front. The rain was falling in torrents. They were charged upon by the Fifth Kentucky, and at once they retreated into the woods just in their rear. General Lightburn sent forward his skirmishers. The rebels opened on them with artillery. He then deployed the other troops of his brigade, and General W. S. Smith sent forward the First brigade and Lee Grasse's battery. Logan moved up Herron's division on the left, and Osterhaus took position behind Morgan L. Smith. After a few shots from our battery, the rear-guard of the enemy again retreated. After following and skirmishing about a mile, our advance reached Rocky Creek, and secured the intersection of the road to Adairsville. An eye-witness of this affair informs us, that "soon after the commencement of the skirmish on the Pine Road, heavy cannonading was heard from Howard's column in the valley east of us. His fire was heavy, especially of artillery, and sounded almost like a general engagement. The Fourth Corps, moving down that road as the center column, had overtaken the enemy and was engaged. The division of General Newton, formerly Sheridan's, was in advance, with the brigade commanded by Colonel Frank T. Sherman, Eighty-eighth Illinois, in the immediate front. Frank's brigade, with Miller's brigade, were heavily engaged for some time, loosing 165 killed and wounded, the Eighty-eighth Illinois loosing 34 and the Seventy-fourth Illinois 55. The enemy were finally driven into their intrenchments at Adairsville.

"The result of the day's work left the center in front of the enemy in Adairsville. The head of General McPherson's column was resting on the Adairsville Road, whence it could strike Johnston from the west, and the Sixteenth Corps was at another cross road from the Rome to the Adairsville Road. Hardee had passed over the mountain to Adairsville where Johnston was in person. Early in the morning the Fifteenth Corps moved by the Rocky Creek Road towards Adairsville, General Dodge moving on the other cross roads. There were indications that Johnston intended to make a stand at that place. Johnston saw the trap and departed in the night time. Sherman's strategy was again successful. His columns had been so marched that in three hours he was able to concentrate them in case the rebels would receive battle.

"The grand army presented a most splendid military pageant as it entered Adairsville. Leaving Adairsville, the right wing passed over a very high mountain, reaching the Kingston Road at Woodville about midnight. The centre and left moved simultaneously on parallel roads. When the right wing left the Rome Road in the morning, the Second cavalry division, General Gerrard, moved forward on the Kingston Road. Near Woodland, his advance, the Fourth Michigan cavalry, found the enemy's cavalry in considerable force, and disposed to wait his advance. The valley in which they were was narrow, and the roadside a considerable part of the way woods, so that only a small force could be used. The two battalions of the Michigan cavalry understood the business and acquitted themselves right gallantly. The rebels concealed themselves in the bushes and behind the fences and houses along the roadside, and fired upon our cavalry. But nothing checked the impetuosity or courage of the troops. It charged the rebels and drove them from every hiding place, and killed and wounded a large number of them. The rebels fled in consternation. The Fourth Michigan lost one killed and eleven wounded. As we rode into Kingston the next morning we saw the evidences of their splendid fighting, dead horses and new made graves marking a distance of more than four miles, over which your Michigan soldiers drove them. On the 18th we moved into and about Kingston. During the same day Jeff. C. Davis, with his division, who left the main army on the 16th at Resaca, entered Rome and captured the foundries and arsenals there, and a large amount of commissary stores. In the night a train of cars arrived over the railroad to Kingston."

Rome is situated at the confluence of the Ostanaula and Etowah Rivers, which form the Coosa River. Kingston and Cassville are three or four miles north of the Etowah, and about twelve miles east of Rome.

Here about two days were devoted to rest, which seemed to be absolutely necessary, after the fatiguing marches, battle and skirmishes heretofore described.

On the 23d, the Fourteenth Army Corps lost twenty-five wagons near Kingston.

After resting and perfecting arrangements for an advance, the forces of Generals Thomas, Schofield and McPherson were ordered across the Etowah River, in the direction of the enemy. They were provided with twenty days rations, and the commissariat and quartermaster's department were to be supplied from the country. Indiscriminate plundering was strictly prohibited, and foraging parties were organized for the purpose of collecting provisions, giving receipts for the same, and distributing them to the army.

At the dawn of daylight on the 23d, the tents of Hooker's corps were struck. Says one who witnessed the movement of this force: "Soon after daylight the star corps, with their long trains of of white-topped wagons, were wending their way through the forests and over the hills and valleys of Georgia. On we went, along the yellow, dirty roads, through plowed fields, where grew hills of young corn, never to be gathered—through green fields of ripening grain—never to be harvested—through gardens and door yards, whence flowers were plucked only to adorn the soldiers dusty caps—over rocky, gravelly, sandy soil, which reflected the scorching heat of the sun, and gave forth clouds of yellow dust—past wells and springs, where there were ten thirsty soldiers eagerly clutching at every cupfull of water—over stony hills, and through shady dells, amidst the grateful foliage of the odorous young pines and broad leafed elms, where woodbines flaunt their gay floral clusters and the more modest forest gems peep above the gravelly slopes and hide behind the graceful fronds of the blooming fern.

"Regiment after regiment, brigade after brigade, division after division—infantry, cavalry and artillery—red, white and blue, start in one glorious galaxy, pursue their resistless course across the sacred soil of Georgia—a grand and hopeful sign to us, but one full of dire portent and ominous of desolation to the wicked instigators of this reckless rebellion.

The bridges leading across the Etowah and Coosa Rivers had been burned by the enemy. This, however, caused but little delay, as the pontoniers soon threw bridges across the rivers. One wing of Sherman's army crossed the Etowah, on the afternoon of the 23d. General Schofield's Corps after crossing the river moved off to the left. General Hascal was in command of Brigadier

General Manson's brigade, as the latter had not recovered from the wound received at the battle of Resaca.

After crossing the river the forces proceeded in line of battle. Our advance skirmished with the enemy during part of the day. Several of our men were wounded by their shells. Cannonading was heard, at intervals, all along the lines.

On the 24th, skirmishing was quite frequent, and during the night, as many as one hundred and twenty-five wagons were captured from the Twenty-third Corps, by Wheeler's troopers.

The enemy under command of the rebel Generals Hood and Polk, were driven into their strong retreat on Pumpkin Vine Creek, in one of the gaps in the Altoona mountains, where they took shelter behind their breastworks. This engagement commenced about two o'clock P. M. on the 25th, and continued with great fury for about two hours.

The enemy were driven through the woods a distance of one mile and a half, with very considerable loss on both sides. At the commencement of the fight, General Geary's First division of the Twentieth Corps engaged the enemy. He was soon reënforced by Generals Williams' and Butterfield's divisions. General Hooker finally ordered a bayonet charge, and the men rushed forward with a shout and drove the enemy out of one of their lines. Towards evening, a severe storm was raging, during which, amid the darkness, several of our soldiers were lost.

The next morning skirmishing was renewed. The enemy was again forced back, and rapidly followed by our forces. Suddenly Geary's Second division received a destructive fire from the woods on the flank. They had been lured into an ambuscade, and masked batteries were opened upon our men with destructive effect. Hooker and staff received a volley which killed one of the escort. Our loss was heavy.

The object of these engagements seemed to have been to hold and keep the enemy engaged, while McPherson with the Fifteenth, Sixteenth and Seventeenth Corps should get on the enemy's flank at Dallas. On the 28th our army was in position in front of the enemy, strongly posted four miles from Dallas.

The next day the enemy massed his forces for an assault on our works, which had been hastily erected. The fighting was terrible, and the slaughter of the enemy great. He was driven back in confusion. At the same time a powerful attack was made on McPherson on the right. This was repulsed, the enemy losing in killed and wounded not less than 2,000, probably many more.

A correspondent of one of our public journals gives the following interesting account of the attack and repulse of the enemy:

"About five in the afternoon the rebels advanced their skirmishers along the whole front of the Army of the Tennessee. Our front was covered with a rifle-pit extending along its whole length, a distance of some two miles, and the right flank by Wilder's brigade of the Second cavalry division. Harrow's Fourth division of the Fifteenth Corps had the extreme right of the line, and Veatch's, the Fourth division of the Sixteenth Corps, the extreme left—the centre, consisting of Sweeney's division of the Sixteenth and Morgan L. Smith's and Osterhaus' division of the Fifteenth Corps.

"The enemy advancing a heavy line of skirmishers, in a short time fell back to the rifle-pits. Our troops of the main army, who were quietly observing the movements of the enemy, at the first volley of the skirmishers, fell instantly into their places behind the breastworks. General and field and staff and line officers sprang to their posts, and in less time than I occupy in narrating, the Army of the Tennessee was in line to receive assault. Two miles of as good men as ever stood in line of battle, all Western regiments but one, confronted Hardee's and Polk's Corps. For the first time in the war, with nearly all the regiments, our men were behind breastworks and being attacked. It had carried many a one such as the rude work of logs before them. It had also charged up to the strong works of Vicksburg and Jackson. But now they were to be charged, and some wondered if as they had always driven the rebels from similar works, they could be held by our Western men.

"Although it was well understood that the movement of the trains had attracted the notice of the rebels, and would very probably induce the belief that our positions were being changed, and that an attack was very probable, yet the attack was so sudden and so rapid that it was necessary to make haste quickly with orders and dispositions.

"General Logan at the first volley mounted his horse, and rode rapidly along to the front. Following close after our skirmishers, as they fell back to rifle-pits, came the rebel lines of battle. With a rebel yell they rushed headlong, charging bravely on the whole line, at the same time under a heavy fire of artillery. Under the orders of their officers, these troops reserved their fire and awaited the shock. Logan rode along the whole line of his corps, hat in hand, his black hair streaming in the air, and at full speed, urging his men at the top of his voice, to "save their fire and give them h—ll." The effect was electrical, the regiments cheered with a will, and one could mark his progress along the line by the shouts of his regiments.

"Soon after General McPherson and his staff rode from his headquarters, on the left of the Sixteenth Corps, along the whole line. The battle was raging furiously, but the men saw their commander, and their cheers arose wildly upon the din of battle. Altogether, that short hour, with the enthusiastic shouts of the Federals, the fierce yells of the rebels, and the continuous crash of small arms, was fearfully exciting.

"The Federal line reserved its fire until the rebels were within thirty yards. The first volley was instantaneous. It seemed to leap from the long line of rifle-pits at the moment of time. Such another single volley of musketry has seldom been heard. The volley from the rear flank followed, and the battle was opened. The rebels fell like grain—scores at a time lay side by side. The battle lasted until night. It was mostly confined to infantry. In the line of the Second division, General Giles A. Smith had placed a section of battery B, First artillery, which, double-shotted with grape, made great havoc. On Harris' line a section of the First Iowa battery was at the front. The remainder of the artillery was on the high ground back of the line of battle. In the close struggle for the rifle-pits, it could not be used without injuring alike friend and foe. How and in what manner the terrible struggle of the rebels to drive in the right wing was conducted, I cannot tell you. All we know is that they repeatedly reformed and renewed the assaults, and with the utmost desperation charged up to the very muzzles of our rifles, and that these ineffectual assaults and struggles were renewed until the rebel force, all cut up, was withdrawn. On the extreme right the rebels, at one turn, gained a slight advantage. The Second brigade was slightly shattered, and a section of the First Iowa battery captured. Just at this time General Logan rode up and ordered the guns to be recaptured. The Sixth Iowa charged the enemy and retook the guns. The brigade suffered severely. Colonel Dickerman, of the One Hundred and Third Illinois, fell mortally wounded. Major Giesy, of the Forty-sixth Ohio, and Lieutenant Colonel Miller, of the Sixth Iowa, fell mortally wounded. In the front of the brigade 272 dead and wounded rebels lay in sight at daylight. Wilder's brigade of mounted infantry, which was on the right flank, was dismounted, and came up and poured in a continuous oblique fire from the sixteen shooting rifles. The rebel loss in his front was heavy. At one place in front of Lightburn's brigade, twenty-one dead rebels lay in one heap. In the front of Veatch's division, a portion of the rebel line was staggered, and its left fell back to the right. As it fell back, General Dodge saw the opportunity and ordered a regiment over the breastworks. The regiment delivered an oblique fire that left over a hundred on the field.

"General Dodge buried 160 in his front. Considered in all respects, the desperate valor of the rebels, the rapidity and pertinacity of the assaults, the coolness and steadiness with which our men and officers received and repulsed them, the slight loss of our army, and the terrible slaughter of the rebels, it was one of the most remarkable battles of the war.

"Our loss did not reach 100. The rebel loss cannot be ascertained by us with certainty. About the close of the engagement a rebel officer shouted to General Morgan L. Smith, that General Hardee wished the firing stopped that he might bring off his wounded. He was answered by General McPherson's order, that if he would send a flag he would answer it. During the night all the rebel wounded that could, crawled back into their lines. As soon as it was light the next morning our men commenced burying the rebel dead and bringing in the rebel wounded, but were frequently fired upon, so that their interment was by no means completed. We buried, however, during the day 450 rebels. At that amount alone, their loss must have reached at least 2,000 in killed and wounded. Estimating six wounded to one killed, I think that 3,000 is a reasonable estimate of the rebel loss in their assault upon the Army of the Tennessee.

"A deserter, who came in to-day, says he heard General Hardee say that he had lost 2,500 of his best men. The rebel officers and men who have fallen into our hands all stated that they had been informed, and believed, that our army was, to a very great extent, composed of 100 days' men. They did not expect to meet the veterans of the Western Army.

"I regret to record a severe casualty to Colonel Ezra Taylor, of Chicago, chief of artillery of the Department of the Tennessee. As he was riding along the lines of the Fifteenth Corps, with General Logan, this afternoon, a rifle ball struck General Logan on the arm, tearing his coat sleeve, and glancing, struck Colonel Taylor. The ball passed through his coat, a thick book, and entering at the right nipple, passed around next to the bones, and lodged under the edge of the shoulder-blade. The wound is severe, but not dangerous. He starts for his home to-night. Colonel Taylor is a faithful, hard-working, and very competent officer. He is much esteemed by his superior officers, and his loss to the service is just now unfortunate."

On the 31st, the enemy made a feeble attack on

our line, and were repulsed. On Thursday noon we entered Dallas.

A letter writer, who was with the army at the time, gives the following account of the situation on June 1st:

"DALLAS, Ga., June 1st.

"Since the night of the 29th of May, when the rebels made so furious an attack on our lines, and were so gallantly repulsed, nothing of special note has occurred. The little excitement attendant on an expected change of the line of attack, involving a retreat from this position, has died away, though the trains of several corps have been already 'hauled out' on the Marietta Road in the direction indicated. McPherson's guns are occasionally heard on our extreme right, and those of Howard and Schofield more frequently on our left. The position of the contending armies is in the high, rolling and heavily timbered region near the sources of those numerous streams which, flowing in opposite directions, supply the waters of the Etowah on the north, and the Chattahoochee on the southeast. The ravines and hollows thus formed are comparatively safe and excellent retreats for our ambulance wagons, saddle horses, &c.

"We are now about twenty-five miles from our railroad base of communications and supplies at Kingston, the rebels being about sixteen miles from their railroad base at Marietta, on the Kingston and Atlanta Railroad.

"Our lines extend in a bold curve from northwest to southeast, the right including Dallas, and the left resting on and including Burnt Hickory. Our lines of fortifications, consisting of successive tiers of breastworks, redoubts, earthworks, &c., erected along this curve about fourteen miles. The position of the rebels confronts ours. Both parties are continually throwing up new works, and constructing additional defenses, forts, &c. The tops of the intervening hills are torn into shreds, or cut clean off by the iron storms. Yesterday a nest of sharp-shooters who, under cover of a house, had been annoying the men of Butterfield's division, came under the observation of that general, and very soon received the attention of the most valuable battery, which demolished the house in a twinkling about the ears of the astonished rebs, and scattered the rascals like chaff. Their sharp-shooters, perched in trees and every possible place of ambuscade, have been and still are a source of great annoyance, and have contributed much to the casualties of our men.

"The head-quarters of several generals have been occasionally moved on account of shells and other missiles, which somehow find their way everywhere. The other day a shell burst at General Thomas' head-quarters, scattering the tents and furniture, and killing or wounding one man, and playing smash generally. Generals Hooker and Butterfield have had equally narrow escapes. One man was killed while getting water from a spring near the head-quarters of the latter.

"Use renders these men cool and even callous in the presence of these messengers of death. Yesterday a man on the skirmish line received a ball in the cheek, which came out behind his ear, through the strong cords of the neck. A stretcher was brought, but he kicked it over, with an oath, walked to the surgeon, and had his wound probed and dressed, and returned to his company, swearing he would 'make the rebs pay for that.' He was from an Eastern regiment."

The rebel General Johnston had selected a position of great natural strength, near his base of supplies, and had one railroad and three good wagon roads over which he could move. His army had been reënforced by all available troops, and he was undoubtedly anxious that Sherman would risk a general engagement. Here Sherman again evinced his good generalship, by determining not to attack Johnston in his intrenchments, but by flank movements to force him into the open field.

Accordingly the movement was ordered to be from the right to the left of our line. The trains were moved east, and in the rear of the troops. The first movement was made with great success on the 3d of June. A division of the Sixteenth Corps moved in the night to a line of rifle-pits and redoubts on a commanding position, about three miles northeast of the extreme right. The division was thus on a position to cover the withdrawal of the remainder of the right wing at daylight. Soon after dawn General Logan commenced moving his corps. It was expected that this movement could not be made without an attack from the enemy. The Fifteenth Corps moved so as to be in constant readiness to resist any attack that might be made. But for some reason, probably ignorance of the movement, our forces were not molested. In fact, it is said that the pickets of the enemy kept up firing in the woods some time after our pickets, under Colonel Parry, of the Forty-seventh Ohio regiment, were withdrawn. Veatch's division, of the Sixteenth Corps, followed the Fifteenth as far as the intrenchments held by Sweeny, and Jeff. C. Davis' division, of the Fourteenth Corps, moved along a parallel road of his own construction, in the same direction with Logan. This movement was made with the greatest celerity and precision, and gave to the army a stronger position and stronger front. As soon as the enemy discovered the movement of our army, he evacuated his works in our front. General Logan's skirmishers found the works abandoned, except by a few pickets, who were captured. The skirmishers of the Fourteenth Corps were firing into the works, which they supposed sheltered thousands of rebels, when, to their great astonishment, they discovered the American flag floating over the enemy's intrenchments.

On the morning of the 6th, at daylight, the Army of the Tennessee marched to Ackworth, and thus Sherman's strategy was successful.

On the 7th, General Sherman sent the following dispatch to the War Department, at Washington:

"I have been to Altoona Pass and find it very admirable for our purpose. It is the gate through the last or most eastern sphere of the Alleghanies. It now becomes as useful to us as it was to the enemy, being easily defended from either direction. The roads hence from Ackworth into Georgia are large and good, and the country more open. The enemy is not in our immediate front, but his signals are seen at Lost Mountain and Kenesaw."

Thus it will be seen that from the 1st of May, when the Army of the Mississippi began to move towards Ringgold, up to this date, the 7th of June, it had made a most wonderful and successful campaign. It had marched over mountains, through gorges and dangerous gaps, forded streams, built bridges, scaled precipices, and constructed roads through the wildest of countries; had fought battles, skirmished almost every day, by moonlight, and amid darkness and howling storms; and had captured every strong-hold from a large and well-officered army, and driven them back within thirty miles of Atlanta.

Previous to this time the public had not regarded Sherman as a military genius or a very cautious general. He was considered to be a bold, fearless, and hard fighter, but very reckless. The manner in which he had conducted the campaign thus far, had removed these impressions, and he has since that time been regarded as one of our ablest generals.

INCIDENTS.

We will close this chapter with the following incidents, which we give upon the authority of various correspondents.

A rebel who had voluntarily given himself up, was asked by one of our soldiers what he thought of Sherman. This was his reply: "Sherman gits on a hill, flops his wings and crows; then yells out, attention! · creation! by kingdoms right wheel! march! *and then we git.*"

Some of the prisoners, with an air of great curiosity inquired in reference to the breech-loading Henry rifle, which can be fired sixteen times without re-loading: "*Where do you get those guns which you load on Sunday, and fire all the week without re-loading?*"

A YANKEE TRICK.

Colonel Wolcott of the Forty-sixth Ohio, played an original and striking trick upon the rebels in his front. They were behind a very heavy earthwork and safe from our sharpshooters. Advancing his regiment he constructed a substantial rifle pit, in which he placed his regiment entirely covered from the rebels, and within short range of their works. He then formed columns some distance in the rear with considerable display, as if about to storm the rebel works. After he had sufficiently attracted their attention, his bugles sounded "forward." The rebels jumped to their works in readiness to resist an assault. The "Johnnies" thus exposed the half of their bodies above the parapet, and instantly received full and square in their faces the volleys of the sixteen shooters of the Forty-sixth. The line fell down and the survivors thunderstruck by the unexpected fire, ran without ceremony out of the works. No doubt they considered it a Yankee trick.

JEFF. C. DAVIS' JOKE.

General Jeff. C. Davis played a serious joke upon the enemy in his front, of which I have not given you the particulars. Davis' division was near the foot of a hill, near the the top of which the rebels had a strong intrenchment. Davis advanced a regiment as skirmishers up the hill through the woods. It moved pretty well up to the work, and finding it too strong to assault, the colonel halted his command, and reported to General Davis that he could not proceed any further without great loss. Davis ordered him to hold his men in that position until he should hear his signal to withdraw. Leaving an interval of the length of his regiment, he put troops on either side and in front of this space in ambush, and sounded the recall. As the regiment commenced falling back leisurely, the rebels came out of their work, and with a tremendous yell, charged down the slope expecting to capture the retreating Yankees. The speed of our men was accelerated and down they rushed to their place in the line, pursued closely by the rebels. The result was a fearful slaughter of the entrapped confederates. Few of the assailants escaped Davis' enfilading fire.

CHAPTER X.

SHERMAN'S GREAT CAMPAIGN FROM CHATTANOOGA TO ATLANTA.

OPERATIONS OF THE ARMY FROM JUNE SEVENTH TO THE CAPTURE OF ATLANTA—SHERMAN'S REPORT—EFFORTS TO BREAK THE ENEMY'S LINES BETWEEN KENESAW AND PINE MOUNTAINS—DEATH OF GENERAL POLK—MCPHERSON'S OPERATIONS—TWO DIRECT ASSAULTS—KENESAW ABANDONED—THE PURSUIT—PASSAGE OF THE CHATTAHOOCHEE—THE BATTLE OF THE TWENTIETH—JOHNSTON RELIEVED—ATTACK ON OUR RIGHT—POSITIONS OF OUR FORCES—SUDDEN ATTACK—DEATH OF MCPHERSON—GRAND MOVEMENT OF THE RIGHT FLANK—KILPATRICK'S OPERATIONS—SHERMAN'S FLANK MOVEMENT AND THE CAPTURE OF ATLANTA—BOMBARDMENT OF ATLANTA—SHERMAN'S CONGRATULATORY ORDER.

The last chapter brings the account of this wonderful campaign to June 7, 1864. In this chapter we propose following him to the capture of Atlanta. The details of this part of the campaign cannot be given in this chapter, but will be given in a subsequent and separate part.

We learn from General Sherman's official report, upon which we base our statements in this chapter, that dispositions were made to break the lines of the enemy between Kenesaw and Pine Mountains. This was on the 11th. General Hooker was placed on the right and front, and General Howard on the left and front of the enemy's position, and General Palmer between it and the railroad. During a sharp cannonading from Howard's right or Hooker's left, General Polk, the renowned bishop of the Episcopal Church, was killed on the 14th.

On the morning of the 14th, Pine Mountain was found abandoned by the enemy. Generals Thomas and Schofield advanced, and found the enemy again strongly intrenched along a line of rugged hills connecting Kenesaw and Lost Mountains. At the same time General McPherson advanced his line, gaining substantial advantage on the left. Pushing operations on the centre as vigorously as the nature of the ground would permit, General Sherman ordered an assault on the centre, when, on the 17th, the enemy abandoned Lost Mountain, and the long line of admirable breastworks connecting it with Kenesaw Mountain. Our forces continued to press at all points, skirmishing in dense forests of timber and across most difficult ravines, until they found the enemy again strongly posted and intrenched, with Kenesaw as his salient point, his right wing being thrown back so as to cover Marietta, and his left behind Nose's Creek, covering the railroad back to the Chattahoochee River. This enabled the enemy to contract his lines, and strengthen them greatly.

On the 27th of June, two direct assaults were made for the purpose of dislodging them, but they failed. On the 1st of July, Sherman ordered General McPherson to throw his whole army, by the right, down to and through Nickajack Creek and Turner's Ferry, across the Chattahoochee. General McPherson commenced this movement on the night of July 2d, and the effect was instantaneous. The next morning Kenesaw Mountain was abandoned, "and," says Sherman, " with the first dawn of morning I saw our skirmishers appear off on the mountain top." We can better imagine than describe the feelings of the officers and their men at that sight. General Thomas' whole line was then moved forward to the railroad, and turned south in pursuit toward the Chattahoochee. Sherman in person, entered Marietta at half-past eight o'clock in the morning, just as the enemy's cavalry had vacated the place.

On the 9th of July, Sherman had secured three good and safe points of passage over the Chattahoochee, with good roads leading to Atlanta. The same day Johnston abandoned his position on the river, burned his bridges, and left Sherman undisputed master north and west of the Chattahoochee at daylight on the 10th of July.

On the 20th of July, all the armies had closed in, converging toward Atlanta. During the afternoon of the 20th, about four o'clock, the enemy sallied from his works in force, and fell in line of battle against our right centre, which was composed of General Newton's division, of General Howard's corps, on the Buckhead Road; of General Hooker's corps, next south, and General Johnson's division, of General Palmer's corps. The blow was sudden and somewhat unexpected, but General Newton had hastily covered his front by a line of rail piles, which enabled him to meet and repulse the attack. General Hooker's whole corps was uncovered, and had to fight on comparatively open ground. After a very severe battle the enemy was driven back to his intrenchments. The action in front of General Johnson was comparatively light, that division being well intrenched. The enemy left on the field over 500 dead, about 1,000 wounded severely, 7 stands of colors, and many prisoners. The loss of our army was not over 1,500 in killed, wounded and missing. On account of the exposed condition of Hooker's corps, the greatest loss fell on it.

Sherman was greatly surprised to find, on the morning of the 22d, that the enemy had abandoned their whole line. He supposed from this that he had resolved to give up Atlanta without further contest; but General Johnston had been relieved of his command, and General Hood substituted in his place. A new policy had been adopted, as the bold attack on our right seemed to indicate. As soon as the movement was discovered, our advancing ranks swept across the strong and well-finished parapet of the enemy, and closed in upon Atlanta, until our forces occupied a line in the form of a general circle of about two miles radius, when we again found him occupying, in force, a line of finished redoubts, which had been prepared for more than a year, covering all the roads leading into Atlanta, and we found him also busy in connecting these redoubts with curtains strengthened by rifle trenches, abattis and *chevaux-de-frize.*

General McPherson, who had advanced from Decatur, continued to follow the railroad, with the Fifteenth Corps, General Logan; the Seventeenth, General Blair, on its left; and the Sixteenth, General Dodge, on its right; but as the general advance of all the armies contracted the circle, the Sixteenth Corps, was thrown out of line by the Fifteenth connecting on the right with General Schofield near the Howard House. General McPherson, the night before, had gained a high hill to the south and east of the railroad, where the Seventeenth Corps had, after a severe fight, driven the enemy, and it gave him a most commanding position, within easy view of the very heart of the city. He had thrown out working parties to it, and was making preparations to occupy it in strength with the batteries. The Sixteenth Corps, was ordered from right to left to occupy this position and make it a strong general left flank. General Dodge was moving by a diagonal path, or wagon track, leading from the Decatur Road, in the direction of General Blair's left flank. General McPherson remained with General Sherman until near noonday, when reports reached them that indicated a movement of the enemy on that flank. McPherson then mounted and rode away with his staff. The day before, Sherman had detached General Garrard's cavalry to go to Covington, on the Augusta Road, forty-two miles east of Atlanta, and from that point to send detachments to break the two important bridges across the Yellow and Ulcofauhatchee Rivers, tributaries of the Ocomulgee. General McPherson had left his wagon train at Decatur, under a guard of three regiments commanded by Colonel, now General Sprague. Soon after McPherson left Sherman at the Howard House, as above stated, General Sherman heard the sound of musketry to our left rear, at first mere pattering shots, but soon they grew in volume, accompanied with artillery, and about the same time the sound of guns was heard in the direction of Decatur. No doubt could longer be entertained of the enemy's plan of action, which was to throw a superior force on our left flank, while he held us with his forts in front, the only question being as to the amount of force he could employ at that point. Sherman hastily transmitted orders to all points of our centre and right to press forward and to give full employment to all the enemy in his lines, and for General Schofield to hold as large a force in reserve as possible, and await developments. Not more than half an hour after General McPherson had left his adjutant general, Lieutenant-Colonel Clark rode up to Sherman and informed him that General McPherson was either dead or a prisoner; and that after he had ridden from him towards General Dodge's columns, and had sent off nearly all his staff and orderlies on various errands, he passed into a narrow path or road that led to the left and rear of General Giles A. Smith's division, which was General Blair's extreme left; that a few minutes after a sharp volley of musketry was heard in that direction, and his horse came out riderless, having two wounds. "*The suddenness of this terrible calamity*," says Sherman, "*would have overwhelmed me with grief, but the living demanded all my thoughts.*" Sherman promptly dispatched a staff officer to General John A. Logan, commanding the Fifteenth Corps, to tell him what had happened; and that he must assume command of the Army of the Tennessee, and hold stubbornly the ground already chosen. Sherman paid this tribute to General McPherson: "He was a noble youth, of striking personal appearance, of the highest professional capacity, and with a heart abounding in kindness that drew to him the affections of all men." His body was recovered, and brought to Sherman in the heat of battle, and sent in charge of his personal staff back to Marietta, and from thence to his home, at Sandusky, Ohio. At Nashville, Louisville, Cincinnati, and all along the route to his final resting place, the highest tributes of respect were paid to the memory and remains of the fallen hero.

THE GRAND MOVEMENT BY THE RIGHT FLANK.

Sherman became satisfied that, to reach the Macon Road, and thereby control the supplies for Atlanta, he would be compelled to move the whole army. Before beginning this movement, he ordered from Chattanooga, four $4\frac{1}{2}$-inch rifled guns, to try their effect on the city of Atlanta. These guns arrived on the 10th, and were put to work day and night, and did execution on the city, causing frequent fires, and creating confusion; yet the enemy seemed determined to hold his forts, even if the city was destroyed. On the 16th of August,

Sherman issued his orders, prescribing the mode and manner of executing the grand movement by the right flank, to begin on the 18th.

This movement contemplated the withdrawal of the Twentieth Corps, General Williams, to the intrenched position at Chattahoochee Bridge, and the march of the main army to the West Point Railroad, near Fairburn, and afterwards to the Macon Road, at or near Jonesboro', with wagons loaded with provisions for fifteen days. About the time of the publication of the orders referred to above, Sherman learned that Wheeler, with a large mounted force, variously estimated from 6,000 to 10,000 men, had passed around by the east and north, and had made his appearance on our lines of communication near Adairsville, and had succeeded in capturing 200 of our beef cattle, and had made a break in the railroad near Calhoun. This was just such a movement as Sherman desired. He had made ample preparations for such a contingency, and this movement left him superior to the enemy in cavalry. Sherman suspended the execution of his orders for the time being, and ordered General Kilpatrick to make up a well-appointed force of about 5,000 cavalry, and move from his camp about Sandtown, during the night of the 18th, to the West Point Road. This force started as ordered, and pushed on to Fairburn, on the West Point Railroad, where it met the enemy and drove him from the ground. Kilpatrick then moved on to Jonesboro', where he did considerable damage, and then rested his force for the night near Lovejoy's. He succeeded in destroying about three miles of the Macon Railroad and one train of cars. The enemy attempted to surround his force and capture them, but they succeeded in cutting their way through their ranks, and moved onward. They crossed the Cotton River on the morning of the 21st, and reached Lithonia, on the Georgia Railroad, east of Atlanta, in the evening of the same day. After resting for the night, the expedition joined the main army on the following morning.

After an interview with General Kilpatrick, Sherman was satisfied that whatever damage he had done would not produce the result desired. He therefore renewed his orders for the movement of the whole army. This, of course, involved the necessity of raising the seige of Atlanta, taking the field with our main force, and using it against its intrenchments. All the army commanders were at once notified to send their surplus wagons, incumbrances of all kinds, and sick, back to the intrenched position at the bridge, and that the movement would begin on the night of the 25th.

Accordingly, all things being ready, the Fourth Corps, General Stanley, drew out of its lines on the extreme left, and marched to a position below Proctor's Creek. The Twentieth Corps, General Williams, moved back to the Chattahoochee. This movement was made without loss, save a few things left in camp by thoughtless officers or men. On the night of the 26th, the Army of the Tennessee drew out, and moved rapidly by a circuit well toward Sandtown, and across Camp Creek. The Army of the Cumberland, moved below Utoy Creek, and General Schofield remained in position. This movement was effected with the loss of but a single man in the Army of the Tennessee. He was wounded by a shell from the enemy. The third move brought the Army of the Tennessee on the West Point Railroad, above Fairburn, the Army of the Cumberland about Red Oak, and General Schofield closed in near Digs and Mims. Sherman then ordered one day's work to be expended in destroying the road, and it was done with a will. Twelve and one-half miles were destroyed, the ties burned, and the rails heated and tortured by the utmost ingenuity of old hands at the work. Several cuts were filled up with the trunks of trees, with logs, rocks, and earth, intermingled with loaded shell, prepared with torpedoes, to explode in case of an attempt to clear them out.

Sherman, in person, inspected this work; and, satisfied with the execution, he ordered the army to move next day eastward, by several roads — General Howard on the right, toward Jonesboro'; General Thomas in the centre, by Shoal Creek Church to Couch's, on the Decatur and Fayetteville Road; and General Schofield on the left, about Morrow's Mills.

On the 31st of August, the enemy came out of his works at Jonesboro', and attacked General Howard. Howard was admirably situated to receive him, and thoroughly repulsed the attack. The attacking party was composed of Lee's and Hardee's corps; and after a contest of more than two hours, withdrew, leaving on the field over 400 dead, and his wounded, of which about 300 were left in Jonesboro'. His losses could not have been much less than 2,500. Hearing the sound of battle at Jonesboro' about noon, orders were renewed to push the other movements on the left and centre, and about four o'clock P. M. the reports arrived simultaneously that General Howard had repulsed the enemy at Jonesboro'; that General Schofield had reached the railroad a mile below Rough-and-Ready, and was working up the road, breaking it as he went; that General Stanley, of General Thomas' army, had taken possession of the road below General Schofield, and was destroying its working south; and that General Bird, of General Davis' Corps, had struck it still lower down, within four miles of Jonesboro'.

Orders were at once given for all the army to turn on Jonesboro', and Howard was ordered to keep the rebels busy, while Thomas should move down from the north, with General Schofield on his left. Sherman also ordered the troops, as they moved down, to continue the thorough destruction of the railroad, because it was then in his hands, and he did not know but that events might divert attention from it. General Garrard's cavalry was directed to watch the roads in the rear, and to the north of the army. General Kilpatrick was sent south, down the west bank of the Flint River, with instructions to attack or threaten the railroad below Jonesboro'. Sherman expected the whole army would close down on Jonesboro' by noon of the 1st of September. General Davis' Corps, having a shorter distance to travel, was on time and deployed, facing the south, his right in connection with General Howard, and his left on the railroad. General Stanley and General Schofield were then moving down along the Rough-and-Ready Road, and along the railroad, breaking it as they moved. When General Davis joined General Howard, General Blair's Corps, on Howard's left, was thrown in reserve, and was immediately sent well to the right, below Jonesboro', to act against that flank, along with General Kilpatrick's cavalry. About four o'clock P. M. General Davis was all ready, and commenced the assault on the lines across open fields, carrying them very handsomely, and taking, as prisoners, the greater part of Govan's brigade, including its commander, with two four-gun batteries. The next morning the enemy was gone. He had retreated south.

Rumors began to reach Sherman, through prisoners, that Atlanta had been abandoned during the night of September 1st; that Hood had blown up his ammunition trains, which accounted for the sounds so plainly heard in the direction of Atlanta, but which, as yet, had not been explained; that Stewart's corps was then retreating towards McDonough, and that the militia had gone off towards Covington. It was then too late for Sherman to interfere and attempt to prevent their escape, and besides he was well satisfied with the substantial victory already gained. Accordingly, he ordered the work of destroying the railroad to cease, and the troops to be held in hand, ready for any movement that further information from Atlanta might warrant.

General Davis' corps had been left above Jonesboro, and General Garrard's cavalry was still further back, and the latter was ordered to send to Atlanta and ascertain the exact truth, and the real situation of affairs. But the same night (September 4th), a courier arrived from General Slocum, reporting the fact that the enemy had evacuated Atlanta, blown up seven trains of cars, and had retreated on the McDonough Road. General Slocum had entered and taken possession on the 2d of September.

The object of the movement against the railroad was, therefore, already reached and concluded. As it was idle to pursue the enemy in that wooded country with a view to his capture, Sherman gave orders, on the 4th, to prepare to move back slowly to Atlanta. On the 5th his forces moved to Jonesboro', five miles, where they remained a day. On the 7th they moved to Rough and Ready, seven miles, and the next day to the camps selected. The Army of the Cumberland were grouped round about Atlanta, the Army of the Tennessee about East Point, and that of the Ohio at Decatur, where the troops occupied clean and healthful camps.

Thus Sherman again accomplished, by wise and honorable strategy, what he could not have otherwise done without the sacrifice of his noble army. Whoever will consider the extent and strength of the fortifications of Atlanta, as represented by the enemy, will not doubt the truth of this statement.

An eye witness of the bombardment of Atlanta, who was within the fortifications at the time, thus speaks of their strength, and the comparative security of the citizens:

"The trenches are impregnable. It might be possible for a heavy massed column to penetrate them, but not without immense loss, and then not to be held. The works, which were admirably located at first, have been materially strengthened, and the assaults of the enemy (Sherman's forces) have only developed our most commanding positions, and demonstrated where the engineer's skill and the miner's labor could be employed to the best advantage.

"In front of the great circular line of intrenchments, for many rods, the fields are broken and irregular, dotted with stumps, and strewn with a complete tangle of tree tops and branches forming a barrier against approach. In front of the batteries, blind pit-falls, miniature stockades, palisades and *chevaux-de-frise* work in all directions, and make a *net work out of whose entanglement a wild fox could barely escape*. By the time a charging line could pass these barriers, under a tornado of grape-shot, shell and minie, the line would be so broken and reduced as to be totally ineffectual.

"The works are almost invulnerable, and every day adds something to their strength, and the soil is unfavorable to mining operations.

"There are also excavations in the soil, roofed with heavy logs, over which is heaped the loose earth to the height of a young Ararat. These little mounds may be seen all over the city. The garden to almost every house which does not boast a cellar is supplied with its artificial bomb-proof. They are perfectly secure against the metal storm, and many of them are quite comfortably furnished with beds and chairs and other furniture. Women and children are huddled together in them for hours at a time, and when the city is furiously shelled at night, the whole community may be said to be under ground. Especially is this the case when the moon is unusually bright, and the approach of the shells cannot be marked by their fiery trail."

We close this chapter with Sherman's congratulatory order to his troops, and his resume of the operations of the campaign:

HEAD-QUARTERS MILITARY DIVISION OF THE MISSISSIPPI,
IN THE FIELD, ATLANTA, Ga.,
THURSDAY, September 8, 1864.

SPECIAL FIELD ORDERS No. 68.

The officers and soldiers of the Armies of the Cumberland, Ohio and Tennessee have already received the thanks of the nation, through its President and Commander-in-Chief; and it now remains only for him who has been with you from the beginning, and who intends to stay all the time, to thank the officers and men for their intelligence, fidelity and courage displayed in the campaign of Atlanta.

On the 1st of May our armies were lying in garrison, seemingly quiet, from Knoxville to Huntsville, and our enemy lay behind his rocky-faced barrier at Dalton, proud, defiant and exulting. He had had time since Christmas to recover from his discomfiture on the Mission Ridge, with his ranks filled, and a new commander-in-chief second to none of the Confederacy in reputation for skill, sagacity and extreme popularity. All at once our armies assumed life and action, and appeared before Dalton; threatening Rocky Face, we threw ourselves upon Resaca, and the rebel army only escaped by the rapidity of his retreat, aided by the numerous roads with which he was familiar, and which were strange to us. Again he took post in Altoona, but we gave him no rest, and by a circuit towards Dallas, and subsequent movement to Ackworth, we gained the Altoona Pass. Then followed the eventful battles about Kenesaw, and the escape of the enemy across the Chattahoochee River.

The crossing of the Chattahoochee and breaking of the Augusta Road was most handsomely executed by us, and will be studied as an example in the art of war. At this stage of our game, our enemies became dissatisfied with their old and skillful commander, and selected one more bold and rash. New tactics were adopted. Hood first boldly and rapidly, on the 20th of July, fell on our right at Peach Tree Creek, and lost; again, on the 22d, he struck our extreme left, and was severely punished, and finally again, on the 28th, he repeated the attempt on our right, and that time must have been satisfied, for since that date he has remained on the defensive. We slowly and gradually drew our lines about Atlanta, feeling for the railroads which supplied the rebel army and made Atlanta a place of importance. We must concede to our enemy that he met these efforts patiently and skillfully, but at last he made the mistake we had waited for so long, and sent his cavalry to our rear, far beyond the reach of recall. Instantly our cavalry was on his only remaining road, and we followed quickly with our principal army, and Atlanta fell into our possession as the fruit of all concerted measures, backed by a brave and competent army. This completed the grand task which had been assigned us by our government, and your general again repeats his personal and official thanks to all the officers and men composing this army, for the indomitable courage and perseverance which alone could give *success.*

We have beaten our enemy on every ground he has chosen, and have wrested from him his own gate city, where were located his foundries, arsenals and workshops, deemed secure on account of their distance from our base, and the seemingly impregnable obstacles intervening. *Nothing* is impossible to an army like this, determined to vindicate a government which has rights wherever our flag has once floated, and is resolved to maintain them at any and all costs.

In our campaign many, yes, very many, of our noble and gallant comrades have preceded us to our common destination, the grave; but they have left the memory of deeds on which a nation can build a proud history. McPherson, Harker, McCook, and others dear to us all, are now the binding links in our minds that should attach more closely together the living, who have to complete the task which still lays before us in the dim future. I ask all to continue as they have so well begun, the cultivation of the soldierly virtues that have ennobled our own and other countries. Courage, patience, obedience to the laws and constituted authorities of our government, fidelity to our trusts and good feeling among each other, each trying to excel the other in the practice of those high qualities, and it will then require no prophet to foretell that our country will in time emerge from this war, purified by the fires of war, and worthy of its great founder, "Washington."

      W. T. SHERMAN, *Major General Commanding.*

Official: L. W. DAYTON, *Aide-de. Camp.*

CHAPTER XI.

SHERMAN'S GREAT CAMPAIGN FROM CHATTANOOGA TO ATLANTA.

ADDITIONAL ACCOUNTS OF THE CAMPAIGN—THE VALUE OF THIS CHAPTER—CAMPAIGN REVIEWED BY A DISTINGUISHED GENERAL.

In addition to the accounts given in the three previous chapters of this campaign, we subjoin another chapter, composed almost entirely of correspondence. Among this correspondence will be found several letters from a distinguished general, who took an active part in the campaign.

This chapter we regard as of great value, and it will be read with great interest, and for this reason. Part of this correspondence will give to the reader a succinct review of the whole campaign, and from other parts he will have descriptions, facts and incidents which we have excluded from the previous chapters, and which will serve the purpose of shedding additional light on this great campaign, and at the same time will be a source of pleasure to the reader and valuable to the future historian.

The following letters from the general, above alluded to, will give to the reader a general review of the entire campaign:

"Marching from Chattanooga on the 5th of May, and from Ringgold on the 7th, Sherman first encountered Johnston at Tunnel Hill, a strong position, but which was used by him merely as an outpost to his still stronger one of 'Buzzard Roost.' This latter is a narrow gorge or pass in the Chatoogata Mountains, flanked on one side by the precipitous sides of Rocky Face Ridge (not unlike the Palisades of the Hudson River), and on the other by the greater but less precipitous elevation called John's Mountain. This gorge was commanded on the Dalton side by an amphitheatre of hills, which, as well as the tops of Rocky Face and John's Mountain, was crowned by batteries, lined with infantry, and terraced by sharpshooters. The railroad and wagon road wind through the gorge, which is absolutely the only passage through the mountains at this place. Taking a leaf from the book of his Yorktown experience, Johnston had skillfully flooded the entrance to the gorge by damming a neighboring mountain stream and covering both railroad and wagon road with water to the depth, in some places, of eight to ten feet. It is scarcely possible to conceive a stronger defensive position; and the rebels had been induced to believe that it was unassailable.

"Two days' reconnoissance and sharp skirmishing proved to General Sherman that an attack in front would cost too great a sacrifice of life, and that it must be turned. The means for this were found in a gap — called 'Snake Creek Gap'— some fifteen miles to the southwest. Our superiority of numbers, and the densely-wooded condition of the country, enabled the gap to be occupied by us, and the manœuvre half completed before it was discovered by Johnston.

"McPherson, with the Fifteenth and part of the Sixteenth Corps, supported by Thomas with the Fourteenth and Twentieth Corps, and Garrard's division of cavalry, effected the flank movement; while Howard, with the Fourth Corps, Schofield with the Twenty-third, and Stoneman's division of cavalry, amused the enemy in front.

"Johnston was, of course, thus forced to abandon his stronghold, and fall back to a new position, to save his railroad and other communications, thus directly menaced.

"This new position was around the town of Resaca, on a range of hills, in a broken and densely-wooded country.

"Guarding against another *turning* operation, the wary Johnston so cared for his flanks that we were forced to attack him in front. For three days we had some very severe fighting; but gaining a little every day, and holding on tenaciously to all he got, Sherman finally possessed himself of certain hills, which commanded the town, railroad bridge, and roads in his rear. Crowning these with our batteries during the night, we were prepared at daylight next morning to render his roads impassable; but the enemy evacuated during the night. Our trophies were eight guns, two colors, several hundred prisoners, and a quantity of provisions and forage.

"Following him up closely, we either drove or turned him out of every succeeding position as far as Marietta, seven miles north of the Chattahoochee, and about fifteen north of Atlanta; while we were close upon him, with the railroad and telegraph fully repaired behind us, and supplies of all sorts at hand in abundance.

"To recapitulate: We have, in a month's time, with a force not *very much* superior to his, forced the enemy back nearly one hundred miles, obliging him to abandon four different positions of unusual strength and proportions; have fought him six times; have captured twelve guns, three colors, over two thousand prisoners, with considerable forage, provisions, and means of transportation; have placed *at least* fifteen thousand of his men *hors de combat;* and have destroyed several important foundries, rolling mills, iron works, &c.,

at Rome and in the Altoona Mountains. All these are substantial proofs of success.

"Johnston now holds an apparently strong position immediately in front of Marietta, which looks like the hardest nut we have yet had to crack. We are in line of battle about one mile in his front, and, as soon as the rain (of which we have had a week's steady outpouring) clears up, we shall try conclusions with him. The probabilities are that we shall have a hard tussle. The accounts of prisoners, deserters, scouts, &c., place Johnston's force at nine divisions, of about seven thousand men each, with an auxiliary force of Georgia militia, variously estimated at from fifteen thousand to twenty-five thousand men. As at present arranged, Hood's Corps is on his left, Hardee's the right, and Polk's the centre, with the militia disposed at various points to the best advantage. The enemy's cavalry, said to number fifteen thousand, is on their flank and *our* rear. I presume Johnston's entire force is not far from eighty thousand men."

"At the date of my last letter (June 12, from Big Shanty) the enemy's line was intrenched upon Lost Mountain, Pine Hill, Kenesaw Mountain (three peaks), and upon a line of ridges connecting these three points, and extending eastward of the last named some two miles, up to and beyond an eminence called Brushy Hill. They also occupied, for about three-quarters of a mile, a line of ridge nearly parallel to the long diameter of Kenesaw, and about half a mile in front of it. You will perceive that their defensive line was irregular, concave to us, with Kenesaw as a sort of citadel or stronghold in a deep reëntrant. The ridge in front of Kenesaw commences about *Wallace's* House, (on the Burnt Hickory and Marietta Road), and extends thence across the railroad behind Noonday Creek about two miles in an east by north direction. Lost Mountain and Kenesaw are about eleven hundred feet high, Pine Hill and Bushy Hill about four hundred feet high, and the ridges everywhere about one hundred and fifty to two hundred feet, or about the same as (and, in fact, not very dissimilar to) Missionary Ridge at Chattanooga. The enemy was everywhere strongly intrenched behind log barricades, protected by earth thrown against them, with a ditch, formidable abatis, and in many places a chevaux-de-frise of sharpened fence rails besides. Their intrenchments were well protected by thick traverses, and at frequent intervals arranged with emplacements and embrasures for field-guns. The thickness of this parapet (which really resembled a *parallel*) was generally six to eight feet *at top* on the infantry-line, and from twelve to fifteen feet thick (at top) where field-guns were posted, or where fire from our artillery was anticipated. The amount of digging and intrenching that Johnston's army has done, and is doing, is almost incredible. From the 12th to the present date, our operations have resulted in wresting Lost Mountain, Pine Hill (the ridge in front of Kenesaw,) and Brushy Hill from the enemy, and forcing back his two wings (Kenesaw Mountain operating as a sort of hinge,) until now his left is behind Olley's Creek, and his right behind the stream which flows between the houses named on the map as McAffee and *Wiley Roberts*. Kenesaw Mountain is now a sharp salient instead of a reëntrant. Of this formidable *point d' appui* we have not yet been able to get possession. It is a rocky eminence, rather precipitous, thickly wooded, and crowned with batteries.

"Our respective lines are about eight or nine miles in length, are from six hundred to seven hundred yards distant from each other, and are strongly intrenched. Skirmishing goes on incessantly, and artillery duels occur two or three times daily. The enemy have at different times made some dozen or more assaults, sometimes getting within fifty yards of our intrenchments, but are always repulsed, and generally with heavy loss to them. On the 27th of June, to gain certain positions, we opened a heavy artillery fire upon their whole line, pressed their two flanks heavily, and made assaults in two places upon their centre. The assaults were unsuccessful; but the Twenty-third Corps, upon our extreme right, gained some important advantages of position, of which we will avail ourselves anon.

"Our losses on this day were about two thousand, of all ranks, Brigadier-General Harker being killed, and Brigadier-Generals Wagner and McCook dangerously wounded.

"Our artillery practice, in all of our operations in this campaign, has been truly admirable, and has proved of indispensable service. We learn from various rebel sources how fatal its effects have been.

"We are now, in every portion of our line, less than three miles distant from Marietta. The enemy, now almost cornered, are thoroughly at bay, and make most determined and obstinate resistance. Every inch we gain is by sheer hard fighting, and it is only by hard fighting that we can hold on to all we get."

"The strategy that gave us Kenesaw Mountain and Marietta on the 3d of July, that forced the enemy out of his next fortified line half-way between Marietta and Chattahoochee on the 5th, and drove the greater portion of his forces across the river, and that finally compelled him to let go his hold of the entire right bank, forced him from the occupation of the immediate left bank, and enabled us to cross and effect a sure lodgment there July 8th to 12th, consisted in strong demonstrations (extending as low down the river as below Campbellton) on the enemy's left, conveying the impression that it was his *left* flank that was to be turned, and that the passage of the river *south* of Atlanta was to be forced, and then rapidly shifting masses of our troops from our extreme right to our extreme left, turning the enemy's *right* flank, and seizing and holding vital strategic points in that direction.

"Crossing the river at Rosswell, and at Phillips' Ferry (five miles below), our left encountered only cavalry and the new levies of militia; while the mass of the enemy's force was watching our feints extending from Power's Ferry (four miles above the railroad-bridge) to Turner's Ferry (some two and a half miles below it). The lodgment once secured on the left bank, bridges were built, and a force was soon thrown over, sufficient not only to hold our own there against all peradventure, but to advance boldly, roll back the enemy's right, and uncover Power's Ferry, which was immediately bridged, and gave us a third and most important crossing. An additional advance of the left gave us Pace's Ferry (only one mile above the railroad bridge), which was securely bridged by a double trestle structure, and which enabled us to cross the remainder of our force. The Army of the Cumberland held our left, the Army of the Ohio the centre, and the Army of the Tennessee the right. Leaving Davis' division of the Fourteenth Corps on the right bank of the Chattahoochee to cover the railroad bridge and watch the approaches from the southwest to our rear, the whole army commenced a grand right wheel, pirouetting upon the river, just above the railroad bridge. In this manner, with our left swinging through Cross-Keys and our centre through Buckhead, we very soon began to menace the Augusta Road, and the enemy's communications everywhere, including the city of Atlanta itself. Our extreme left found but little else than cavalry to encounter, with a few horse-artillery guns, and a very light force of supporting infantry—thus plainly indicating that in the enemy's mind the delusion that his left and not his right was still the real point of attack, and that Atlanta was to be approached by us from the southwest instead of from the northwest, had not been dispelled. Under these circumstances, our left and left-centre were enabled to pass with but little trouble the naturally strong defensive lines of Nance's and Peach Tree Creek. Becoming now awakened to his real position, the enemy commenced extending towards his right, falling gradually back upon Atlanta so as to shorten his line, and was thus compelled to relax his grasp of the Chattahoochee near Turner's Ferry. Having now obtained entire control of both banks of the river covered by our line, and for some miles both above and below, Davis' division was crossed to the left bank and joined its corps. The right wheel of our army was still continued, and it soon gave us possession of Decatur and the Atlanta and Augusta Railroad, passing through that town. The railroad was destroyed by us for many miles, and this line of communication rendered useless to the enemy. Driving the enemy before us gradually, as he fitfully struggled from one defensive intrenched position to another, we at length forced him within the defences of Atlanta itself, and on the 21st our troops took their position in front of them. At that date the Army of the Tennessee (our left) fronted the southeast of the city, with its centre across the Augusta Railroad and its left about two miles east of the Macon Railroad; the Army of the Ohio covered the eastern front, and the Army of the Cumberland the northeastern, which included the railroad to Chattanooga, and covered our bridges and other communications across the Chattahoochee. On the afternoon of the 20th of July, while the left division (Ward's) of the Twentieth Corps and the right division (Newton's) of the Fourth Corps were advancing to occupy a position from which the enemy had been driven the night previous, the enemy turned upon them and advanced in heavy masses to attack. Our men, though the greater portion were but slightly protected by the usual log or rail breastworks, and some of them were entirely in the open field, stood up to the work most manfully, and successfully repulsed, with heavy loss to the enemy, all of the repeated attacks made upon them. Night closed upon the enemy in full retreat, and our own line well advanced beyond the position it had when first attacked. Our loss was a trifle less than two thousand. We buried six hundred of the enemy's dead, and captured four hundred prisoners and seven regimental flags. The enemy's entire loss, as since admitted by their newspapers, was six thousand.

"On the 22d of July, about eleven o'clock A. M., the enemy availed himself of somewhat similar circumstances attending the Fifteenth and Seventeenth Corps, and attacked them furiously in flank and front as they were getting into position. Our men, attacked thus suddenly, and by overwhelming numbers, were heavily pressed, and at two points recoiled. An unclosed gap between the two corps, and another created by the disorder of a division of the Fifteenth Corps, gave the enemy an opportunity to penetrate our line, get possession of some of our guns, and take several hundred prisoners. .

The Sixteenth Corps being promptly moved up to the threatened points, our best ground was speedily recovered, four of our guns retaken, and our lines securely reëstablished. The enemy very persistently repeated his attacks several times (one particular hill, the key to the position, being assaulted seven times), but were handsomely repulsed, and before sunset were driven everywhere from the field in confusion. Our losses were three thousand seven hundred and sixty men killed, wounded and missing, thirteen guns, and two colors. Of the enemy we buried, or delivered to them next morning under flag of truce, three thousand one hundred dead, and captured two thousand two hundred prisoners and eighteen regimental colors. Their entire loss, by all ordinary rules of computation, could not be less than twelve thousand. Our severest loss on this day was General McPherson, who fell instantly killed by a volley from a portion of the enemy's force which had penetrated a piece of woods within our lines. A gallant and experienced soldier, a refined and cultivated gentleman, he died universally regretted.

"On the 28th of July the enemy assaulted another portion of our line, where they again encountered the Fifteenth Corps. As usual, they moved up in heavy force and made repeated assaults, but were again unsuccessful, and were driven back to their intrenchments, leaving the ground behind them strewed with their dead and wounded. Our losses were eight hundred and fifty-six killed, wounded and missing. We buried over six hundred of the enemy's dead, and captured four regimental colors, and have good reason to put their entire loss at five thousand. Since we crossed the Chattahoochee the enemy must have lost twenty thousand. While these events were transpiring, several cavalry expeditions were sent out for the destruction of railroads, supplies, &c., &c. Major General Rousseau broke the railroad for thirty miles between West Point and Montgomery, captured two hundred prisoners and five hundred horses and mules, and returned with a loss of less than thirty men. Brigadier General Garrard broke the Atlanta and Augusta Railroad for fifteen miles near Covington, burned two important railroad bridges, two locomotives and trains of loaded cars, two thousand bales of cotton, and several dépôts, and captured one hundred and fifty prisoners and three hundred horses and mules. His loss was only two men. Brigadier General McCook, starting from below Campbellton, crossed the Chattahoochee, broke several miles of the Atlanta and West Point and Atlanta and Macon Railroads, burned six hundred loaded wagons of the enemy's supply and reserve train, and killed a large number (said to be eight hundred) of mules. This expedition captured several hundred prisoners, including Brigadier General Ross, but, becoming surrounded by an overwhelming force of the enemy, General McCook was obliged to cut his way through, abandoning all his prisoners, and losing five hundred men. Major General Stoneman is still out on another important and hazardous expedition, but has not yet been heard from.

"Meanwhile, the enemy obstinately defend Atlanta, which we find to be entirely surrounded by strong earthworks, armed with a numerous and powerful artillery, and garrisoned by a force quite strong enough to render the question of assault one to be not lightly considered. The fate of the city is nevertheless as certain as any thing in war *can* be; and it must soon fall into our hands.

"During the whole of this summer's campaign in Northern Georgia the services of the artillery have been conspicuous. The Western soldier seems to be peculiarly adapted for this special service: brave, self-reliant, and a good marksman, he stands steadily to his gun in the most critical times, and delivers his fire coolly and with good effect. The three years' experience which this Western volunteer artillery has had, has given its officers and men a vast store of valuable practical knowledge. It is no unusual thing for a field-battery to take up its position, intrench itself securely, and open an effective fire, in the shortest possible time, unaided by the advice of superior officers or the assistance of engineer or other troops. We have abundance of rebel testimony in proof of the accuracy and vigor of our artillery fire.

"I write in great haste — under a broiling sun — with only the shelter of a tent-fly."

"Artillery Head-Quarters,
"Military Division of the Mississippi,
"Atlanta, September 10, 1864.

"I think my last letter to you closed with some accounts of the cavalry raids of Generals McCook and Stoneman, the uncaptured portions of whose forces had about that time just returned to our lines. The object of these two expeditions — one issuing from our right flank, the other from our left — was the destruction of a portion of the railroad to Macon, and the consequent interruption, if not the complete severance, of the enemy's sole remaining line of communication and supply.

"Stoneman, after completing his portion of the work, was granted permission by General Sherman (the request for this indulgence having been urgently pressed by General Stoneman) to attempt the liberation of our officers imprisoned at Macon, and of our thirty thousand enlisted men at Andersonville.

"Although Stoneman failed altogether in the latter portion of his programme, both raids were almost as successful as cavalry raids usually are, *i. e.*, much damage was inflicted upon the enemy, with considerable loss to ourselves; the enemy, as usual, repairing his damage within the week or ten days following.

"Failing to dislodge Hood from Atlanta in this way, General Sherman next resorted to a further extension of his right, hoping to outflank him in that direction. The Twenty-third Corps, supported by the Fourteenth, was, on the 6th of August, moved out to the south of Utay Creek. The enemy had probably anticipated a movement of this sort, for the Twenty-third Corps, on approaching the enemy's supposed flank, suddenly developed a strongly intrenched line, with the customary 'abatis' and 'head-log' stretching away southward, in the direction of East Point, as far as the eye could reach. Hascall's division of the Twenty-third Corps was moved up to try its strength, the Fourteenth Corps on its left, meantime, making a feigned assault to prevent the accumulation of too large a force in front of Hascall.

"The natural difficulties of the ground, and the impenetrable nature of the artificial obstructions, prevented Hascall's success; and, with a loss of about two hundred men, compelled him to return to his lines.

V.

"Next day a more determined assault was made, the enemy's line carried, and our dead and wounded of the previous day recovered. This line was now discovered to be an exterior one, run out in a southwesterly direction for nearly a mile at an obtuse angle to his main line, and was held by a single division. The possession of this exterior work enabled General Sherman to close at all points directly upon the enemy's main line of defense. This line was now plainly developed to be a series of redoubts of great thickness of parapet and good command, connected throughout by a continuous infantry parapet, covered by abatis, *chevaux-de-frise*, and entanglements of various other kinds;—the whole completely surrounding Atlanta, and thence extending the ridge all the way to East Point (six miles), covering the track jointly between two points by the Atlanta and Macon and the Atlanta and West Point Railroads.

"Under such circumstances, it is plain that Hood, with the advantage of interior lines, and acting strictly on the defensive behind his strong intrenchments, could, with an inferior force, successfully hold his position.

"The fertile genius of Sherman was fully equal to the occasion. A careful survey and consideration of the situation satisfied him that Hood's lines could not be assaulted, even successfully, without a sacrifice of life to his own troops not justified by the circumstances. He therefore determined to bring strategy to his aid. His conceptions here were characterized by his usual boldness, promptness and independence. He determined to withdraw his whole army from the immediate front of Atlanta, and, leaving one corps at the Chattahoochee River to guard his tête-de-pont, covering the railroad bridge, and the pontoon and trestle bridges within the space of a mile north and south of it, to throw the remainder of his troops to the southwest and south of the city, across the Macon Railroad—the West Point Railroad to be thoroughly destroyed en route. The plan was submitted to the lieutenant general, who, though deeming it hazardous, gave it his full approval, and preparations were accordingly at once made for putting it into execution.

"Meantime, to divert the enemy's attention from our real purposes, but principally to prevent that accumulation of supplies within the city which it was well understood was being made, General Barry, chief of artillery, was authorized to place in certain favorable positions some rifled siege-guns, and to keep up from them a continuous fire day and night until the preparations for the main movement were completed. This was done, and for twelve days the constant dropping of $4\frac{1}{2}$-inch shells and case-shot materially interfered with the running of railroad trains and the accumulation of supplies, and was the immediate cause, by the occasioning of several destructive conflagrations, of the destruction of much of the enemy's public property. General Kilpatrick, during the same interval, was instructed to make a raid across the enemy's communications, which resulted in the temporary breakage of some miles of railroad, the dispersion of a brigade of the enemy's cavalry, and the capture of one hundred prisoners, three flags, and one piece of artillery. On the 25th of August, all the necessary preparations having been completed, the grand movement was appointed to commence.

"Our line at that time was held as follows: The Fourth Corps, with its left resting upon the Georgia Railroad, formed our extreme left; next, on the right, was the Twentieth Corps, its right resting on Proctor's Creek; the Sixteenth, Seventeenth and Fifteenth Corps, forming the Army of the Tennessee, came next; then the Fourteenth Corps; and, finally, the Twenty-third Corps, which formed our extreme right. Garrard's cavalry division covered our left flank, and Kilpatrick's our right. During the night of the 25th of August, the Fourth Corps drew out from its intrenchments, and, moving by the rear of the Twentieth Corps, crossed Proctor's

Creek, and was massed behind the left centre of the Army of the Tennessee; the Twentieth Corps was also withdrawn from its intrenchments, and took position at the railroad bridge across the Chattahoochee; Garrard's cavalry fell back behind Peach Tree Creek. By daylight of the 26th, this portion of the movement was completed, and the north and east sides of Atlanta uncovered.

"The enemy, quite taken by surprise, were evidently at a loss to understand the movement, and seemed to believe that we had commenced to retreat. During the next night the Fourth Corps pushed on in the direction of 'Red Oak,' on the Atlanta and West Point Railroad, and the Army of the Tennessee and the Fourteenth Corps were withdrawn from their intrenchments, and moved, the former in the direction of 'Fairburn,' the latter in that of 'Red Oak.' The whole front of Atlanta was now uncovered, except that portion occupied by the Twenty-third Corps, which alone remained in its intrenchments. The enemy, still bewildered and apparently uncertain of our intentions, sent out a skirmish line to reconnoitre. It moved but little beyond our abandoned works, except in the direction of the railroad bridge, where it found us in force and strongly intrenched. During the next day the Twenty-third Corps withdrew from its intrenchments, and formed the left of our new line, which now advanced, reached and crossed the West Point Railroad, and intrenched for the night, facing east and north. The next day was spent in destroying the West Point Railroad, which was most effectually done from Red Oak to Fairburn, and some miles beyond, every tie being burned, and every rail twisted and warped. The enemy seemed now to be awakened to a suspicion that an extensive infantry raid upon the Macon Railroad was in process of execution, and probably believed that it was to be effected by perhaps the half, or even a smaller portion, of our whole force. He was evidently innocent of the belief that our whole army was moving upon his communications. Hood sent Hardee's corps, followed by S. D. Lee's, to Jonesboro', remaining in Atlanta with Stewart's corps and the militia. On the 30th of August Sherman put his army again in motion, in a south-easterly direction, aiming to strike the Macon Railroad from 'Rough and Ready' to Jonesboro'. The Army of the Tennessee, marching from Fairburn, crossed Flint River in the latter part of the day, driving the enemy's cavalry before it, and had approached to within half a mile of Jonesboro', when it encountered Hardee, and Lee's corps strongly intrenched in a favorable position, and where night overtook it. The remainder of the army, *en échelon* towards the left, did not succeed in getting up to the railroad. Kilpatrick's cavalry covered our right front and flank, and Garrard's our left flank and rear. About noon on the next day (August 31) Hardee, acting probably under the belief that but a small portion of our infantry was opposed to him, sallied from his works around Jonesboro', and assaulted the lines of the Fifteenth and Sixteenth Corps. The assault was general, but it lacked that enthusiasm and dash which ordinarily accompany the headlong attack of rebel troops, and it was repulsed by our men with little difficulty. The enemy fell back to his lines after two more attempts to assault, leaving his dead and many of his wounded in our hands. His loss in killed, wounded and prisoners was more than two thousand, while ours was not as many hundreds. The Fourth, Fourteenth and Twenty-third Corps reached the railroad during the course of the day, and thoroughly destroyed it, from 'Rough and Ready' to within two miles of Jonesboro'. During the afternoon of the next day, the Fourteenth Corps came up and formed on the left of the Army of the Tennessee. The Fourth and Twenty-third being still at the rear, with but slight prospect of their getting up before dark to strike the enemy in rear, General Sherman ordered the Fourteenth Corps to move forward to the assault without delay. Its position enabled it to take the rebel line flank. Davis, forming his troops with the divisions of Baird and Morgan in line, and the division of Carlin in support, moved handsomely up, crossed several hundred yards of open field under a heavy fire, and came down with a run upon the enemy, whose works our men mounted with a ringing cheer, and rolled up his whole right flank like a scroll. Unfortunately, our remaining troops did not get up in season, and darkness setting in, Hardee was enabled to get away. But for this his whole corps would have been swept off like chaff. As it was, however, Davis captured two four-gun batteries, and Brigadier General Gowan and his entire brigade of Cleburn's division, the crack fighting division of Hood's army.

"About midnight, heavy explosions and the brilliant illumination of burning supplies in the direction of Atlanta, twenty miles in our rear, gave us to understand that Hood had at last comprehended his situation and danger, and that, to save his army from being cut in two and crushed in detail, he had evacuated his stronghold, and *Atlanta was ours.*

"At daylight next morning (September 2), it was discovered that Hardee had fallen back seven miles, to 'Lovejoy's Station,' where good fortune had given him a naturally strong position, which he speedily intrenched, and where Hood effected the junction of his disunited forces the same day.

"Atlanta captured, our task was done, and, as General Sherman announced in his orders of the day, was '*well done.*' After destroying the Macon Railroad for six miles toward Lovejoy's, the different corps at once took up their positions covering their hard won acquisition. Here they are now engaged resting from their continuous labor of four months, and reorganizing and refitting for a new campaign, and, let us hope, new conquests.

" It would follow too soon upon the momentous events of this glorious summer campaign in Georgia, to discuss it critically, even with the brevity necessary for a magazine article; but those whose good fortune it has been to participate in it, however humbly, feel an honest pride in believing that its story will hold as high a place in history as that of any other in the present war."

CHAPTER XII.

SHERMAN AND THE OCCUPATION OF ATLANTA.

SHERMAN A MILITARY GENIUS — OPINIONS OF HIS CAMPAIGN — THE LONDON TIMES AND LONDON STAR — MEASURES FOR HOLDING ATLANTA — CITIZENS ORDERED FROM ATLANTA — SHERMAN AND HOOD — THEIR CORRESPONDENCE — AN ATLANTA EXILE — PERMANENT OCCUPATION INTENDED — OPERATIONS OF FORREST AND OTHERS — HOOD'S NORTHERN MOVEMENT — ATTACK AND REPULSE AT ALTOONA — THE PURSUIT — HOOD CROSSES THE TENNESSEE — SHERMAN'S PLANS — BATTLES OF FRANKLIN AND NASHVILLE — SHERMAN RETURNS TO ATLANTA — A FACETIOUS LETTER.

The operations of General Sherman's army, which resulted in the capture of Atlanta, and which have been partially recorded in the three previous chapters, make some of the most wonderful pages in the history of war. The army endured long marches, great hardships and bloody battles, seemingly without a murmur of complaint. The artifices to mislead the enemy were so successful, Sherman's marches were so well guarded, his army so well fed, his battles so well fought and won, that both officers and soldiers deserve the highest credit and praise, and Sherman has proved himself a military genius.

The southern people were made to believe that so far as Johnston and Hood were concerned, they had succeeded in "drawing Sherman on;" that they had accomplished the very thing they had intended from the start, and now that they had him "just where they wished," they would break up his long line of communications, compel him to evacuate Atlanta and then fall upon him and destroy his army. The people of the North, and the army, regarded the campaign as one of the greatest, most successful and decisive of the war. Even foreign nations and foreign papers — some of which were not remarkably friendly to our government or army, and which have from the beginning of the war, predicted the downfall of the great republic — were constrained to admit that Sherman's campaign was a great success.

The London *Times*, a paper of more influence than any other in England, and more hostile to our government than any other paper published beyond the ocean, thus speaks of this wonderful campaign:

"Nobody imagined that a Northern army could penetrate so far into the South and maintain itself so securely as Sherman's army has now done for months together. Neither the distance from the base of his operations, nor the difficulties of obtaining supplies, nor any of the numerous embarrassments incidental to a position in a hostile country, have impeded his proceedings. He can hold his own in the heart of Georgia and encounter the Confederates on equal terms. He may yet be repulsed, but he has shown that there is nothing impracticable in an expedition which would have been thought desperate at an earlier period of the war. The capture of Atlanta may fairly be regarded as crowning with success the campaign of the Northwestern Army of the Union. The results of the achievements are still to be seen; nor is it, indeed, yet certain that General Sherman will be able to retain his prize, but it is a prize nevertheless, for it represents the object which the Federal commander proposed to himself from the beginning of his expedition. Never, since the commencement of the war, has a Federal force plunged so intrepidly into Confederate territory. The Confederates have lost an important position and been unsuccessful in a campaign. They have not, however, lost an army, nor any considerable quantity of munitions or stores. The Federals have taken a turn in a State hitherto inaccessible to their armies, and can boast of an army quartered in Georgia.

"One of the great objects of the campaign in Georgia was the destruction of the Confederate army, and that has not been attained. General Hood remains in command of a force which, though it is not a match for Sherman's army, is nevertheless strong, well organized and *safe.*"

Such are the forced admissions of the London *Times*, a paper that has constantly wielded a large influence in favor of the enemies of the Republic. Let not the reader, however, imagine that our cause and our great generals had not a more candid, unprejudiced and sensible advocate among the people of England, than the London *Times*.

We take pleasure in here recording the just and truthful remarks of the London *Star*, a paper not unfriendly to our country and her brave and successful armies:

"Sherman's army has occupied Atlanta. The latter is one of those victories which form the turning points of great wars. It has been the object of the campaign of an army of probably 80,000 men, under one of the best generals of the North, who, with rare pertinacity and caution has advanced, step by step into the enemy's country, and who has won by assaults, now by strategy, beaten back the Southern army until at length the city at which he aimed has fallen into his grasp. The steady advance of the North on those Western fields of conflict has been as uniform as their failures in Eastern

Virginia—before the existing campaign—have been conspicuous.

"From Cairo to Atlanta constitutes a record of the most brilliant success which any army could hope to achieve. That obstacles and defeats have been encountered only makes the persistence, which has at length obtained victory, shine out with greater lustre. Kentucky was cleared of the great rebel armies in 1862; Tennessee was fought for and won in 1863, and the summer campaign of 1864, more arduous than either of the preceding, has rolled back the Confederates from the North of Georgia and placed Atlanta, the Birmingham of the West, at the feet of the conqueror.

"The success of Sherman may be measured by the hazardous nature of his campaign and the physical difficulties which he had to surmount, as well as by the strength of the army opposed to him and the value of his acquisitions. So bold was his advance, and so eminently perilous, that the Southern people not only refused to believe in the possibility of its success, but chuckled complacently at what they believed to be the profound policy of Johnston in retreating to draw Sherman still further from his base. Many in this country whose zeal for the South constantly leads them into blunders, eagerly swallowed this version of an advance which all sensible writers treated as a most threatening invasion, and even after Sherman had shown, by repeated battles and continued advances that he was not an assailant to be despised, these unfortunate prophets have never ceased to consign him weekly, to destruction.

"No doubt they will now inform us that Hood has given up Atlanta as a strategic measure for the purpose of drawing Sherman on to Macon, at which point a most dreadful fate awaits him. Hood, however, is not a scientific but a fighting general, and he and Sherman had another fierce conflict at the Macon Road, in which the Confederates were severely handled. This is another proof of the hopeless inferiority of the Confederate to that of the Union army."

We must now resume the narrative. As soon as Sherman had occupied Atlanta, he began to strengthen and protect his communications with Chattanooga and the North; well knowing that the enemy would attempt to destroy them and thus compel the evacuation of Atlanta. He also somewhat strengthened the fortifications of Atlanta, and that his plans might be kept from the enemy, he issued an order compelling all citizens to leave the place, giving them the choice of going South or North. This was denounced by the enemy and their friends in the North and in England, as an unheard of cruelty. In this order, the wisdom of which is not now doubted, General Sherman said: "Citizens are requested to leave Atlanta and proceed either North or South. The government will furnish transportation South as far as Rough and Ready; North as far as Chattanooga. All citizens may take their movable property with them. Transportation will be furnished for all movables. Negroes who wish to do so may go with their masters, other male negroes will be put in government employ, and the women and children sent outside the lines."

That this order might be carried out, an agreement was entered into between Sherman and Hood for a truce to last ten days.

The correspondence that follows will give full information on this subject, and will go very far to justify the course of General Sherman:

THE DEPOPULATION OF ATLANTA—CORRESPONDENCE OF GENERAL SHERMAN.

REPLY TO GENERAL HOOD.

HEADQUARTERS MILITARY DIVISION OF THE
MISSISSIPPI, AND IN THE FIELD,
ATLANTA, GA., Sept. 10, 1864.

General J. B. HOOD, commanding Army of the Tennessee, Confederate Army:

GENERAL:—I have the honor to acknowledge the receipt of your letter of this date at the hands of

Messrs. Ball and Crew, consenting to the arrangements I had proposed to facilitate the removal South, of the people of Atlanta who prefer to go in that direction. I enclose you a copy of my orders, which will, I am satisfied, accomplish my purpose perfectly. You style the measures proposed "unprecedented," and appeal to the dark history of war for a parallel as an act of "studied and ungenerous cruelty." It is not unprecedented, for General Johnston himself very wisely and properly removed the families all the way from Dalton down, and I see no reason why Atlanta should be excepted. Nor is it necessary to appeal to the dark history of war when recent and modern examples are so handy. You yourself burned dwelling houses along your parapet, and I have seen to-day, fifty houses that you have rendered uninhabitable because they stood in the way of your forts and men. You defended Atlanta on a line so close to the town that every cannon shot and many musket shots from our line of investments, that overshot their mark, went into the habitations of women and children. General Hardee did the same at Jonesboro', and General Johnston did the same last summer at Jackson, Miss. I have not accused you of heartless cruelty, but merely instance these cases of very recent occurrence, and could go on and enumerate hundreds of others, and challenge any fair man to judge which of us has the heart of pity for the families of a "brave people." I say it is kindness to these families of Atlanta to remove them now at once from scenes that women and children should not be exposed to; and the brave people should scorn to commit their wives and children to the rude barbarians who thus, as you say, violate the laws of war, as illustrated in the pages of its dark history. In the name of common sense, I ask you not to appeal to a just God in such a sacrilegious manner,—you, who in the midst of peace and prosperity, have plunged a nation into civil war, "dark and cruel war," who dared and badgered us to battle, insulted our flag, seized our arsenals and forts that were left in the honorable custody of a peaceful ordnance sergeant, seized and made prisoners of war the very garrisons sent to protect your people against Negroes and Indians, long before any overt act was committed by the (to you) hateful Lincoln Government, tried to force Kentucky and Missouri into the rebellion in spite of themselves, falsified the vote of Louisiana, turned loose your privateers to plunder unarmed ships, expelled Union families by the thousand, burned their houses, and declared by act of your Congress the confiscation of all debts due Northern men for goods had and received. Talk thus to the marines, but not to me, who have seen these things, and who will this day make as much sacrifice for the peace and honor of the South as the best born Southerner among you. If we must be enemies, let us be men, and fight it out as we propose to-day, and not deal in such hypocritical appeals to God and humanity. God will judge us in due time, and he will pronounce whether it be more humane to fight with a town full of women and the families of a "brave people" at our back, or to remove them in time to places of safety among their own friends and people.

I am, very respectfully, your obedient servant,
 (Signed,) W. T. SHERMAN,
Major-General Commanding.
Official copy:
Signed, L. M. DAYTON, *A. D. C.*

FROM THE AUTHORITIES OF ATLANTA.

ATLANTA, Ga., September 11, 1864.
Major General W. T. SHERMAN:

SIR—The undersigned, mayor and two members of council for the city of Atlanta, for the time being the only legal organ of the people of the said city to express their wants and wishes, ask leave most earnestly, but respectfully, to petition you to reconsider the order requiring them to leave Atlanta. At first view, it struck us that the measure would involve extraordinary hardship and loss; but since we have seen the practical execution of it, so far as it has progressed, and the individual condition of many of the people, and heard the statements as to the inconveniences, loss and suffering attending it, we are satisfied that the amount of it will involve in the aggregate consequences appalling and heart-rending.

Many poor women are in the advanced state of pregnancy; others having young children, whose husbands, for the greater part, are either in the army, prisoners, or dead. Some say: "I have such a one sick in my house; who will wait on them when I am gone?" Others say: "What are we to do? we have no houses to go to, and no means to buy, build or rent any; no parents, relatives or friends to go to." Another says: "I will try and take this or that article of property; but such and such things I must leave behind, though I need them much." We reply to them: "General Sherman will carry your property to Rough and Ready, and then General Hood will take it thence on." And they will reply to that: "But I want to leave the railroad at such a place, and cannot get conveyance from thence on."

We only refer to a few facts to illustrate in part how this measure will operate in practice. As you advanced, the people north of us fell back, and before your arrival here a large portion of the people here had retired South; so that the country south of this is already crowded, and without sufficient houses to accommodate the people, and we are informed that many are now staying in churches and other out-buildings. This being so, how is it possible for the people still here (mostly women and children) to find shelter, and how can they live through the winter in the woods—no shelter or subsistence—in the midst of strangers, who know them not, and without the power to assist them much, if they were willing to do so.

This is but a feeble picture of the consequences of this measure. You know the woe, the horror and the suffering cannot be described by words. Imagination can only conceive of it; and we ask you to take these things into consideration. We know your mind and time are continually occupied with the duties of your command, which almost deters us from asking your attention to the matter; but thought it might be that you had not considered the subject in all of its awful consequences, and that, on reflection, you, we hope, would not make this people an exception to all mankind; for we know of no such instance ever having occurred —surely not in the United States. And what has this helpless people done, that they should be driven from their homes, to wander as strangers, outcasts and exiles, and to subsist on charity?

We do not know as yet the number of people still here. Of those who are here, a respectable number, if allowed to remain at home, could subsist for several months without assistance; and a respectable number for a much longer time, and who might not need assistance at any time.

In conclusion, we most earnestly and solemnly petition you to reconsider this order, or modify it, and suffer this unfortunate people to remain at home and enjoy what little means they have.

Respectfully submitted,

JAMES M. CALHOUN, *Mayor.*

E. E. RAWSON,
S. C. WELLS, } *Councilmen.*

GENERAL SHERMAN'S REPLY.

HEAD-QUARTERS MILITARY DIVISION OF THE
MISSISSIPPI, AND IN THE FIELD,
ATLANTA, Ga., Sept. 12, 1864.

JAMES M. CALHOUN, Mayor; E. E. RAWSON and S. C. WELLS, representing City Council of Atlanta:

GENTLEMEN—I have your letter of the 11th, in the nature of a petition to revoke my orders removing all the inhabitants from Atlanta. I have read it carefully, and give full credit to your statements of the distress that will be occasioned by it, and yet shall not revoke my order, simply because my orders are not designed to meet the humanities of the case, but to prepare for the future struggles, in which millions, yes, hundreds of millions of good people outside of Atlanta have a deep interest. We must have *Peace*, not only in Atlanta, but in America. To secure this, we must stop the war that now desolates our once happy and favored country. To stop war, we must defeat the rebel armies that are arrayed against the laws and Constitution which all must respect and obey. To defeat these armies, we must prepare the way to reach them in their recesses, provided with the arms and instruments which enable us to accomplish our purpose.

Now, I know the vindictive nature of our enemy, and that we may have many years of military operations from this quarter, and therefore deem it wise and prudent to prepare in time. The use of Atlanta for warlike purposes is inconsistent with its character as a home for families. There will be no manufactures, commerce or agriculture here for the maintenance of families, and sooner or later want will compel the inhabitants to go. Why not go *now*, when all the arrangements are completed for the transfer, instead of waiting till the plunging shot of contending armies will renew the scene of the past month? Of course, I do not apprehend any such thing at this moment; but you do not suppose that this army will be here till the war is over. I cannot discuss this subject with you fairly, because I cannot impart to you what I propose to do; but I assert that my military plans make it necessary for the inhabitants to go away, and I can only renew my offer of services to make their exodus in any direction as easy and comfortable as possible. You cannot qualify war in harsher terms than I will. War is cruelty, and you cannot refine it; and those who brought war on our country deserve all the curses and maledictions a people can pour out. I know I had no hand in making this war, and I know I will make more sacrifices to-day than any of you to secure peace. But you cannot have peace and a division of our country. If the United States submits to a division now, it will not stop, but will go on till we reap the fate of Mexico, which is eternal war. The United States does and must assert its authority wherever it has power; if it relaxes one bit to pressure, it is gone, and I know that such is not the national feeling. This feeling assumes various shapes, but always comes back to that of *Union*. Once admit the Union, once more acknowledge the authority of the National Government, and instead of devoting your houses and streets and roads to the dread uses of war, I and this army become at once your protectors and supporters, shielding you from danger, let it come from what quarter it may. I know that a few individuals cannot resist a torrent of error and passion, such as has swept the South into rebellion; but you can point out, so that we may know those who desire a government, and those who insist upon war and its desolation.

You might as well appeal against the thunderstorm as against these terrible hardships of war. They are inevitable; and the only way the people of Atlanta can hope once more to live in peace and quiet at home, is to stop this war—which can alone be done by admitting that it began in error, and is perpetuated in pride. We don't want your negroes, or your horses, or your houses, or your land, or anything you have; but we do want and will have a just obedience to the laws of the United States. That we will have; and if it involves the destruction of your improvements, we cannot help it. You have heretofore read public sentiment in your newspapers that live by falsehood and excitement, and the quicker you seek for truth in other quarters, the better for you.

I repeat then, that by the original compact of government, the United States had certain rights in Georgia, which have never been relinquished, and never will be; that the South began war by seizing forts, arsenals, mints, custom houses, &c., long before Mr. Lincoln was installed, and before the South had one jot or tittle of provocation. I myself, have seen in Missouri, Kentucky, Tennessee and part of

Mississippi, hundreds and thousands of women and children fleeing from your armies and desperadoes, hungry and with bleeding feet. In Memphis, Vicksburgh and Mississippi, we fed thousands upon thousands of the families of rebel soldiers left on our hands, and whom we could not see starve. Now that war comes home to you, you feel very differently; you deprecate its horrors, but did not feel them when you sent car loads of soldiers and ammunition, and moulded shell and shot, to carry war into Kentucky and Tennessee, and desolate the homes of hundreds and thousands of good people, who only asked to live in peace at their old homes, and under the government of their inheritance. But these comparisons are idle. I want peace, and believe it can only be reached through Union and war, and I will ever conduct war purely with a view to perfect and early success.

But, my dear sirs, when that peace does come, you may call on me for anything. Then will I share with you the last cracker, and watch with you to shield your homes and families against danger from every quarter. Now you must go and take with you the old and feeble; feed and nurse them, and build for them in more quiet places proper habitations, to shield them against the weather, until the mad passions of men cool down, and allow Union and Peace once more to settle on your old homes at Atlanta.

Yours in haste,
W. T. SHERMAN, *Major-General.*

A FALSEHOOD CORRECTED.

ATLANTA, September 24, 1864.

To the Louisville Agent of the New York Associated Press:—

Your press dispatches of the 21st embrace one from Macon of the 14th, announcing the arrival of the first train of refugees from Atlanta, with this addition, "that they were robbed of everything before being sent into the rebel lines." Of course, that is false; and it is idle to correct it so far as the rebels are concerned, for they purposed it as a falsehood, to create a mischievous public opinion. The truth is, that during the truce, 446 families were moved south, making 705 adults, 860 children and 479 servants, with 1,651 pounds of furniture and household goods on the average for each family, of which we have a perfect recollection by name and articles. At the end of the truce, Colonel Warner of my staff, who had general supervision of the business, received from Major Clan, of General Hood's staff, the following letter:

"Rough and Ready, Sept. 21, 1864.

"Colonel:—Our official communication being about to close, you will permit me to bear testimony to the uniform courtesy you have shown on all occasions to me and my people, and the promptness with which you have corrected all irregularities arising in our intercourse. Hoping at some future time to be able to reciprocate your courteousness, and in many instances your positive kindness, I am with respect, your obedient servant,

"U. T. CLAN,

"*Major and A. A. G., General Hood's Staff.*

"Lieutenant Colonel Willard Warner, of General Sherman's Staff."

I would not notice this, but I know the people of the North, liable to be misled by a falsehood calculated for special purposes, and by a desperate enemy, will be relieved by this assurance, that not only care, but real kindness has been extended to families who lost their homes by the act of their male protectors.

(Signed,)   W. T. SHERMAN,
Major-General Commanding.

The following letter from one of the exiles of Atlanta, will be read with interest. How much of it may be regarded as apocryphal, will be left to the judgment of the reader:

[From the Eatonton Countryman.]

EATONTON, GA., November 4, 1864.

J. A. TURNER, ESQ.—

DEAR SIR: At your request, I have written down all the points of interest furnished me by my friend, connected with her leaving Atlanta, &c. I have written it hastily, and leave it for you to condense as you may deem proper. Hoping its publication may prove of some interest to your readers, I proceed as follows:

I had the pleasure of meeting with a very intelligent lady, a few days since, one of the exiles from Atlanta under the late order of General Sherman banishing the citizens from that place, who furnished me with some facts which may prove of interest to your readers. As soon as the Yankees obtained possession of the city, the officers began to hunt up comfortable quarters, and the lady of whom I speak found herself under the necessity of taking three of them as boarders, or of submitting to the confiscation of her house to the purpose of sheltering our foe. Those who boarded with Mrs. —— proved to be very gentlemanly fellows, and rendered her service in protecting her from the intrusion of the private soldiers, besides aiding her in disposing of her cows and hogs when she was compelled to leave. A neighbor of hers, whose husband had rendered himself obnoxious to the

Yankees by his services to the South, was ordered by a Yankee general to vacate her premises in two hours, and a guard was stationed to prevent her from moving her effects.

Referring to this evacuation of the trenches around the city, he asked the lady if they did not all think he was retreating, and when she replied that some did think so, he laughed heartily at the idea, and remarked: "I played Hood a real Yankee trick that time, didn't I? He thought I was running away, but he soon had to pull up stakes and run himself." (I wonder whose turn it is to laugh now!)

The lady from whom these facts were obtained says that Sherman had a vast number of applications from ladies, and others, in reference to their moving, and that, so far as she could learn, he was patient, gentlemanly and obliging, as much so as he could be to them consistently with his prescribed policy.

This lady appealed to General Sherman, who immediately ordered the removal of the guard, and permitted her to remove or sell any or all of her furniture, and other valuables, at her discretion. The lady with whom I conversed was under the necessity of calling upon General Sherman, after the publication of his banishment, and she represents him as being very kind and conciliatory in his deportment towards her and others who visited him. He expressed much regret at the necessity which compelled him to order the citizens of Atlanta from their homes; but stated, in justification of his course, that he intended to make Atlanta a second Gibraltar; that, when he completed his defensive works, it would be impregnable; and as no communication could be held with their friends in the South, they (the citizens) would suffer for food; that it was impossible for him to subsist his army, and feed the citizens too, by a single line of railroad; and that, as he intended to hold Atlanta at all hazards, he thought it was humanity to send them out of the city, where they could obtain necessary supplies.

He took the little child of my friend in his arms, and patted her rosy cheeks, calling her a 'poor little exile,' and saying he was sorry to drive her away from her comfortable home, but that war was a cruel and inexorable thing, and its necessities compelled him to do many things which he heartily regretted. In conversation with the lady, he paid a just and well-merited tribute to the valor of our arms. He remarked that it would be no disgrace to us if we were finally subjugated — as we certainly would be — as we had fought against four or five times our number with a degree of valor which had excited the admiration of the world; and the

United States Government would gain no honor or credit if they succeeded in their purpose, as they had thus far failed with five men in the field to our one.

He regarded the Southern soldiers as the bravest in the world, and admitted that in a fair field fight we could whip them two to our one; but he claimed for himself and his compeers the credit of possessing more strategic ability than our generals. "You can beat us in fighting, madam," said he, "but we can out-manœuvre you; your generals do not work half enough; we work day and night, and spare no labor nor pains to carry out our plans."

He permitted her to bring out her horse and rockaway, although his army was greatly needing horses at the time, and also to send her provisions to some suffering relatives within his lines. She speaks in high terms of the discipline of the Yankee army; says that the privates are more afraid of their officers than our slaves are of their masters, and that during her stay there was no disorderly conduct to be seen anywhere; but that quiet and good order prevailed throughout the city.

An instance of Yankee kindness deserves to be mentioned here. A widow lady, whose husband had been a member of the Masonic fraternity, died, shortly after the occupation of the city by the enemy. The Yankee officers gave her a decent and respectable burial, and then took her three orphan children and sent them to their own homes, to be educated at some Masonic institution in the North.

From the facts which I report, on the authority of a lady of unquestioned veracity and respectability, it will be seen that our barbarous foes are not entirely lost to all the dictates and impulses of humanity. Would to God that the exhibition of it were more frequent in their occurrence.

Respectfully, yours,

GEORGE G. N. MACDONELL.

It was generally believed that Sherman intended to hold Atlanta permanently, as a base of future operations. But whoever will consider the various lines of communication, and their total length, will see at a glance that he never could have entertained such an idea for a moment. The distance from Louisville, Ky., on the Ohio River, to Nashville, is 185 miles; from Nashville to Chattanooga, 151 miles; and from Chattanooga to Atlanta, 136 miles. Total distance, 472 miles. Over this long route supplies were carried to Atlanta. Thus it is evident that it would take a very large force to guard and keep open this line of communications. The enemy, however, supposed this was Sherman's purpose, and at once set to work with their cavalry on the lines of communication.

A strong force, under command of General Forrest, appeared in Northern Alabama, where they compelled the garrison at Athens, Ala., under command of Colonel Campbell, after a fight of two hours' duration, to surrender. The garrison consisted of five hundred men of the Sixth and Eighth Indiana cavalry. A detachment of three hundred men, sent from Decatur, Ala., to reënforce the garrison at Athens, were, after a most obstinate engagement, captured. Forrest then destroyed several miles of the Tennessee and Alabama Railroad between Decatur and Athens, and all the bridges on the road. He then advanced towards Pulaski, Tenn., a village seventy-five miles south of Nashville. General L. H. Rousseau advanced to meet Forrest with the force of infantry and cavalry under his command. He was hard pressed by the enemy, and was compelled to fall back slowly. Rousseau subsequently readvanced and maintained his position. While Rousseau was engaged with Forrest near Pulaski, a detachment from the rebel forces passed around Pulaski, and severed the communication between that place and Nashville. In the mean time, guerrillas in Kentucky captured two trains of cars on the route from Louisville to Nashville. They burned nineteen cars.

On the 29th of October, three days after Rousseau met Forrest at Pulaski, Wheeler and Roddy were north of Decatur, Alabama, making their way towards the Railroad between that place and Chattanooga for the purpose of destroying the Railroad between Huntsville and Stevenson, and then effect a junction with Forrest at Tullahoma, Tennessee. Gen. Rousseau changed his operations to the Chattanooga Railroad, at Tullahoma.

But we cannot stop to notice all the efforts of the enemy to interrupt the communications of Sherman. These, undoubtedly, were the forerunners of Hood's great movement North. The Richmond papers threw out dark mysterious hints of some grand event that was about to be enacted that would compel Sherman to evacuate Atlanta and retreat back to Chattanooga, or else his army would be annihilated. So confident were the enemy of the success of their new scheme that their President, Jeff. Davis, in a public speech made at Macon, Georgia, on Sabbath, September 25th, announced the determination of Hood to march into Tennessee to sever the wonderfully attenuated lines of communications held by Sherman.

General Sherman had anticipated this movement, and made all necessary arrangements to carry out his plans, the grandest movement of the war. He sent detachments under various commanders at different points along the Railroad between Atlanta and Chattanooga, and all his spare forces to General Thomas.

About the time that Davis made his famous speech at Macon, General Hood transferred his army from Lovejoy's Station, in the region of Jonesboro' twenty miles South of Atlanta, on the Macon Railroad to the West Point Railroad, near Newman. On the 29th and 30th of September the enemy crossed the Chattahoochee, threw himself on the Railroad running from Chattanooga to Atlanta, occupied Dallas and threatened Rome and Kingston. On the 5th of October, Hood struck at the important post of Altoona. His General, S. G. French, in command of the advance division of Stewart's corps made the assault and was handsomely repulsed by our forces under the command of the gallant General Corse, a most skillful and intrepid officer.

In the meantime, Sherman had left Atlanta in possession of the Twentieth Corps, General Slocum commanding, impregnably fortified and with abundant supplies; and with two corps he moved North after Hood. He followed him closely like a pursuing foe. When Hood's general was assaulting Altoona, General Sherman was at Kenesaw Mountain, from the summit of which he signalled to General Corse at Altoona, over the heads of Hood's troops, to hold out until he relieved him.

He pressed Hood's rear so heavily that he was compelled to abandon the attack and move northward on the parallel roads east of the railroad.

In reference to this affair, Generals Sherman and Howard issued the following orders:

GENERAL CORSE'S DEFENCE OF ALTOONA PASS.

MAJOR GENERAL SHERMAN'S ORDER.

HEADQUARTERS MILITARY DIVISION OF THE MISSISSIPPI, }
IN THE FIELD, KENESAW MOUNTAIN, Oct. 7, 1864. }

SPECIAL FIELD ORDERS, No. 86.

The General Commanding, avails himself of the opportunity, in the handsome defence made of "Altoona," to illustrate the most important principle in war, that fortified posts should be defended to the last, regardless of the relative numbers of the party attacking and attacked.

Altoona was garrisoned by three regiments, commanded by Colonel Tourtelotte, and reënforced by a detachment from a division at Rome, under command of Brigadier-General J. M. Corse, on the morning of the 5th, and a few hours after was attacked by French's division, of Stewart's corps, two other divisions being near at hand and in support. General French demanded a surrender, in a letter, to "avoid a useless effusion of blood," and gave but five minutes for answer. General Corse's answer was emphatic and strong that he and his command were ready for the "useless effusion of blood" as soon as it was agreeable to General French.

This was followed by an attack which was prolonged for five hours, resulting in the complete repulse of the enemy, who left his dead on the ground, amounting to more than two hundred, and four hundred prisoners, well and wounded. The "effusion of blood" was not "useless," as the position at Altoona was and is very important to our present and future operations.

Y

The thanks of this army are due, and are hereby accorded to General Corse, Colonel Tourtelotte, officers and men, for their determined and gallant defence of Altoona, and it is made an example to illustrate the importance of preparing in time, and meeting the danger, when present, boldly, manfully and well.

This army, though unseen to the garrison, was coöperating by moving toward the road by which the enemy could alone escape, but unfortunately were delayed by the rain and mud; but this fact hastened the retreat of the enemy.

Commanders and garrisons of the posts along our railroads are hereby instructed that they must hold their posts to the last minute, sure that the time gained is valuable and necessary to their comrades at the front.

By order of Major-General SHERMAN:

L. M. DAYTON, *A. D. C.*

L. H. EVERTS, *Captain and A. A. G.*

MJAOR-GENERAL HOWARD'S ORDER.

HEADQUARTERS DEPARTMENT AND ARMY TENNESSEE, NEAR KENESAW MOUNTAIN, October 9.

GENERAL FIELD ORDERS, No. 13.

While uniting in the high commendation awarded by the General-in-Chief, the Army of the Tennessee would tender through me its most hearty appreciation and thanks to Brigadier-General J. M. Corse for his promptitude, energy and eminent success in the defence of Altoona Pass, against a force so largely superior to his own; and our warmest congratulations are extended to him, to Colonel Tourtelotte, and the rest of our comrades in arms who fought at Altoona, for the glorious manner in which they vetoed "the useless effusion of blood."

O. O. HOWARD, *Major-General.*

Official

M. R. FLINT, *A. D. C.*

On the 12th of October, Hood, with one corps of his army, invested Dalton, and the two other corps were engaged in tearing up the railroad obstructing Snake Creek Gap, in order to delay Sherman, who was rapidly pursuing. Threatening Chattanooga for a moment, Hood suddenly broke away and marched westerly to Lafayette, and southwesterly to Gadsden. Thus in the campaign of a month's duration Hood had succeeded in severing the railroad between Chattanooga and Atlanta. At the end of the month, however, Sherman's forces, by great industry and skill, reöpened the road.

Anticipating Hood's movement to cross the Tennessee, troops were placed at Bridgeport and other points along the river. With the remainder of the army, Sherman moved to Galesville in pursuit of the enemy, at which place he remained for several days. This place, it will be remembered, is in Northern Alabama, near the Georgia line. Hood remained for more than a week at Gadsden, where he threw up fortifications. While in this position, it is said, upon pretty good authority, that Hood's army had a *"happy time."* Beauregard had brought reënforcements to Hood. Whereupon the chief officers, Generals Hood, Beauregard, S. D. Lee, Cheatham, Clayton, Cleburn and Bate made speeches promising to "*wipe Sherman out from the list of Yankee officers.*"

On the 23d of October Hood began to move his forces northwesterly through Lookout Mountain towards Gunter's Landing and Decatur, on the Tennessee River. In the meantime, the army of General Dick Taylor had quickly moved up the Mobile and Ohio Railroad from Eastern Louisiana to Corinth, and thence to Tuscumbia.

About the 1st of November portions of Hood's army crossed the river at Muscle Shoals, between Florence and Decatur, and at other points along the river. His forces were attacked at various points. The Union gunboats took part in these engagements, and in some instances succeeded in repulsing the enemy, and for the time defeated their efforts to cross the river. The gunboats Undine and transports Venus and Cheseman were captured at Fort Herman, on the river, after a hard fight with the enemy's shore batteries. Most of the crew were killed or wounded. At Johnsonville, eight steamboats, loaded with government stores, were burned by the Union forces, to prevent them from falling into the hands of the enemy. The place was evacuated, and soon occupied by Forrest, who captured two of our gunboats that were left to defend the town.

Here Sherman and Hood parted, and forever. The enemy and the people of the entire country seemed to be unable to comprehend Sherman's movements, and were greatly perplexed. Sherman said of Hood: "*Let him go North; our business is down South. If he will cross the river and march North, I will give him his rations.*"

General Thomas was appointed to the command of all the troops in Tennessee and Kentucky, and had a force large enough to meet the enemy and manage him.

About the time that Hood was crossing the Tennessee, Sherman sent the following characteristic telegram:

"Hood has crossed the Tennessee. Thomas will take care of him and Nashville, while Schofield will not let him into Chattanooga or Knoxville. Georgia and South Carolina are at my mercy, and I shall strike. Do not be anxious about me. I am all right."

While Sherman was engaged in the pursuit of Hood north, the enemy that were south of Atlanta, supposing that place abandoned, started with a grand flourish of trumpets to recapture what they had lost. They approached at two points, and after an engagement, which lasted about thirty minutes, they were disappointed and chagrined, and compelled to march back in greater haste than they advanced, leaving on the field upwards of twenty of their number killed and wounded.

Hood continued his march north until he reached Franklin, within about twenty miles of Nashville, where his columns were terribly shattered by the troops of General Schofield in the battle at that place. From thence he marched to and invested Nashville, from which position he was subsequently driven by the forces of that noble old soldier, General Thomas, after losing a large part of his army and most of his artillery. Thus ended the inglorious campaign of Hood to Sherman's rear.

We shall next see Sherman on his grand march from Atlanta to Savannah.

A FACETIOUS LETTER FROM SHERMAN.

When Sherman was at Atlanta, Ga., last fall, a Southern clergyman sent to him a complaint that his horse had been carried off by a United States soldier. The general sent back this humorous reply:

DEAR SIR—Your letter of September 14th is received. I approach a question involving a title to a "horse" with deference for the laws of war. That mysterious code, of which we talk so much and know so little, is remarkably silent on the "horse." He is a beast so tempting to the soldier, to him of the wild cavalry, the fancy artillery, or the patient infantry, that I find more difficulty in recovering a worthless, spavined beast, than in paying a million of "greenbacks;" so that I fear I must reduce your claim to one of finance, and refer you to the great Board of

Claims in Washington, that may reach your case by the time your grand-child becomes a great-grand-father.

Privately, I think it was a shabby thing in the scamp of the Thirty-first Missouri, who took your horse; and the colonel or his brigadier should have restored him. But I cannot undertake to make good the sins of omission of my own colonels or brigadiers, much less those of a former generation. "When this cruel war is over," and peace once more gives you a parish, I will promise, if near you, to procure out of one of Uncle Sam's corrals a beast that will replace the one taken from you wrongfully, but now it is impossible. We have a big journey before us, and need all we have, and. I fear, more too; so look out when the Yanks are about, and hide your beasts, for my experience is that all soldiers are very careless in a search for title. I know that General Hardee will confirm this, my advice.

With great respect, yours truly,

W. T. SHERMAN, Major General.

CHAPTER XIII.

SHERMAN'S GRAND MARCH FROM ATLANTA TO SAVANNAH.

MOVEMENT TOWARDS ATLANTA — PREPARATIONS FOR THE MARCH — THE ARMY — ORDERS OF SHERMAN AND SLOCUM — CONCENTRATION OF FORCES — THE "GATE CITY BURNED" — COMMUNICATION CUT OFF — UNDER A CLOUD — THE ENEMY DECEIVED — THE REBEL PRESS — THE GENERAL LINES OF THE MARCH — PROGRESS OF THE ARMY — FIGHT AT GRISWOLDVILLE — ENCAMPED ON HOWELL COBB'S FARM — MILLEDGEVILLE OCCUPIED — INCIDENT — MARCH TO MILLEN AND SAVANNAH — SCOUTS SENT OUT — HOWARD'S DISPATCH TO THE NAVY — FORT MC ALISTER CAPTURED — JOURNAL OF THE MARCH — INVESTMENT AND CAPTURE OF SAVANNAH — POETRY — SHERMAN'S ORDERS — CORRESPONDENCE — BRITISH CONSUL AT SAVANNAH.

In the last chapter we left Hood on the banks of the Tennessee, preparing for the invasion and conquest of the middle portions of that State, while Sherman, to the astonishment of the enemy and the whole country, was marching back towards Atlanta.

Sherman announced his plans, in part, to his friend Captain Pennock of the United States Navy, in the following letter:

KINGSTON, GA., Nov. 3d, 1864.
Capt. PENNOCK, U. S. N., Mound City:

In a few days I will be off for salt water, and hope to meet my old friend D. D. Porter again. Will you be kind enough to write and tell him to look out for me about Christmas, from Hilton Head to Savannah?

W. T. SHERMAN, *Major-General.*

At the time this letter was written Sherman was making every preparation for his great triumphal march through Georgia. All valuable property was removed to Chattanooga. The bridge across the Chattahoochee was burned, the railroad was torn up for miles and the rails heated and twisted so as to be unfit for future use, and large quantities of them were sent to Chattanooga.

Sherman issued the order for his march at Kingston, Ga., Nov. 9th, 1864, from which we learn that the army was to be divided into two wings; the right commanded by Major-General O. O. Howard; the left by Major-General H. W. Slocum. The right wing was composed of the Fifteenth and Seventeenth Corps; the left of the Fourteenth and Twentieth Corps. In addition to these forces there was, also, a large body of cavalry, commanded by

General Kilpatrick, and a brigade of artillery for each corps, and one battery of horse artillery for the cavalry. The Fourteenth Corps was commanded by Brevet Major-General Jeff. C. Davis; the Fifteenth by Brevet Major-General Osterhaus; the Seventeenth by Major-General Blair, and the Twentieth by Major-General Slocum.

The whole army, estimated by the enemy at thirty-five thousand actually numbered nearly sixty thousand well equipped soldiers, accustomed to long marches, fierce battles and glorious victories. They marched without tents or a general train of supplies. They were ordered to supply themselves from the country through which they marched. The frequent orders and exhortations of the rebel authorities compelling the Southern people to cease the culture of cotton, their late king, and raise breadstuffs, was an assurance to Sherman and his soldiers that they would find bread on the route.

We here subjoin the order of Generals Sherman and Slocum, documents well worth reading and preserving. They shed light on all of this grand movement:

SHERMAN'S ORDERS FOR HIS MARCH.

HEADQUARTERS, MILITARY DIVISION OF THE MISSISSIPPI,
IN THE FIELD, KINGSTON, GA., Nov. 9, 1864.

SPECIAL FIELD ORDERS, No. 120.

1. For the purpose of military operations this army is divided into two wings, viz: The right wing, Major-General O. O. Howard

commanding, the Fifteenth and Seventeenth Corps; the left wing, Major-General H. W. Slocum commanding, the Fourteenth and Twentieth Corps.

2. The habitual order of march will be, whenever practicable, by four roads, as nearly parallel as possible, and converging at points hereafter to be indicated in orders. The cavalry, Brigadier-General Kilpatrick commanding, will receive special orders from the Commander-in-Chief.

3. There will be no general trains of supplies, but each corps will have its ammunition and provision train, distributed habitually as follows: Behind each regiment should follow one wagon and one ambulance; behind each brigade should follow a due proportion of ammunition wagons, provision wagons and ambulances. In case of danger, each army corps should change this order of march by having his advance and rear brigade unincumbered by wheels. The separate columns will start habitually at seven A. M., and make about fifteen miles per day, unless otherwise fixed in orders.

4. The army will forage liberally on the country during the march. To this end, each brigade commander will organize a good and sufficient foraging party, under the command of one or more discreet officers who will gather, near the route traveled, corn or forage of any kind, meat of any kind, vegetables, corn meal, or whatever is needed by the command; aiming at all times to keep in the wagon trains at least ten days' provisions for the command, and three days' forage. Soldiers must not enter the dwellings of the inhabitants or commit any trespass; during the halt or a camp they may be permitted to gather turnips, potatoes and other vegetables, and drive in stock in front of their camps. To regular foraging parties must be entrusted the gathering of provisions and forage at any distance from the road traveled.

5. To army corps commanders is entrusted the power to destroy mills, houses, cotton gins, &c., and for them this general

principle is laid down: In districts and neighborhoods where the army is unmolested, no destruction of such property should be permitted; but should guerrillas or bushwhackers molest our march, or should the inhabitants burn bridges, obstruct roads, or otherwise manifest local hostility, then army corps commanders should order and enforce a devastation more or less relentless, according to the measure of such hostility.

6. As for horses, mules, wagons, &c., belonging to the inhabitants, the cavalry and artillery may appropriate freely and without limit; discriminating, however, between the rich, who are usually hostile, and the poor or industrious, usually neutral or friendly. Foraging parties may also take mules or horses to replace the jaded animals of their trains, or to serve as pack mules for the regiments or brigades. In all foraging, of whatever kind, the parties engaged will refrain from abusive and threatening language, and may, when the officer in command thinks proper, give written certificates of the facts, but not receipts; and they will endeavor to leave with each family a reasonable portion for their maintenance.

7. Negroes who are able-bodied and can be of service to the several columns, may be taken along; but each army commander will bear in mind that the question of supplies is a very important one, and that his first duty is to see to those who bear arms.

8. The organization at once of a good pioneer battalion for each corps, composed, if possible of negroes, should be attended to. This battalion should follow the advance guard, should repair roads and double them if possible, so that the columns will not be delayed after reaching bad places. Also, army commanders should study the habit of giving the artillery and wagons the road, and marching their troops on one side; and also, instruct the troops to assist wagons at steep hills or bad crossings of streams.

9. Captain O. M. Poe, Chief Engineer, will assign to each wing of the army a pontoon train, fully equipped and organized, and

the commanders thereof will see to its being properly protected at all times.

By order of Major-General W. T. SHERMAN.
L. M. DAYTON, *Aid-de-Camp.*

GENERAL SLOCUM'S ORDER TO HIS WING OF THE ARMY.

HEADQUARTERS TWENTIETH CORPS,
ATLANTA, GA., Nov. 7, 1864.

CIRCULAR.

When the troops leave camp on the march about to commence, they will carry, in haversack, two days' rations salt meat, two days' hard bread, ten days' coffee and salt, and five days' sugar. Each infantry soldier will carry sixty rounds of ammunition on his person. Every effort should be made, by officers and men, to save rations and ammunition; not a round of ammunition should be lost or unnecessarily expended. It is expected that the command will be supplied with subsistence and forage mainly from the country. All foraging will be done by parties detailed for the purpose by brigade commanders, under such rules as may be prescribed by brigade and division commanders. Pillaging, marauding and every act of cruelty or abuse of citizens will be severely punished. Each brigade commander will have a strong rear guard on every march, and will order the arrest of all stragglers. The danger of straggling on this march should be impressed upon the mind of every officer and man of the command. Not only the reputation of the corps, but the personal safety of every man will be dependent, in a great measure, upon the rigid enforcement of discipline and the care taken of the rations and ammunition.

By command of Major-General SLOCUM.
H. W. PERKINS, *A. A. G.*

The troops were all concentrated in and near Atlanta. The city was set on fire in order to destroy everything that might be of use to the enemy.

An eye witness of the burning of Atlanta on the day and night of the 15th of November, thus describes that scene:

"Atlanta is entirely deserted of human beings, excepting a few soldiers here and there. The houses are vacant; there is no trade or traffic of any kind; the streets are empty. Beautiful roses bloom in the gardens of fine houses, but a terrible stillness and solitude cover it all, depressing the hearts even of those who are glad to destroy it. In your peaceful homes at the North you cannot conceive how these people have suffered for their crimes.

"A grand and awful spectacle is presented to the beholder in this beautiful city, now in flames. By order, the chief engineer had destroyed, by powder and fire all the storehouses, dépôt buildings and machine shops. The heaven is one expanse of lurid fire; the air is filled with flying, burning cinders; buildings covering over two hundred acres are in ruins or in flames; every instant there is the sharp detonation or the smothered burning sound of exploding shells and powder concealed in the buildings, and then the sparks and flame shoot away up into the black and red roof, scattering the cinders far and wide.

"These are the machine shops where have been forged and cast rebel cannon, shot and shell, that have carried death to many a brave defender of our nation's honor. These warehouses have been the receptacle of munitions of war, stored, to be used for our destruction. The city, which next to Richmond, has furnished more material for prosecuting the war than any other in the South, exists no more as a means for the enemies of the Union.

"A brigade of Massachusetts soldiers are the only troops now left in the town. They will be the last to leave it. To-night I heard the really fine band of the Thirty-third Massachusetts playing 'John Brown's soul goes marching on,' by the light of the burning buildings. I have never heard that noble anthem when it was so grand, so solemn, so inspiring."

On the 14th and 15th, the march began in earnest. As Cortez burned his ships behind him, and thus cut off all possibility of a retreat, so Sherman broke up his communications; cut loose from all support and marched, relying upon his noble soldiery and his own genius for a successful issue of the campaign.

For days and weeks he was not heard from except through the enemy's channels. The general, his brave army and their movements were covered with a dark cloud from the view of their friends. No one seemed to know where they were or whither they were marching, or what had befallen them. All over the North, men daily and almost hourly inquired, where is Sherman? His bold movement, imperfectly comprehended, was regarded as full of peril and hazardous in the extreme. Nevertheless not a few believed most confidently, that he would make a successful march either to the Gulf or to the Atlantic coast. General Grant had said, "I expect more of Sherman than of any other man in the country."

This movement was as incomprehensible to the enemy as to us, and far more perplexing to them. They regarded it as a retreat, and not as the deliberate plan of a great military genius. Their views, as expressed by their public presses, are curious, and should be preserved, as a record of the times, and the manner in which they were either deceived or undertook to deceive the public in regard to Sherman's movements.

We here insert a few extracts from the enemy's press, as a monument of Sherman's great achievement, and their amazing folly.

EXTRACTS FROM THE REBEL PRESS.

[From the Augusta Constitutionalist, November 20th.]

We must retard, harass, starve, destroy the army of Sherman. The opportunity is ours. The hand of God is in it. The blow, if we can give it as it should be given, may end the war. We urge our friends in the track of the advance to remove all forage and provisions, horses, mules, negroes and stock, and burn the balance. Let the invader find the desolation he would leave behind him staring him in the face. You must do it yourself, or the enemy will do it.

Let the cry of Beauregard, who is now with us, go up through the State—to arms! to arms!

It is fully believed that General Sherman, finding his way North entirely closed, and a bold and defiant army confronting him has determined upon making a bold retreat to the rear, where no army of consequence could impede his movement.

In our judgment it is the Anabasis of Sherman. It is plain his only object can be the making of a certain and secure base. He must move fast and obtain his object speedily, or he is lost.

His movement is occasioned by the fact that Forrest has destroyed his stores at Johnsonville, and cut his communication on the north.

Sherman has many weary miles to march in obtaining his object. It is absurdity to talk about his making a winter campaign with no communication with his Government. He is retreating—simply retreating. He will destroy as he goes, but that makes it none the less so.

[From the Augusta Constitutionalist, November 22d.]

To our country friends we again reiterate the advice—the advice of our generals and congressmen, the advice which common sense would give:—cut trees across all the roads in front of the enemy, burn the bridges, remove everything possible in time, and before the enemy arrives, burn and destroy what cannot be removed—leave nothing upon which he can subsist; and hide the millstones and machinery of all mills. The cattle of the country should be driven off, and the hogs unpenned and hastened into the woods and swamps. By such a course our own citizens, without guns, can conquer the enemy. It is not possible for him to haul provisions and forage; and could his line of march be retarded by roads blocked with fallen trees, and streams (however small, for slight streams retard artillery) made bridgeless, the food for horses and men removed or destroyed, his army at once becomes an easy conquest to the troops, and veterans at that, which already begin to swarm about the supposed points in his line of march.

It is the duty of the officers in command to see that this road is made difficult, and forage and provisions removed and destroyed. Squads of men should be scouring the country in front of his advance, with orders to urge the people first to remove forage and dismantle and secrete millstones and machinery; and if they fail through unwillingness to do it, then to burn and destroy what cannot be removed.

The Russians destroyed the Grand Army of Napoleon of five hundred thousand men by destroying the country about them by the full use of fire applied to their own cities, houses and granaries; and, in forcing his rapid and disastrous retreat from their country, gave the first great blow to that master in the art of war which conquered France, and placed the great leader a prisoner on the island of St. Helena. Let Georgians imitate their unselfishness and love of country for a few weeks, and the army of Sherman will have the fate of Napoleon.

If Sherman lives and forages upon the country, it will be, first, the mean and cowardly selfishness of the people; and, second, the inertness and indifference of Confederate officers. It is the natural duty of the former, as Georgians, to destroy rather than the enemy should eat it; the sworn duty of the latter, as true officers of the Confederacy, to see that this be the case.

[From the Savannah News, November 22d.]

The present war has afforded practical demonstrations of all the theories of military tactics — of surprises, concentration, celerity of movement, strategic feints, retreats, intrepid onsets and protracted sieges—and to-day we are witnessing a re-enactment of that great military disaster, the forced retreat of a victorious army through a hostile country. As Napoleon was forced to retreat from his conquest of Moscow, so is his feeble and heartless imitator, Sherman, forced to return from Atlanta, the capture of which cost him the loss of a larger army than that which he now commands. The great aim of the abolition despotism at Washington in the commencement of the spring campaign was the capture of Richmond and Atlanta. The conquest of one or both of these great Confederate centres was deemed essential to the maintenance of Black Republican ascendancy, and hence the main efforts of the Lincoln Government were directed to the accomplishment of those objects. More than a hundred thousand lives were vainly sacrificed in the attempt to reach Richmond, and to-day Lee's heroic veterans hold the remnant of Grant's army cowering before their impregnable lines. Sherman, after months of hard fighting, and after the sacrifice of nearly a hundred thousand troops, succeeded against a vastly inferior force in obtaining possession of our great railroad centre. But he found it a barren victory. The ruin which he had wrought was no compensation for the sacrifice he had made—the tenantless houses, the devastated fields and acres of burial grounds with which he had surrounded himself, offered no subsistence for the remnant of his army. He found, too late, that conquest was not victory, and that the army whom he had vainly endeavored to subdue, still unconquered and defiant, had not only escaped his grasp, but had assumed a position which threatened his destruction. Cut off from his base of supplies, the country in the track of his advance being exhausted, surrounded on every side by a hostile people, starvation staring him in the face, he was forced to look for a retreat from his perilous position. His movement towards Chattanooga, as well as the appearance of a large fleet of supply ships off Mobile a few days since, leave no doubt that he designed to seek a water base and the cover of gunboats at Mobile; but the active operations of Forrest, and the concentration of forces under Hood in lower Alabama, rendered such a retreat impossible. Every other avenue of escape being closed, his last and only desperate hope is to make his way through the interior of the State to the Atlantic coast While his main body will be compelled to advance slowly through that section of the State where he hopes to find subsistence, his light troops and cavalry will occupy a wide breadth of country, threatening our principal towns, and by feints in all directions, for a time, perhaps, succeed in deceiving us in regard to his real point of destination, and thus prevent a concentration of our forces.

A few days, however, will develop his designs, when, if our united efforts are properly directed, he will reap the reward of his reckless temerity in utter annihilation. We have only to arouse our whole arms-bearing people—hover on his front, his flanks and rear—remove from his reach or destroy everything that will subsist man or beast—retard his progress by every means in our power, and, when the proper time comes, fall upon him with the relentless vengeance of an insulted and outraged people, and there need be no doubt of the result. As the great Napoleon found his Moscow, so will the brutal Sherman find his Atlanta.

[From the Savannah News, November 22d.]

Now is the time for the men of Georgia to rally to her defense, in response to the call of the Governor. He has done his duty—the men of the State must now perform theirs. If they do, our State will be delivered from impending ruin. Be prompt to the rescue.

The patriots—the genuine lovers of their own soil—of their wives, children and neighbors, and of liberty, will not hesitate to rush to arms. Let all who are able to do any good at the front, and who try to dodge or shirk their duty in this solemn and important hour, be marked. The man who now refuses to defend us is unworthy of property, liberty or country.

> "He who dallies is a dastard,
> And he who doubts is damned."

[From the Register, November 22d.]

General Fry issues an order this morning, calling on all the men in Augusta to prepare immediately for the defense of their homes, by uniting themselves with some local organization. We have no need to say a word of the importance of this call. It can no longer be doubted that an insolent foe is in the very heart of our beloved Empire State, burning, pillaging and desolating the country he passes over. Our homes are threatened with the same fate that has thrust thousands from their homes in the upper portion of the State. The enemy is coming with his hell hounds, thirsty for lunder, and the torch is red in his hands. He would leave our beautiful city a smouldering heap of blackened ruins, our firesides desolate, our women and children thrust out of house and home, our altars 'esecrated, and our whole country a barren waste. Georgians, can there be need of an appeal to rouse you to your duty in this trying hour? We think not. If you are not insensible to all the principles of patriotism, you will rally now—rally as one man to meet the coming foe.

You will not have to stand alone to oppose the coming storm. Soldiers are already arriving,—others are on their way from Virginia. Shall they come and find you inactive? Nay; let every arm now grasp its weapon, and every effort be made to throw obstructions in the pathway of the foe. On you alone depends your safety. Remain inactive, and the consequence may prove fatal; do your duty, and the overthrow of the enemy is sure.

[From the Richmond Examiner, November 26th.]

The news from Georgia, now the most interesting of all, is exceedingly meagre and untrustworthy; but no doubt can now be entertained of Sherman's design or of his destination. When Davis sent, and Hood took, the only army apparent in the country off his shoulders, and carried it through the mountains to stick it in the mud between Tuscumbia and Florence, Sherman determined to make an attempt on the lines of communication between Virginia, the Carolinas, and the rest of the Confederate States. His work in Northern Georgia was done, and for ulterior operations any point on the seacoast would be a better base than Chattanooga. He risked much in appearance, but perhaps little in reality, by destroying his communications. A marching army can transport ammunition for at least three pitched battles, and for supplies this season of the year he might partly rely on the country through which he proposed to pass. If he could take Macon or Augusta by the way, he would accomplish great things; but the destruction of these towns was not his main object. His design was to destroy the railroads, as far as he could, which ran from Southern and Western Georgia to Virginia and the Carolinas, and to rest his army at Beaufort and Port Royal. That he would go to that point rather than Savannah, is nearly certain; for if he directed his course to Savannah or to Charleston, he would find fortified and well defended cities, and his troops, exhausted by a long march, both in strength and ammunition, would be wholly unfit to reduce either place. But the enemy already has possession of Beaufort. He would have no fighting to do there, and he would find transports laden with every species of supply awaiting his arrival. It is, therefore, reasonable to believe that Beaufort is the point of destination, and that if he fails at Augusta, he will make his way thither as fast as the Confederate troops will permit him. If the reader will glance at the map, he will perceive that when Sherman has passed from Chattanooga to Atlanta, and thence to Beaufort, he will have severed every railroad between Georgia and Virginia. This severance will be easily repaired; but if he can establish himself permanently at Beaufort, he may be able

A*

to operate against those roads repeatedly. Furthermore, Beaufort lies between Charleston and Savannah, and can be conveniently used as the base of land operations against either city. It is evidently highly important that Sherman should never take Augusta or Macon, and should never reach Beaufort.

[From the Richmond Whig, November 28th.]

We do not intend to inform the Yankee newspapers where Sherman now is, but we feel no hesitation in assuring them that he is not in Charleston or Savannah, or either in Macon or Augusta; and that not one of those cities has been threatened by his forces. We can tell them likewise that his march has been even more leisurely than he anticipated; and that, so far from accomplishing the modest fifteen miles a day, provided for in his orders, he has not attained much more, on an average, than the half of that rate. It is now fifteen days since he left Atlanta. In a week he was to be in possession of Macon, and in twelve days of Augusta, and in a few days more of some other important point; but where is he now? We leave it to the Yankee papers to guess, supplying them only with the information that he has not found sweet potatoes very abundant in Georgia, and that hog and hominy have not been served up for the entertainment of his bedeviled troops."

From Atlanta two railroads, the Georgia and the Georgia Central, run in a southeasterly direction to the Atlantic coast. The Georgia Railroad passes through Augusta, to Charleston; Georgia Central, through Macon to Savannah. From Atlanta to Macon the distance is 103 miles; from Macon to Savannah 190 miles. The distance from Atlanta to Augusta is 171 miles; from Augusta to Charleston 137 miles. These two great railroads were the general lines of Sherman's march of wonderful distances. He moved out of Atlanta while that place was yet in flames, in two columns. The right wing, under Howard, marched straight down the Macon and Western Railroad, south of the "Gate City," first striking East Point, where the Atlantic and West Point Railroad crosses it, and from thence to Rough and Ready, at which point, after sharp skirmishing with the enemy's cavalry, under command of Iverson, who had made several amusing demonstrations, which was ycleped by the enemy as "the siege of Atlanta," reached Jonesboro, on Wednesday, the 16th, and encamped for the night. At this place the railroad buildings were destroyed.

At Jonesboro there was a division of our forces. On the 18th the infantry occupied Griffin, on the

Atlantic and Macon Railroad. The cavalry passed from McDonough, where they had burned the court house and other public buildings, and reached this same road at Forsythe, and thus destroyed the communications between Atlanta and Macon. The enemy fell back to Macon, where their principal forces were concentrating, supposing that it was Sherman's intention to attack that stronghold. Instead, however, of marching to the fortifications of Macon, the column turned due east, following the general direction of the Georgia Central Railroad. The advanced cavalry occupied Hillsboro and Monticello, and destroyed everything in both places that could be of value to the enemy. The infantry encamped that night at Indian Spring, near the town of Jackson. This part of the army, the right wing, spent the 19th in preparing bridges to cross the Ocomulgee River. On the 20th the passage of the stream was effected, and the army marched from there to Gordon on the Georgia Central Railroad, south west of Milledgeville, the capital of the State. At this point great damage was done to the Central Road, and the railroad running from thence to Milledgeville.

From here General Walcott, in command of a detachment of cavalry and a brigade of infantry, was thrown forward to Griswoldville, towards

Macon, in the rear of the army, merely for demonstrative purposes. The enemy, five thousand strong, advanced upon our troops, who had thrown up temporary breastworks, with a section of a battery in position. The cavalry fell slowly back on either flank of the brigade, protecting them from attack in flank and rear. The enemy consisted of Hardee's old corps, which was brought up from Savannah, and chiefly State militia. "With that ignorance of danger common to new troops," said an eye-witness, "the rebels rushed upon our veterans with the greatest fury. They were received with grape shot and musketry at point blank range, our soldiers firing coolly while shouting derisively to the quivering columns to come on, as if they thought the whole thing a nice joke. The enemy resumed the attack, but with the same fatal result, and were soon in full flight, leaving more than three hundred killed and wounded on the field. Our loss was some forty killed and wounded. A pretty severe lesson."

Meanwhile the left wing of the army, Slocum's column, passed through Decatur, Covington and Madison, and having destroyed everything that could be of advantage to the enemy, marched on towards Milledgeville, the capital. Before reaching the latter place, it is said that Sherman camped on one of the plantations of Howell Cobb. Said one who was with the army at the time: "We found his granaries well filled with corn and wheat, part of which was distributed and eaten by our animals and men. A large supply of syrup made from sorghum, which we found at nearly every plantation on the march, was stored in an outhouse. This was also disposed of to the soldiers, and the poor decrepit negroes, which this humane, liberty-loving major general left to die in this place a few days ago. Becoming alarmed, Cobb removed all the able-bodied mules, horses, cows and slaves. He left behind some fifty old men — cripples, and women and children — with scarcely enough clothing to cover their nakedness, with little or no food, and without means of procuring any. We found them cowering over the fire-places of their miserable huts, where the wind whirled through the crevices between the logs, frightened at the approach of the Yankees, who, they had been told would kill them. A more forlorn, neglected set of human beings I never saw."

General Sherman distributed provisions among them, and assured them that we were their friends, and not their foes.

Slocum, with the Twentieth Corps, on the 22d of November, entered Milledgeville. A correspondent of one of our public journals thus speaks of this event:

"MILLEDGEVILLE, November 24.

"We are in full possession of the capital of the State of Georgia, and without firing a gun in its conquest. On Friday last the Legislature, which had been in session, hearing of our approach, hastily decamped without any adjournment. The legislative panic spread among the citizens to such an extent as to depopulate the place, except of a few old gentlemen and ladies and the negroes, the latter welcoming our approach with ecstatic exclamations of joy: 'Bress the Lord! tanks be to Almighty God; the Yanks is come; de day ob jubilee hab arribed; and then accompanied their words with rather embarrassing hugs, which those nearest the sidewalks received quite liberally.

"General Slocum, with the Twentieth Corps, first entered the city, arriving by way of Madison, having accomplished his mission of destroying the railroads and valuable bridges at Madison. The fright of the legislators, described by witnesses, must have been comical in the extreme. They little imagined the movement of our left wing, hearing first of the advance of Kilpatrick on the extreme right toward Macon, and supposed that to be another raid. What their opinion was when Howard's army appeared at McDonough it would be difficult to say, and their astonishment must have approached insanity when the other two columns were heard from — one directed toward Augusta and the other swiftly marching straight upon their devoted city.

"It seemed as if they were surrounded upon all sides except toward the east, and that their doom was sealed. With the certain punishment for their crimes looming up before them, they sought every possible means of escape. Private effects, household furniture, everything, was conveyed to the depôt, and loaded into cars until they were filled and heaped, and the flying people could not find standing room.

"Any and every price was obtained for a vehicle. A thousand dollars was cheap for a common buggy, and men rushing about the streets in agony of fear lest they should 'fall victims to the ferocity of the Yankees.'

"Several days of perfect quiet passed, after this exodus, when, on a bright, sunshiny morning, a regiment entered the city with a band playing the national airs, which music had many a day since been hushed in the capital of Georgia.

WHAT SHERMAN DID AT MILLEDGEVILLE.

"But few of the troops were marched through the city. Some two or three regiments were detailed under the orders of the engineers to destroy certain property designated by the general commanding. The magazines, arsenals, depôt buildings, factories of one kind and another with storehouses containing large amounts of government property, and some 1,700 bales of cotton burned. Private houses were respected everywhere—even those of noted rebels; and I heard of no instance of pillage or insult to the inhabitants. One or two of the latter, known as having been in the rebel army, were made prisoners of war, but the surgeons at the hospitals, the principal of the insane asylum, and others, expressed their gratitude that such perfect order was maintained throughout the city.

" General Sherman is at the executive mansion, its former occupant having with extremely bad grace fled from his distinguished visitor, taking with him the entire furniture of the building. As General Sherman travels with a *menage*, (a roll of blankets, and haversack full of hard-tack,) which is as complete for a life out in the open air as in a palace, the discourtesy of Governor Brown was not a serious inconvenience.

" General Sherman's opening move in the present campaign has been successful in the highest degree. At first moving his army in three columns, with a column of cavalry on his extreme right, upon eccentric lines, he diverted the attention of the enemy, so that he concentrated his forces at extreme points, Macon and Augusta, leaving unimpeded the progress of the main body. In this campaign, the end of which does not yet appear, it is not the purpose of the general to spend his time before fortified cities, nor yet to encumber his wagons with wounded men. His instructions to Kilpatrick were to demonstrate against Macon, getting within five miles of the city."

On the appearance of our army in Milledgeville, the proprietor of the principal hotel of that city fled, leaving the building and its valuable contents in the hands of an old lady. The silver ware and other valuables were deposited in a closet by this old lady, and securely locked as she supposed. It is said that one of the officers of the army borrowed the key, in his official capacity, and after discovering the contents of the closet, neglected to lock the door, but returned the key. The rank and file, in accordance with the maxim that "all is fair in love and war," plunged into the closet, and half an hour thereafter a chaste variety of spoons, knives and forks, silver ware and crockery, was flourishing in the arms of a hundred soldiers.

As a general rule, our soldiers were not permitted to enter private houses, or disturb the property of private families. They were allowed to help themselves freely to the productions of the country, such as sweet potatoes, chickens, turkeys, ducks, beef, and whatever might be necessary for the comfort of the "inner man." Few of the "boys in blue" made the march on empty stomachs.

Keeping the general direction of the two railroads, as heretofore indicated, the two wings of the army moved on, overcoming the obstacles in their way without much difficulty and without any very serious fighting. The enemy learned, when it was too late, that Sherman would not delay his columns for the sake of capturing the city of Macon, where they had a strong force concentrated behind breastworks and fortifications. Nor could the enemy tell as the army moved east, whether Sherman aimed at Augusta and Charleston or Savannah. The deception was kept up until the whole army was concentrated at Millen, with the exception of the cavalry, a portion of which, under Kilpatrick, occupied Waynesboro, between Millen and Augusta for the purpose of keeping up the deception. The army then turned South and marched down the peninsula between the Savannah and Ogeechee Rivers. On the afternoon of the 8th of December, the signal guns of the navy, in Ossabaw Sound, were distinctly heard, which sent a thrill of gladness through the hearts of our brave soldiers.

On the evening of December the 9th, General Howard sent Captain Duncan and two scouts to open up communications with General Foster and Admiral Dahlgren. The captain descended the Ogeechee River in a small boat on the 12th, and delivered the following dispatch to Admiral Dahlgren:

HEADQUARTERS, ARMY OF THE TENNESSEE,
NEAR SAVANNAH CANAL, Dec., 9, 1864.

To the Commander of the United States Naval Forces in the vicinity of Savannah, Georgia—

SIR: We have met with perfect success thus far. The troops are in fine spirits and near by.

Respectfully,
O. O. HOWARD, *Major-General,*
Commanding Right Wing of the Army.

On Tuesday, December 13th, the second division of the Fifteenth Corps captured Fort McAllister. This work is situated on the Ogeechee River fifteen miles from Savannah, at the point where the river is crossed by the Savannah, Albany and Gulf Railroad, and about six miles from Ossabaw Sound. The capture of this fort opened complete communications between the army and the navy.

Sherman sent to the War Department the following dispatch, announcing the capture of Fort McAllister and the success of his march to the sea:

"To-day, at 5 P. M., General Hazen's division

of the Fifteenth Corps, carried Fort McAllister by assault, capturing its entire garrison and stores. This opened to us the Ossabaw Sound, and I passed down on a gun-boat to communicate with the fleet. Before opening the communication we had completely destroyed all railroads leading into Savannah, and invested the city. The left is on the Savannah River, ten miles above this city, and the right on the Ogeechee, at King's Bridge.

"The army is in splendid order, the weather fine, and supplies abundant. Our march was most agreeable and not molested by guerillas. We reached Savannah three days ago, but owing to Fort McAllister we could not communicate; but now we have Fort McAllister, we can go ahead. We have captured two boats on Savannah River, and prevented their gunboats from coming down. The estimated population of Savannah is 25,000, and the garrison 15,000. Gen. Hardee commands.

"We have not lost a wagon on the trip, but have gathered in a large supply of negroes, mules and horses. Our teams are in better condition than when we started. My first duty will be to clear the army of superfluous negroes, mules and horses.

"I have utterly destroyed over two hundred miles of rail, and consumed all stores and provisions that were essential to the armies of Lee and Hood.

B*

"The quick work made with McAllister, and the opening of communication with our fleet, and consequent independence for supplies, dissipates all their boasted threats to head me off and starve the army.

"*I regard Savannah as already gained.*

"Yours truly,

(Signed,) "W. T. SHERMAN,

"*Major-General.*"

In this connection, the reader will be pleased with the following extracts from the journal of one who accompanied the grand triumphal march of Sherman, from which he will be able to gather a history of the more important events and incidents of the march not heretofore recorded in these pages:

MARCHING ON.

NEAR TONNILLE STATION, ON THE GEORGIA CENTRAL RAILROAD, Nov. 27.

Since writing the above, the enemy have moved forward all along the line. The rebels seem to have understood, but too late, that it was not Sherman's intention to make a serious attack upon Macon. They have, however, succeeded in getting Wheeler across the Oconee at a point below the railroad bridge. We first became aware of their presence in our front by the destruction of several small bridges across Buffalo Creek, on the two roads leading to Sandersville, over which were advancing the Twentieth and Fourteenth Corps.

We were delayed but a few hours. The passage was also contested by the rebel cavalry under Wheeler, and they fought our front all the way, and into the streets of Sandersville. The Twentieth Corps had the advance, deploying a regiment as skirmishers, forming the remainder of the brigade in line of battle on either side of the road. The movement was executed in the handsomest manner, and was so effectual as not to impede the march of the column in the slightest degree, although the roll of musketry was unceasing. Our loss was not serious, twenty odd killed and wounded.

NEAR THE OCONEE.

As the Twentieth Corps entered the town they were met by the Fourteenth, whose head of column arrived at the same moment. While these two corps had met with the obstructions above mentioned, the army, under Gen. Howard, was attempting to throw a pontoon across the Oconee at the Georgia Central Railroad Bridge. Here they met a force under the command of General Wayne, which was composed of a portion of Wheeler's cavalry, militia, and a band of convicts who had been liberated from the penitentiary upon the condition that they would join the army.

The most of these desperadoes have been taken prisoners, dressed in their State Prison clothing. General Sherman has turned them loose, believing that Gov. Brown had not got the full benefits of his liberality. The rebels did not make a remarkably stern defense of the bridge, for Howard was able to cross his army yesterday, and commenced breaking railroad again to-day. In fact, all of the army, except one corps, are engaged in the same work. Morgan, with his army, was hardly able to reach this point when he met Gen. Hardee, who has managed to get around here from Macon. Our troops struck the railroad at the station a few hours after the frightened band escaped.

THANKSGIVING DAY KEPT.

We have been told that the country was very poor east of Oconee, but our experience has been a delightful gastronomic contradiction of the statement. The cattle trains are getting so large that we find difficulty in driving them along. Thanksgiving Day was very generally observed in the army; the troops scorning chickens in the plentitude of turkeys with which they had supplied themselves.

SUPPLIES ABUNDANT.

Vegetables of all kinds, and in unlimited quantities, were at hand, and the soldiers gave thanks as soldiers may, and were merry as soldiers can be. In truth, so far as the gratification of the stomach goes, the troops are pursuing a continuous thanksgiving.

In addition to fowls, vegetables and meats, many obtain a delicious syrup made from sorghum, which is cultivated on all the plantations, and stored away in large troughs and hogsheads. The mills here and there furnish fresh supplies of flour and meal, and we hear little or nothing of "hard-tack," that terror to weak mastication. Over the sections of country lately traversed I find very little cultivation of cotton. The commands of Davis appear to have been obeyed; and our large droves of cattle are turned nightly into the immense fields of ungathered corn to eat their fill, while the granaries are crowded to overflowing with both oats and corn.

We have also reached the sand regions, so that the fall of rain has no terrors; the roads are excellent, and would become firmer from a liberal wetting. The rise of the river will not bother us much, for each army corps has its pontoons, and the launching of its boats is the matter of an hour.

THE COUNTRY PEOPLE

all through this section were found to be extremely ignorant. Rich men there are, whose plantations line the roads for miles; men and women who own, or did own, hundreds of slaves, and raised every year their thousand bales of cotton; but their ignorance is only equalled by that twin sister of ignorance, intolerance. I can understand, as I never did before, why it was that a few persons, who every year represented the South in Congress, were able to wield that influence as a unit. Many of the people claim to have been Unionists from the beginning of the war. It seems hard, sometimes, to strip such men as clear of all eatables as do our troops, who have the art cultivated to the most eminent degree; but, as Gen. Sherman often says to them: "If it is true that you are Unionists, you should not have permitted Jeff. Davis to dragoon you, until you are as much his slaves as once the niggers were yours."

Gen. Sherman invites all able-bodied negroes (others could not make the march,) to join the column, and he takes especial pleasure when they join the procession, on some occasions telling them they are free; that Massa Lincoln has given them their liberty, and that they can go where they please; that if they earn their freedom they should have it; but that Massa Lincoln has given it to them anyhow. Thousands of negro women join the column, some carrying household truck; others, and many of them there are, who bear the heavy burden of children in their arms, while older boys and girls plod by their sides. All these women and children are ordered back, heart-rending though it may be to refuse them liberty.

But the majority accept the advent of the Yankees, as the fulfillment of the millennial prophecies. The "day of jubilee," the hope and prayer of a lifetime, has come. They cannot be made to understand that they must remain behind, and they are satisfied only when General Sherman tells them — as he does every day — that we shall come back for them some time, and that they must be patient until the proper hour of deliverance comes.

THE MARCH TO THE OGEECHEE.

Nov. 29, NEAR JOHNSON'S, ON THE SOUTH SIDE OF THE GEORGIA RAILROAD.

We have not heard from the army on the north side of the railroad since it left us at Sandersville; nor from Kilpatrick until to-day, and then indirectly through a negro, who reports that the son of his master rode all the way from Louisville in great haste, reporting that Wheeler was fighting the Yankees, who were advancing on Augusta. General Sherman's second step in this campaign will have been equally successful with the first, if he is able to cross the Ogeechee to-morrow without much opposition. Davis' and Kilpatrick's movement has been a blind, in order to facilitate the passage over the Ogeechee of the main body of the army, which for two days past has been marching on parallel roads south of the railroad.

Thus far we have reason to believe that the rebels are ignorant of our principal movement, and are trembling with the fear that Augusta is our objective.

Kilpatrick is doing the same work which he accomplished with such high honor when covering our right flank in the early days of the campaign. His column now acts as a curtain upon the extreme left, through which the enemy may in vain attempt to penetrate. He has a yet grander aim in view. If he succeeds, his name will not only stand at the head of our great cavalry generals, but it will be uttered with the prayers and blessings of the wives and children of the prisoners whom he may liberate at Millen, which is the point he aims for, and where have been incarcerated many thousands of our brave comrades. Kilpatrick started on the same day that our army left Milledgeville, the 25th instant.

ON THE MARCH.

All day long the army has been marching through magnificent pine woods—the savannahs of the South, as they are termed. I have never seen, and I can't conceive, a more picturesque sight than the army winding along through these grand old woods. The pines rise, naked of branches, eighty and ninety feet, and then are crowned with a tuft of pure green. The trees are wide apart, so that frequently two trains of wagons and troops in double columns are marching abreast. In the distance may be seen a troop of horsemen, some general and his staff, turning about, here and there, their gay uniforms and red and white flags contrasting harmoniously with the bright, yellow grass underneath and the deep evergreen. War has its romance and its pleasures, and nothing could be more delightful, nor can there be more beautiful subjects for the artist's pencil than a thousand sights which have met my eye for days past, and which can never be seen outside the army.

STATION ON GEORGIA CENTRAL RAILROAD, }
Wednesday, November 30th, 1864. }

With the exception of the Fifteenth Corps, our army is across the Ogeechee, and without fighting a battle This river is a line of great strength to the rebels, and they might have made its passage a costly effort for us, but they have been outwitted and outmanœuvred. I am more convinced than ever that if General Sherman intends taking his army to the seaboard, it is evidently his policy to avoid a battle, or any contest which will delay him in the establishment of a new base of operations and supplies; if he is able to establish this new base, and at the same time destroy all the lines of communication from the rebel armies, with the great cities, so that they will be as much isolated as if those strongholds were in our hands, he will have accomplished the greatest strategic victory in the war, and all the more welcome because bloodless.

We have heard to-day from Kilpatrick and from Millen. Kilpatrick made a splendid march, fighting all the way to Waynesboro, destroying the railroad bridge crossing Briar Creek, between Augusta and Millen. It is with real grief that I write he was unable to accomplish the release of our prisoners. It appears that for some time past the rebels have been removing our soldiers from Millen; the officers have been sent to Columbia, S. C., and the privates further south, somewhere on the Gulf Railroad.

THE PASSAGE OF THE OGEECHEE.

We have had very little difficulty in crossing the Ogeechee. The Twentieth Corps moved down the railroad, destroying it to the bridge. The Seventeenth Corps covered the river at this point, where a light bridge was only partially destroyed. It was easily repaired, so that the infantry and cavalry could pass over it, while the wagons and artillery used the pontoons. The Ogeechee is about sixty yards in width at this point. It is approached on the northern or western side through swamps, which would be impassable were it not for the sandy soil which packs solid when the water covers the roads, although in places there are treacherous quicksands which we are obliged to corduroy.

This evening I walked down to the river. A novel and vivid sight was it to see the fires of pitch pine flaring up into the mist and darkness, the figures of men and horses looming out of the dense shadows in gigantic proportions. Torchlights are blinking and flashing away off in the forests, while the still air echoed and reëchoed with the cries of the teamsters and the wild shouts of the soldiers. A long line of the troops marched across the front bridge, each soldier bearing a torch; their light reflected in quivering lines in the swift running stream.

IN A FOG.

Soon the fog, which settles like a blanket over the swamps and forests of the river bottoms, shut down upon the scene, and so dense and dark was it, that torches were of but little use, and men were directed here and there by the voice.

AN ORIGINAL CHARACTER.

At this station we came across an old man named Wells, who was the most original character I ever met. He was depôt-master in the days when there was a railroad here. He is a shrewd old man, and seemed to understand the merits of the war question perfectly. He said:

"They say you are retreating, but it is the strangest sort of a retreat I ever saw. Why, dog bite them, the newspapers have been lying in this way all along. They allers are whipping the Federal armies, and they allers fall back after the battle is over. It was that ar' idee that first opened my eyes. Our army war allers whipping the Feds, and we allers fell back. I allers told 'em it was a d—d humbug, and now by —— I know it, for here you are right on old John Wells' place; hogs, potatoes, corn and fences all gone. I don't find any fault. I expected it all."

"Jeff. Davis and the rest," he continued, "talk about splitting the Union. Why if South Carolina had gone out by herself, she would have been split in four pieces by this time. Splitting the Union! Why d—n it, the State of Georgia is being split right through from end to end. It is these rich fellows who are making this war, and keeping their precious bodies out of harm's way. There's John Franklin went through here the other day, running away from your army. I could have played dominoes on his coat tails. There's my poor brother, sick with small-pox at Macon, working for eleven dollars a month, and hasn't got a cent of the d—d stuff for a year. 'Leven dollars a month and eleven thousand bullets a minute. I don't believe in it, sir.

"My wife came from Canada, and I kind o' thought I would sometime go there to live, but was allers afraid of the ice and cold; but I can tell you this country is getting too cussed hot for me. Look at my fence rails burning there. I think I can stand the cold better.

"I heard as how they cut down the trees across your road, up country, and burn the bridges; why, (dog bite their hides!) one of your Yankees can take up a tree and carry it off, tops and all; and there's that bridge you put across the river in less than two hours — they might as well try to stop the Ogeechee as you Yankees.

"The blasted rascals who burnt this yere bridge thought they did a big thing; a natural born fool cut in two had more sense in either end than any of them.

"To bring back the good old times," he said, "it'll take the help of Divine Providence, a heap of rain, and a deal of elbow grease, to fix things up again."

SHERMAN'S MANŒUVRES.

SCARBORO', Ga., December 3.

Pivoted upon Millen, the army has swung slowly round from its eastern course, and is now moving in six columns upon parallel roads southward.

Until yesterday it was impossible for the rebels to decide whether or not it was General Sherman's intention to march upon Augusta. Kilpatrick had destroyed the bridge above Waynesboro, and, falling back, had again advanced, supported by the Fourteenth Army Corps, under General Davis. South of this column, moving eastward through Birdsville, was the Twentieth Corps, commanded by General Slocum. Yet, further south, the Seventeenth Corps, General Blair in command, followed the railroad, destroying it as he advanced. West and south of the Ogeechee the Fifteenth Corps, General Osterhaus in immediate command, but under the eye of General Howard, has moved in two columns.

Until now Davis and Kilpatrick have been a cover and shield to the real movements. At no time has it been possible for Hardee to interpose any serious obstacle to the advance of the main body of our army, for our left wing has always been a strong arm thrust out in advance, ready to put in chancery any force which might attempt to get within its reach.

The rebel councils of war appear to have been completely deceived, for we hear it reported that Bragg and Longstreet are at Augusta, with 10,000 men, made up of militia, two or three South Carolina regiments, and a portion of Hampton's Legion, sent there for one month. It is possible, now, that the curtain has been withdrawn, and as it may appear that we are marching straight for Savannah, their generals, with their ten thousand, may attempt to harass our rear; but they can accomplish nothing but the loss of a few lives, without checking our progress.

The work so admirably performed by our left wing, so far as to oblige the rebels in our front constantly to retreat, by threatening their rear, now becomes the office of the Fifteenth Corps, our right wing on the right bank of the river. Its two columns are moving one day's march in advance of the main body of the army, marching down the peninsula between the Savannah and Ogeechee Rivers. The necessity and value of these flank movements, first of the right wing with Kilpatrick's cavalry, then of Davis and Kilpatrick on the left, and now of Howard on our right, is because we cannot run over and demolish any and all the rebel forces in Georgia. They could not for a moment stand before this army upon any ordinary battle-ground, but a very small force of infantry and cavalry at a river could delay a column half a day, and perhaps longer, and as our soldiers have got tired of chickens, sweet potatoes, sorghum, &c., and have been promised oysters on the half shell, oysters roasted, stewed, &c., in short, oysters, they don't care to be delayed.

The railroad, which has been receiving our immediate attention within the last week, is altogther the best we have seen in the State, though the rail itself is not so heavy as the T rail on the Augusta and Atlanta Road.

We daily traverse immense corn fields, covering from one hundred to one thousand acres. These were once devoted to the cultivation of cotton, and it is surprising to see how the planters have carried out the orders or wishes of the rebel government in this respect. There has been a large amount of cotton destroyed in this campaign, but it must have been but a small portion even of the limited crop raised, as the destruction has chiefly been away from the railroads. As near as we can learn, two-thirds of the cotton has been sent over the Georgia Central Railroad to Augusta by way of Millen; from thence a limited amount has been transported to Wilmington for trans-Atlantic shipment; the balance yet remains in the vicinity of Columbia, South Carolina.

One thing is most certain, neither the West nor the East will draw any supplies from the counties in this State traversed by our army for a long time to come; our work has been the next thing to annihilation.

CONCENTRATION AT OGEECHEE—A FIGHT.

OGEECHEE CHURCH, December 6.

The army for two days past has been concentrating at this point, which is the narrowest part of the peninsula. General Howard is still on the west side of the Ogeechee, but is within supporting distance, and has ample means of crossing the river should it be necessary, which is not at all probable. Kilpatrick has again done noble work. On Sunday last, while marching toward Alexander, for the purpose of more thoroughly completing the destruction of the railroad bridge crossing Briar Creek, we found Wheeler on his way near Waynesboro. He fought him several times, punishing him severely in each instance, driving his infantry and cavalry before him through Waynesboro and beyond the bridge, which was completely destroyed. He rejoined the main body of our army then marching southward.

A significant feature of this campaign, which has not before been mentioned in this diary, received a marked illustration yesterday. Except in a few instances, private residences have not been destroyed. Yesterday we passed the plantation of a Mr. Stubbs. The house, cotton-gin, press, cornricks, stables, everything was in flames, and in the dooryard lay the the dead bodies of several bloodhounds, that had been used to track and pull down negroes and our escaped prisoners. And wherever our army has passed, everything in the shape of a dog has been killed. The soldiers and officers are determined that no more flying fugitives, white men or negroes, shall be followed by track hounds that come within reach of their powder and ball.

THE ARMY FURTHER SOUTH.

DECEMBER 8.

The army has been advancing slowly and surely, but as cautiously as if a strong army were in our front. The relative position of the troops has not materially changed since last writing, except that we are all further South. From fifteen to twenty miles lies Savannah, it is to be supposed, in some perturbation at the certainty of our approach. If the rebels intend fighting in defence of the city, it will be behind their fortifications, for as yet we have only skirmished with parties of cavalry, and they have not seen the head of our infantry column.

A BOLD MOVEMENT.

General Howard has just returned from a very successful movement. Fearing that we should detach a force for the purpose of destroying the Gulf Road, which they are using to its utmost capacity just now, they pushed a force across the Ogeechee. While this body were covered by a strong riverside line, General Corse, of Altoona memory, shoved his division between the Little and Great Ogeechee, thirteen miles in advance of the main columns to the canal, which runs from the Ogeechee to the Savannah River. He bridged the canal, crossed it with his division, and now holds a position out of which Hood's army could not drive him.

This bold step had forced the rebels to evacuate the line of works stretching from river to river, and they have now fairly sought refuge in the fortifications proper of Savannah.

HEARING THE SIGNAL GUNS OF THE GUNBOATS.

All the afternoon we have heard the signal guns of our gunboats, supposed to be in Ossabaw Sound. My heart thrills with gladness to think that we are within speaking distance of our brethren of the brave navy, and that we are hereafter to act in unison with, we hope, more purpose than has been the result with most expeditions on the Atlantic coast. The next three days promises to be full of interest, for we shall now seek to establish a base in connection with our fleet.

CLOSING IN UPON SAVANNAH.

DECEMBER 9.

We are gradually closing in upon the city. General Howard holds the position gained on the other side of the canal yesterday, and has advanced the larger part of his command in its support. Portions of our army are now within eight miles of Savannah. General Blair's column lost several officers and men, some of them by honorable fighting, as the rebels withstood the advance with pertinacity.

One officer and several men were severely wounded by the explosion of shells and torpedoes buried and concealed in the road, which was an attempt at cowardly murder. The prisoners were marched over the road, and removed two of these treacherous, death-dealing instruments.

General Davis is to-night at Cherokee Hill, having crossed the Charleston Road, partially destroying the bridge spanning the Savannah. He has also been opposed by the rebels, but, as with the other columns, the opposition only accelerated the progress of the troops, who hurry forward on the double-quick at the sound of the guns, eager to get into the fight. To-morrow we may expect to have concentrated our army so as to form a continuous line about the city.

STRONG LINES OF REBEL WORKS.

December 10.

The army has advanced some six miles to-day, and have everywhere a strong line of works, which appear to be held by a large force; with 32-pound guns in position, their line, although extended, is more easily defended, because of a succession of impassable swamps, which stretch across the peninsula. All the openings between these morasses and the roads which lead through them, are strongly fortified, and the approaches have been contested vigorously, but with little loss to us. General Sherman seems to avoid the sacrifice of life, and I doubt his making any serious attack until he has communication with the fleet.

We have connected our lines, so that the corps are within supporting distance of each other. The soldiers are, meanwhile, in most cheerful spirits, with that *insousciance* which is the most characteristic feature of our troops.

CAPTURE OF FORT M'ALLISTER.

DECEMBER 13.

At Fort McAllister. To-day I have been a spectator of one of those glorious sights where the actors, passing through the most fearful ordeal of fire which befalls the soldier, come out successful, and are always after heroes.

The Second division of the Fifteenth Corps have marched to-day fifteen miles; and, without the assistance of artillery, have crossed an open space of six hundred yards, under a fierce fire of twenty-one heavy guns, crawling through a thick abatis, crossed a ditch of great depth, at whose bottom were driven thick palisades, torn them away, surmounted the crest and palisades, shot and bayoneted the gunners, who refused to surrender, at their posts, and planted the stars and stripes upon the work in triumph. The assault was made with a single line, which approached the fort from all sides but that of the river, at the same instant, never for an instant wavering, no man lurking shelter, but facing the fire manfully.

The explosion of torpedoes at this point did not deter them. General Sherman's old division and corps had been told that he had said, "Carry the place by assault to-night, if possible." They resolved to fulfill their old commander's wish, and they did it. Perhaps in the history of this war there has not been a more striking example of the evidence of quick, determined action. Had we waited, put up intrenchments, shelled the place, and made the usual approaches, we should have lost many more lives, and time was invaluable. As it is, our entire loss is not more than ninety men killed and wounded, and we have gained a necessity—a base of supplies. Our whole army are eager to emulate such a glorious example, and this *esprit du corps* has been raised to the grandest height.

General Sherman did not feel that his march to the sea was completed until Savannah was captured. That city fell, as Jericho of old did, without resistance. Its gates were opened, and the conqueror marched in.

After the capture of Fort McAllister, Sherman began the systematic investment of the city. The enemy made the best use of every natural advantage against us. The rice fields below the city were flooded by means of the canals, rendering an advance from that quarter difficult. The swamps north and west were perplexing barriers. These were difficulties only in the way of an assault. Our lines, however, were greatly annoyed in the gradual approach by torpedoes, which the enemy had ingeniously disposed. They were so perfectly covered as to be almost unnoticeable, and so arranged that the slightest pressure of the foot upon the small plug sufficed to explode them.

This danger Sherman overcome, by ordering the rebel prisoners in his hands to go before our advancing lines, find the torpedoes, and dig them up — dig up the death traps which perhaps their own hands had planted.

The investment of the city was as complete as it could be made by the 20th of December. Every outlet of the city was completely in our possession, except the causeway just below Hutchinson's Island, and every effort was made to secure that.

On the morning of the 20th of December, Sherman sent by flag of truce his demand for the surrender of the city, closing his dispatch with the words of General Hood, in his demand for the surrender of Dalton and the negro troops: "If this demand is not complied with, I shall take no prisoners." Of course this was intended as irony on the part of Sherman.

General Hardee, in his reply, boasted that he had men and supplies enough to hold the city, and that he would not surrender.

Arrangements were completed for the assault and bombardment. Even the guns of the enemy which had been captured with the surrounding forts, had been removed and placed in position to aid us in the attack.

General Hardee anticipated the assault, and on the night of the 20th evacuated, passing over the Union Causeway under the protection of his iron-clads and the batteries of the lower end of Hutchinson's Island. The rear guard of the fugitives fired the navy-yard, and the iron-clads were blown up.

On the following morning, December 21st 1864, the beautiful city of Savannah was surrendered by the mayor and council of the city, with the request that private property and the rights of citizens should be respected.

Thus ended the most remarkable march in the annals of history. European journals, and among these the London *Times* admit that the march of Sherman from Chattanooga to Savannah, is absolutely without a parallel. " As the pilgrims landed and sent liberty and a glorious form of nationality Westward, along their northern lines of march, so the West sounded back to the ocean again that sublime hymn of universal freedom which our fathers sung on Plymouth Rock, when they dedicated this continent to God."

This wonderful march, and those who took part in it, will be remembered. The pen of the historian and the lays of the minstrel will keep this great event fresh in the memory of men. Even now and thus beautifully, has this story been woven into verse:

SHERMAN'S MARCH TO THE SEA.

Our camp-fires shone bright on the mountain
    That frowned on the river below,
While we stood by our guns in the morning,
    And eagerly watched for the foe,
When a rider came out from the darkness
    That hung over mountain and tree,
And shouted, "Boys up and be ready,
    For Sherman will march to the sea."

When cheer upon cheer for bold Sherman
    Went up from each valley and glen,
And the bugle reëchoed the music
    That came from the lips of the men;
For we know that the stars on our banner
    More bright in their splendor would be,
And that blessing from North-land would greet **us**
    As Sherman marched down to the sea.

D*

Then forward, boys, forward, to battle,
    We marched on our wearisome way,
And we strewed the wild hills of Resaca—
    God bless those who fell on that day.
Then Kenesaw, dark in its glory,
    Frowned down on the flag of the free:
But the East and the West bore our standard
    As Sherman marched down to the sea.

Still onward we pressed till our banner
    Swept out from Atlanta's grim walls,
And the blood of the patriot dampened
    The soil where the traitor's flag falls.
But we paused not to weep for the fallen
    Who slept by each river and tree;
Yet we twined them wreaths of the laurel
    As Sherman marched down to the sea.

Proud, proud was our army that morning,
    That stood by the cypress and pine,
When Sherman said: "Boys, you are weary
    This day fair Savannah is thine."
Then sang we a song for our chieftain
    That echoed o'er river and lea,
And the stars on our banner shone brighter
    When Sherman marched down to the sea.

After the escape of General Hardee with his 13,000 troops, and the surrender by the mayor of the city, our army marched in, to the evident delight of the citizens. In numerous instances men and women looked upon the old flag and wept, and some hailed it with lively demonstrations of joy.

The fruits of the capture were as follows: The city; all its fortifications intact, with the adjoining rivers and harbors; about 1,200 prisoners; 152 guns; 38,000 bales of cotton; large quantities of ammunition and rice; thirteen locomotives, and 200 railroad cars. The forts captured were McAllister, on the Ogeechee; Lawton and Lee, on the Savannah River, near the city, and Jackson, on the river, two miles below the city.

With the following orders of General Sherman, and one or two short extracts from correspondence, we close this chapter:

SHERMAN'S CONGRATULATORY ORDER TO HIS ARMY.

HEAD-QUARTERS MILITARY DIVISION OF THE MISSISSIPPI,
IN THE FIELD, SAVANNAH, Ga., January 8.

SPECIAL FIELD ORDERS No. 6.

The general commanding announces to the troops composing the Military Division of the Mississippi, that he has received from the President of the United States and from Lieutenant General Grant, letters conveying the high sense and appreciation of the campaign just closed, resulting in the capture of Savannah and the defeat of Hood's army in Tennessee.

In order that all may understand the importance of events, it is proper to revert to the situation of affairs in September last. We held Atlanta, a city of little value to us, but so important to the enemy that Mr. Davis, the head of the rebellious faction in the South, visited his army near Palmetto, and commanded it to regain it, as well as to ruin and destroy us by a series of measures which he thought would be effectual.

That army, by a rapid march, first gained our railroad near Big Shanty, and afterward about Dalton. We pursued, but it marched so rapidly that we could not overtake it, and General Hood led his army successfully far toward Mississippi, in hopes to decoy us out of Georgia. But we were not then to be led away by him, and purposed to control and lead events ourselves. Generals Thomas and Schofield, commanding the department to our rear, returned to their posts, and prepared to decoy General Hood into their meshes, while we came on to complete our original journey.

We quietly and deliberately destroyed Atlanta and all the railroads which the enemy had used to carry on war against us; occupied his State capital, and then captured his commercial capital, which had been so strongly fortified from the sea as to defy approach from that quarter.

Almost at the moment of our victorious entry into Savannah came the welcome and expected news that our comrades in Tennessee had also fulfilled, nobly and well, their part; had decoyed General Hood to Nashville, and then turned on him, defeating his army thoroughly, capturing all his artillery, great numbers of prisoners, and were still pursuing the fragments down into Alabama. So complete a success in military operations, extending over half a continent, is an achievement that entitles it to a place in the military history of the world.

The armies serving in Georgia and Tennessee, as well as the local garrisons of Decatur, Bridgeport, Chattanooga and Murfreesboro, are alike entitled to the common honor, and each regiment may inscribe on its colors at pleasure the words "Savannah" or "Nashville."

The general commanding embraces in the same general success the operations of the cavalry column, under Generals Stoneman, Burbridge and Gillem, that penetrated into Southwestern Virginia, and paralyzed the efforts of the enemy to disturb the peace and safety of the people of East Tennessee. Instead of being put on the defensive, we have, at all times, assumed the bold offensive, and completely thwarted the designs of the enemies of our country. By order of

Major General W. T. SHERMAN.

L. W. DAYTON, *Aide-de Camp.*

REGULATIONS BY GENERAL SHERMAN.

HEAD-QUARTERS MILITARY DIVISION OF THE MISSISSIPPI, IN THE FIELD, SAVANNAH, Ga., January 14.

It being represented that the Confederate army and armed bands of robbers, acting professedly under the authority of the Confederate government, are harassing the people of Georgia, and endeavoring to intimidate them in the efforts they are making to secure to themselves provisions, clothing, security to life and property, and the restoration of law and good government in the State, it is hereby ordered and made public:

First. That the farmers of Georgia may bring into Savannah, Fernandina or Jacksonville, Fla., marketing, such as beef, pork, mutton, vegetables of any kind, fish, &c., as well as cotton in small quantities, and sell the same in open market, except the cotton, which must be sold by or through the Treasury agents, and may invest the proceeds in family stores, such as bacon and flour, in any reasonable quantities, groceries, shoes and clothing, and articles not contraband of war, and carry the same back to their families. No trade store will be attempted in the interior, or stocks of goods sold for them, but families may club together for mutual assistance and protection in coming and going.

Second. The people are encouraged to meet together in peaceful assemblages to discuss measures looking to their safety and good government, and the restoration of State and National authority, and will be protected by the National Army, when so doing; and all peaceable inhabitants who satisfy the commanding officers that they are earnestly laboring to that end must not only be left undisturbed in property and person, but must be protected as far as possible consistent with the military operations. If any farmer or peaceable inhabitant is molested by the enemy—viz: the Confederate army of guerrillas—because of his friendship to the National Government, the perpetrator, if caught, will be summarily punished, or his family made to suffer for the outrage; but if the crime cannot be traced to the actual party, then retaliation will be made on the adherents to the cause of the rebellion. Should a Union man be murdered, then a rebel selected by lot will be shot: or if a Union family be persecuted on account of the cause, a rebel family will be banished to a foreign land. In aggravated cases, retaliation will extend as high as five for one. All commanding officers will act promptly in such cases, and report their action after the retaliation is done. By order of

Major General W. T. SHERMAN.

L. W. DAYTON, *Assistant Adjutant General*.

RECEPTION OF THE UNION ARMY.

Beyond all question, the Union army has been more cordially received in Savannah than in any other place which has fallen into our hands.

The city contains about 25,000 inhabitants. Several thousand refugees are at present residing there. A large class of the population will be entirely dependent upon the Federal authorities for food, and doubtless until some plan of caring for them can be set in operation, considerable suffering will occur. A few days, however, will suffice to bring up all needed supplies both for the army and any civilians whom the authorities may see fit to aid.

DESCRIPTION OF THE CITY.

Savannah, as all readers know, is on the south side of the river bearing its name, and eighteen miles from the sea. The general level of the city is some forty-five feet above the water. It is regularly laid out, the streets are very broad and handsomely shaded, while the extensive private yards, and the great number of parks and public squares, give to the place the aspect of an infinite succession of suburban residences. It is one of the most beautiful cities in the country. A tropical air is thrown over it all by the character of the trees, flowers and shrubs. Few trees are selected for the streets and yards that are not evergreen, and flowers in endless variety greeted our Northern boys. Live oaks, magnolias, orange and bay trees are to be seen everywhere. In some of the streets four rows of trees are planted, forming leaf-arched avenues across the entire city, two for carriages on each side of the way, and a splendid promenade in the centre. Many of these are huge forest trees, while all are large, and the effect is most impressive. There are many very elegant public buildings, and there is little of that decayed look which the war has brought over most of the Southern cities.

Among the finest public buildings are the Custom House and the Exchange, the Armory and

State Arsenal, St. John's and the Independent Presbyterian Churches. There is a large and valuable collection of works in the State Historical Society, and the same is true of the Public Library.

REVOLUTIONARY REMAINS.

These are numerous, and excite strange emotions. An elegant monument stands in Chippewa Square, erected to the memory of Pulaski, who fell in the attack upon the city, when it was held by the British in 1779.

In Monument Square there is a beautiful Doric obelisk designed to commemorate the deeds of Greene and Pulaski. General Lafayette laid the corner stone of this structure in 1825. The base of the pedestal is ten feet by seven, and about twelve feet high. The shaft surmounting this is about forty feet high.

Mounds and ditches still remain near the swamp southeast of the city, and a fort built by General Greene can still be traced. Tatnall's tomb is in the cemetery of Bonaventure, and many of the soldiers of that olden time are mouldering there with him. If such ground could be cursed, how deep the stain which would rest upon it from all the traitor graves which now mar the beauty of the spot! Sleeping side by side are those who bled to establish our Government, and those who have died seeking its overthrow. Yet the flag that waved over those old forts when the nation's life began, floats above them again, the earnest of a nobler life, dawning even now. The flag that Greene loved, and which Pulaski looked upon while dying, and which floated over Tatnall's ships, Sherman's men, from their far off Western homes, have borne across a continent and set it up again on the fields of its old renown. It shall wave there long after traitors have received their merited reward of infamy.

BONAVENTURE.

This cemetery, situated near Fort Jackson, is a most wonderful spot. Originally it was a private estate, laid out with great taste, and well stocked with shade trees and ornamental shrubs. These trees now form shaded avenues miles in extent, and hung, as they are, so thickly with the long gray moss, they look as if

> "Eternity had snowed its years upon them,
> And the white winter of their age had come."

Yet through these marks of age the greenness of perpetual spring smiles constantly, even as the glory of the Resurrection outshines the dimness of the graves of the sleepers below. There are walks here that remind one of the Bosphorus, with its cypress and its gloom. There are bright groves of orange and bay, brilliant flowers and birds of golden plumage and sweet song. The far-off murmur of the sea is ever faintly heard; birds do not cease to sing or flowers to bloom. Here nature never dies, and were it not for man's decay we might almost imagine that our footsteps were leading us over the beautiful walks of Paradise.

GENERAL SHERMAN AND THE BRITISH CONSUL AT SAVANNAH.

[Washington Correspondence of the New York Herald.]

On the arrival of General Sherman at Savannah, he saw a large number of British flags displayed from buildings, and had a curiosity to know how many British consuls there were there. He soon ascertained that these flags were on buildings where cotton had been stored away, and at once ordered it to be seized. Soon after that, while the general was busily engaged at his head-quarters, a pompous gentleman walked in, apparently in great haste, and inquired if he was General Sherman? Having received an affirmative reply, the pompous gentleman remarked, "that when he left his residence the United States troops were engaged in removing his cotton from it, where it was protected by the British flag."

"Stop, sir," said General Sherman; "not your cotton, sir, but my cotton; my cotton in the name of the United States Government, sir. I have noticed," continued General Sherman, "a great many British flags here, all protecting cotton. I have seized it all in the name of my Government."

"But sir," said the consul, indignantly, "there is scarcely any cotton in Savannah that does not belong to me."

"There is not a pound of cotton here, sir, that does not belong to me, for the United States," responded Sherman.

"Well, sir," said the consul, swelling himself up with the dignity of his office, and reddening in his face, "my Government shall hear of this. I shall report your conduct to my Government, sir."

"Ah! pray, who are you, sir?" said the general.

"Consul to Her British Majesty, sir."

"Oh! indeed," responded the general. "I hope you will report me to your Government. You will please say to your Government, for me, that I have been fighting the English Government all the way from the Ohio River to Vicksburg, and thence to this point. At every step I have encountered British arms, and British goods of every description, at every step, sir. I have met them, sir, in all shapes; and now, sir, I find you claiming all the cotton, sir. I intend to call upon my Government to order me to Nassau at once."

"What do you propose to do there?" asked the Consul, somewhat taken aback.

"I would," replied the general, "take with me a quantity of picks and shovels, and throw that cursed sand hill into the sea, sir. You may tell your Government that, sir. I would shovel it into the sea, sir; and then I would pay for it, sir—if necessary. Good day, sir."

It is needless to add that General Sherman was not again troubled with the officious representative of Her Majesty's Government.

CHAPTER XIV.

SHERMAN'S CAMPAIGN IN THE CAROLINAS.

THE CONSUMMATION OF THE GREAT PLAN — MOVEMENTS OF THE TWO WINGS OF THE ARMY UNDER HOWARD AND SLOCUM — TRANSFER OF THE FORTS AND CITY TO GEN. FOSTER — CAPTURE OF FORT FISHER BY PORTER AND TERRY — DETERMINATION OF SHERMAN — STRATEGY AT THE SALKEHATCHIE — WADING THROUGH DEEP WATER — PURSUIT OF THE ENEMY TO BRANCHVILLE — DESTRUCTION OF THE RAILROAD — OFFICIAL REPORT OF SHERMAN — RESULT OF THE CAMPAIGN — FALL OF CHARLESTON — HORRORS OF THE EVACUATION — INCIDENTS.

This campaign may be called the climax of this colossal war. Heretofore we have spoken of the campaigns from Chattanooga to Atlanta, and from Atlanta to Savannah. The truth is, they were but parts of one great whole. The movement of Sherman, which commenced on the 1st day of May, 1864, and ended with the surrender of Johnston's army and all the Confederate forces from the Chattahoochee to the Potomac on the 26th day of April, 1865, extending through almost an entire year, was but one campaign; was but the carrying out of the plan of Sherman when he marched from Chattanooga; a campaign that has no parallel in the annals of history.

And now, in leading the reader through the final part of this most wonderful campaign, we can do nothing more than give to him its great outlines. In doing this, and for the sake of recording nothing but veritable history, we will follow somewhat closely the official report of General Sherman, adding to parts of it interesting details and incidents therein omitted.

Less than one month was consumed at Savannah in making proper dispositions of captured property and other local matters, and in preparations for the march North through the "sacred soil of South Carolina."

By the 15th of January, 1865, Sherman and his splendid army were ready for the march. Preliminary to this, General Howard, commanding the right wing, was ordered to embark his forces at Thunderbolt; transport them to Beaufort, and thence by the 15th of January, make a lodgment on the Charleston Railroad at Pocotaligo. This was accomplished punctually, at little cost, by the Seventeenth Corps, Major-General Blair, and a dépôt for supplies was established near the mouth of Pocotaligo Creek, with easy water communications back to Hilton Head. As our troops advanced toward the Charleston Railroad they met the enemy, who fell back after a short skirmish. The next day an attempt was made to flank the enemy's position, but they hastily evacuated their works, leaving three guns behind them. This position was gained with the loss of about ten men killed and wounded. The attempt of General Foster to carry this same position about a month previously, cost him twelve or fifteen hundred men.

THE LEFT WING.

The left wing, commanded by Major-General Slocum, and the cavalry commanded by Major-General Kilpatrick, were ordered, in the meantime, to rendezvous near Robertsville and Coosawachie, South Carolina, with a dépôt of supplies at Pureysburg, or Sister's Ferry, on the Savannah River. General Slocum had a good pontoon bridge constructed opposite the city, and the "Union Causeway," leading through the low rice fields opposite Savannah was repaired and corduroyed, but before the time appointed to start the heavy rains of January had swollen the river, broken the pontoon bridge and overflooded the whole bottom so that the causeway was four feet under water, and Slocum was compelled to look higher up for a passage over the Savannah River. He moved up to Sister's Ferry, but even there the river, with its overflowed bottoms was nearly three miles wide, so that he did not succeed in getting his whole wing across until the first week in February.

In the meantime, General Grant had sent to Sherman, Grover's Division of the Nineteenth Corps, to garrison Savannah, and had drawn the Twenty-third Corps, Major-General Schofield's command, from Tennessee and sent it to reënforce the commands of Major-Generals Terry and Palmer, operating on the coast of North Carolina, to prepare the way for the march of Sherman.

On the 18th of January, Sherman transferred the forts and city of Savannah to Major-General Foster, commanding the Department of the South. Sherman then imparted to Foster his plans of operation and instructed him how to follow his movements inland by occupying, in succession, the city of Charleston and such other points along the seacoast as would be of any value to us.

The combined naval and land forces under Admiral Porter and General Terry had, on the 16th of January, captured Fort Fisher and the Rebel forts at the mouth of Cape Fear River, and thus gave to Sherman another point of security on the sea-coast.

Sherman had already resolved, in his own mind, and had advised General Grant that he would undertake, "at one stride," to make Goldsboro, and open communications with the sea by the Newbern

Railroad. He ordered Colonel W. W. Wright, Superintendent of Military Railroads to proceed, in advance to Newbern, and to be prepared to extend the railroad out from Newbern to Goldsboro by the 15th of March. On the 19th of January, all preparations were finished and the orders for the march given. The Chief Quartermaster and Commissary, Generals Easton and Beckwith, were ordered to complete the supplies at Sister's Ferry and Pocotaligo, and then follow the movements of the army coastwise, looking for its arrival at Goldsboro, North Carolina, about the 15th of March, where they were to open communications with Sherman from Morehead City.

On the 22d of January, General Sherman in person, embarked at Savannah for Hilton Head, where he held a conference with Admiral Dahlgren of the United States Navy, and Major-General Foster commanding the Department of the South, and the next day proceeded to Beaufort, riding out thence on the 24th to Pocotaligo, where the Seventeenth Corps, Major-General Blair was encamped. At that time the Fifteenth Corps was somewhat scattered. Wood's and Hazen's divisions were at Beaufort. John E. Smith's was marching from Savannah by the coastward, and Corse was still at Savannah, cut off by storms and the freshet in the river.

On the 25th a demonstration was made against the Combahee Ferry and the Railroad Bridge across the Salkehatchie, merely to amuse the enemy, who had evidently adopted that river as his defensive line against our supposed *objective point*, the City of Charleston. General Sherman reconnoitered the line in person, and saw that the heavy rains had swollen the river so that water stood in the swamps for a breadth of more than one mile, at a depth of from one to twenty feet. Not having the remotest intention of approaching Charleston, a comparatively small force was able, by seeming preparations to cross over, to keep in their front a considerable force of the enemy who seemed disposed to contest our supposed advance on Charleston.

On the 27th, General Sherman rode to the camp of General Hatch's division of Foster's command, on the Tullafuiney and Coosawatchie Rivers and directed those places to be evacuated, as no longer of any use to us. That division was then moved to Pocotaligo to keep up the feints already begun, until we should, with the right wing, move higher up and cross the Salkehatchie about River's or Broxton's Bridge.

On the 29th Sherman learned that the roads back of Savannah had at last become sufficiently clear of the flood to admit of General Slocum putting his wing in motion, and that he was already approaching Sister's Ferry, whither a gun-boat, the Pontiac, Captain Luce, kindly furnished by Admiral Dahlgren, had preceded him to cover the crossing. In the meantime, three divisions of the Fifteenth Corps had closed up at Pocotaligo, and the right wing had loaded its wagons and was ready to start. Sherman, therefore, directed General Howard to move one corps, the Seventeenth, along the Salkehatchie as high up as River's Bridge, and the other, the Fifteenth, by Hickory Hill, Bosser's Cross-Roads, Anglesey Post Office and Beaufort's Bridge. Hatch's division was ordered to remain at Pocotaligo, feinting at the Salkehatchie Railroad Bridge and Ferry until our movement turned the enemy's position and forced him to fall behind the Edisto.

The Seventeenth and Fifteenth Corps drew out of camp on the 31st of January, but the real march began on the 1st of February. All the roads northward had for weeks been held by Wheeler's cavalry who had, by details of negro laborers, felled trees, burned bridges and made obstructions to impede our march. But so well organized were the pioneer battalions and so strong and intelligent our men, that obstructions seemed only to quicken their progress. Felled trees were removed, and bridges rebuilt by the heads of columns before the rear could close up. On the 2d of February the 15th Corps reached Toper's Cross Roads, and the Seventeenth was at River's Bridge. From Toper's Cross Roads Sherman communicated with General Slocum, still struggling with the floods of the Savannah River at Sister's Ferry. He had two divisions of the Twentieth Corps, General Williams, on the east bank, and was enabled to cross over on his pontoons the cavalry of Kilpatrick. General Williams was ordered to Beaufort Bridge, by way of Lawtonville and Allendale, Kilpatrick to Blackville, by way of Barnwell, and General Slocum was ordered to hurry the crossing at Sister's Ferry as much as possible, and overtake the right wing on the South Carolina Railroad. General Howard, with the right wing, was directed to cross the Salkehatchie and push rapidly for the South Carolina Railroad, at or near Midway. The enemy held the line of the Salkehatchie in force, having infantry and artillery intrenched at River's and Beaufort's bridges. The Seventeenth Corps was ordered to carry River's Bridge, and the Fifteenth Corps Beaufort's Bridge. The former position was carried promptly and skilfully by Mower's and Giles A. Smith's divisions of the Seventeenth Corps, on the 3d of February, by crossing the swamp, nearly three miles wide, with water varying from knee deep to shoulder deep. The weather was bitter cold, and Generals Mower and Smith led their divisions in person, on foot, waded the swamps, made a lodgment below the bridge, and turned on the rebel brigade which guarded it, driving it in disorder and confusion towards Branchville. Our casualties were one officer and seventeen men killed, and seventy wounded, who were sent to Pocotaligo.

For this success great credit should be given to Generals Mower and Smith, who promptly carried out General Sherman's orders in the face of great difficulties. To march a whole day, and that, too, a bitter, cold day in mid-winter, through water up to the arm-pits in places, required endurance, such as none but brave and true soldiers could or would endure. Such men cannot well fail of success.

A correspondent, who examined the position abandoned by the enemy, speaks of it as follows:

"FEBRUARY 5.

"I have examined the works at Beaufort Bridge to-day, which were evacuated by the rebels as soon as we made the crossing at River's Bridge. It is a place of remarkable strength, both in its natural advantages and the strong line of works which defend the passage. A brigade with a single section of artillery could have held an army at bay. So it would seem, at least, when one wades and stumbles over the narrow road which leads for half a mile through the swamp. When you come out of the dense jungle, and before crossing the main branch of the stream, you see before you, upon its border, a line of well-built works extending for a quarter of a mile on either side. Here are three embrasures, which were pierced for heavy guns, while the parapet is surmounted by the protecting head-log. If the enemy had not been flanked below, and could have held this place, it would have cost us hundreds of lives. As it is, we gained the peninsula formed by the Salkehatchie and Edisto Rivers. We have the choice of going to Augusta or Charleston. The latter place we can capture with less trouble than Savannah gave us, supposing we made a direct attack, for we can make an excellent base at Bull's Bay. I know that the general expects to capture Charleston by operating a hundred miles away from its walls — a strategy which has not always been practised in this war.

"General Williams is up with two of the divisions of the Twentieth Corps. Kilpatrick and his cavalry are at Allandale, and the balance of the left wing have crossed the Savannah. The army here has made a short move to-day, and we are within a single day's march of the Charleston and Augusta Railroad. We hear that the rebels intend defending it at several points, but they cannot protect the whole line, and we will flank them somewhere."

After the line of the enemy on the Salkehatchie was broken, they retreated hastily behind the Edisto River, at Branchville, and our whole army was pushed rapidly to the South Carolina Railroad, at Midway, Bamberg, or Lowry's Station and Graham's Station. The Seventeenth Corps, by threatening Branchville, forced the enemy to burn the railroad bridge, and Walker's Bridge below, across the Edisto. All hands were at once set to work to destroy the railroad track. From the 7th to the 10th of February this work was thoroughly prosecuted by the Seventeenth Corps, from Edisto up to Bamberg, and by the Fifteenth Corps, from Bamberg up to Blackville. In the meantime General Kilpatrick had brought his cavalry rapidly by Barnwell to Blackville, and had turned toward Aiken, with orders to threaten Augusta, but not to be drawn needlessly into serious battle. This he skilfully accomplished, skirmishing heavily with Wheeler's cavalry, first at Blackville, and afterwards at Williston and Aiken. General Williams, with two divisions of the Twentieth Corps, marched to the South Carolina Railroad, at Graham's Station, on the 8th, and General Slocum arrived at Blackville on the 12th of the month. The destruction of the railroad was continued by the left wing from Blackville up to Windsor. By the 11th of February all the army was on the railroad from Midway to Johnson's Station, thereby dividing the enemy's forces, which still remained at Branchville and Charleston on the one hand, and at Aiken and Augusta on the other.

For a clear and satisfactory account of the rest of the campaign, we refer to the official report of General Sherman, which we here insert word for word:

GENERAL SHERMAN'S OFFICIAL REPORT.

We then began the movement on Orangeburg. The Seventeenth Corps crossed the south fork of the Edisto River at Binnaker's Bridge, and moved straight for Orangeburg, while the Fifteenth Corps crossed at Holman's Bridge, and moved to Poplar Springs in support. The left wing and cavalry were still at work on the railroad, with orders to cross the South Edisto at New and Guignard's Bridges, move to the Orangeburg and Edgefield Road, and there await the result of the attack on Orangeburg. On the 12th the Seventeenth Corps found the enemy intrenched in front of the Orangeburg Bridge, but swept him away by a dash, and followed him, forcing him across the bridge, which was partially burned. Behind the bridge was a battery in position, covered by a cotton and earth parapet, with wings as far as could be seen. General Blair held one division (Giles A. Smith's) close up to the Edisto, and moved the other two to a point about two miles below, where he crossed Force's division by a pontoon bridge, holding Mower's in support. As soon as Force emerged from the swamp, the enemy gave ground, and Giles A. Smith's division gained the bridge, crossed over, and occupied the enemy's parapet. He soon repaired the bridge, and by four in the afternoon the whole corps was in Orangeburg, and had begun the work of destruction on the railroad. Blair was ordered to destroy this railroad effectually up to Lewisville, and to push the enemy across the Congaree, and force him to burn the bridges, which he did on the 14th; and without wasting time or labor on Branchville or Charleston, which I knew the enemy could no longer hold, I turned all the columns straight on Columbia. The Seventeenth Corps followed the State Road, and the Fifteenth Corps crossed the North Edisto from Poplar Springs, at Schilling's Bridge, above the mouth of "Cawcaw Swamp" Creek, and took a country road, which came into the State Road at Zeigtor's. On the 15th the Fifteenth Corps found the enemy in a strong position at Little Congaree Bridge (across Congaree Creek), with a *tete-de-pont* on the south side, and a well constructed fort on the north side, commanding the bridge with artillery. The ground in front was very bad, level and clear, with a fresh deposit of mud from a recent overflow. General Charles R. Woods, who commanded the leading division, succeeded, however, in turning the flank of the *tete-de-pont* by sending Stone's brigade through a cypress swamp to the left; and, following up the retreating enemy promptly, he got possession of the bridge and fort beyond. The bridge had been partially damaged by fire, and had to be repaired for the passage of artillery, so that night closed in before the head of the column could reach the bridge across the Congaree River, in front of Columbia. That night the enemy shelled our camps from a battery on the east side of the Congaree, above Granby. Early next morning (February 10), the head of the column reached the bank of the Congaree, opposite Columbia, but too late to save the fine bridge which spanned the river at that point. It was burned by the enemy. While waiting for the pontoons to come to the front, we could see the people running about the streets of Columbia, and occasionally small bodies of cavalry, but no masses. A single gun of Captain De Grass' battery was firing at their cavalry squads, but I checked his firing, limiting him to a few

F*

shots at the unfinished State House walls, and a few shells at the railroad depôt, to scatter the people who were seen carrying away sacks of corn and meal that we needed. There was no white flag or manifestations of surrender. I directed General Howard not to cross directly in front of Columbia, but to cross the Saluda at the Factory, three miles above, and afterward Broad River, so as to approach Columbia from the north. Within an hour of the arrival of General Howard's head of column at the river opposite Columbia, the head of column of the left wing also appeared, and I directed General Slocum to cross the Saluda at Zion Church, and thence to take roads direct for Winnsboro, breaking up *en route* the railroads and bridges about Alston.

Colonel Howard effected a crossing of the Saluda near the Factory on the 16th, skirmishing with cavalry, and the same night made a flying bridge across Broad River, about three miles above Columbia, by which he crossed over Stone's brigade, of Wood's division, Fifteenth Corps. Under cover of this brigade, a pontoon bridge was laid on the morning of the 17th. I was in person at this bridge, and at 11 o'clock in the forenoon learned that the Mayor of Columbia had come out in a carriage and made a formal surrender of the city to Colonel Stone, Twenty-fifth Iowa infantry, commanding Third brigade, First division, Fifteenth Corps. About the same time a small party of the Seventeenth Corps had crossed the Congaree in a skiff, and entered Columbia from a point immediately west. In anticipation of the occupation of the city, I had made written orders to General Howard touching the conduct of the troops. These were to destroy absolutely all arsenals and public property not needed for our own use, as well as all railroads, depôts and machinery useful in war to an enemy, but to spare all dwellings, colleges, schools, asylums and harmless private property. I was the first to cross the pontoon bridge, and, in company with General Howard, rode into the city. The day was clear, but a perfect tempest of wind was raging. The brigade of Colonel Stone was already in the city, and was properly posted. Citizens and soldiers were on the streets, and general good order prevailed. General Wade Hampton, who commanded the Confederate rear guard, had, in anticipation of our capture of Columbia, ordered that all cotton, public and private, should be moved into the streets and fired, to prevent our making use of it. Bales were piled everywhere, the rope and bagging cut, and tufts of cotton were blown about in the wind, lodged in the trees and against houses, so as to resemble a snowstorm. Some of these piles of cotton were burning, especially one in the very heart of the city, near the Court House, but the fire was partially subdued by the labor of our soldiers. During the day the Fifteenth Corps passed through Columbia, and out on the Camden Road. The Seventeenth did not enter the town at all; and as I have before stated, the left wing and cavalry did not come within two miles of the town.

Before one single public building had been fired by order, the smouldering fires set by Hampton's order were rekindled by the wind, and communicated with the buildings around. About dark they began to spread, and got beyond the control of the brigade within the city. The whole of Wood's division was brought in, but it was found impossible to check the flames, which, by midnight, had become unmanageable, and raged until about four o'clock in the morning, when, the wind subsiding, they were got under control. I was up nearly all night, and saw Generals Howard, Logan, Wood and others laboring to save houses and protect families thus suddenly deprived of shelter, and of bedding and wearing apparel. I disclaim, on the part of my army, any agency in this fire; but, on the contrary, claim that we saved what of Columbia remains unconsumed. And, without hesitation, I charge General Wade Hampton with having burned his own city of Columbia, not with a malicious intent, or as the manifestation of a silly "Roman stoicism," but from folly and want of sense, in filling it with lint, cotton and tinder. Our officers and men on duty worked well to extinguish the flames, but others not on duty, including the officers who had long been imprisoned there, rescued by us, may have assisted in spreading the fire after it had once begun, and may have indulged in unconcealed joy to see the ruin of the capital of South Carolina. During the 18th and 19th the arsenal, railroad depôts, machine shops, foundries and other buildings were properly destroyed by detailed working parties, and the railroad track torn up and destroyed down to Kingsville and the Wateree Bridge, and up in the direction of Winnsboro.

At the same time the left wing and cavalry had crossed the Saluda and Broad Rivers, breaking up the railroad about Alston, and as high up as the bridge across Broad River on the Spartanburg Road, the main body moving straight for Winnsboro, which General Slocum reached on the 21st of February. He caused the railroad to be destroyed up to Blackstakes Dépôt, and then turned to Rocky Mount, on the Catawba River. The Twentieth Corps reached Rocky Mount on the 22d, laid a pontoon bridge, and crossed over during the 23d. Kilpatrick's cavalry followed, and crossed over in a terrible rain during the night of the 23d, and moved up to Lancaster, with orders to keep up the delusion of a general movement on Charlotte, N. C., to which General Beauregard and all the cavalry of the enemy had retreated from Columbia. I was also aware that Cheatham's corps, of Hood's old army, was aiming to make a junction with Beauregard at Charlotte, having been cut off by our rapid movement on Columbia and Winnsboro. From the 23d to the 26th we had heavy rains, swelling the rivers, and making the roads almost impassable. The Twentieth Corps reached Hamburg Rock on the 26th, and waited there for the Thirteenth Corps to get across the Catawba. The heavy rains had so swollen the river that the pontoon bridge broke, and General Davis had very hard work to restore it, and get his command across. At last he succeeded, and the left wing was all put in motion for Cheraw. In the meantime the right wing had broken up the railroad to Winnsboro, and thence turned for Pea's Ferry, where it was crossed over the Catawba before the heavy rains set in, the Seventeenth Corps moving straight on Cheraw *via* Young's Bridge, and the Fifteenth Corps by Tiller's and Kelly's Bridges. From this latter corps detachments were sent into Camden to burn the bridge over the Wateree, with the railroad dëpôt, stores, etc. A small force of mounted men, under Captain Duncan, was also dispatched to make a dash and interrupt the railroad from Charleston to Florence, but it met Butler's division of cavalry, and, after a sharp night skirmish on Mount Elon, was compelled to return unsuccessful. Much bad road was encountered at Lynch's Creek, which delayed the right wing about the same length of time as the left wing had been at the Catawba. On the 2d of March the leading division of the Twentieth Corps entered Chesterfield, skirmishing with Butler's division of cavalry, and the next day, about noon, the Seventeenth Corps entered Cheraw, the enemy retreating across the Pedee, and burning the bridge at that point. At Cheraw we found much ammunition and many guns, which had been brought from Charleston on the evacuation of that city. These were destroyed, as also the railroad trestles and bridges down as far as Darlington. An expedition of mounted infantry was also sent down to Florence, but it encountered both cavalry and artillery, and returned, having only broken up in part the branch road from Florence to Cheraw.

Without unnecessary delay, the columns were again put in motion, directed on Fayetteville, N. C., the right wing crossing the Pedee at Cheraw, and the left wing and cavalry at Sneedsboro. General Kilpatrick was ordered to keep well on the left flank, and the Fourteenth Corps, moving by Love's Bridge, was given the right to enter and occupy Fayetteville first. The weather continued unfavorable and roads bad, but the Fourteenth and Seventeenth Corps reached Fayetteville on the 11th of March, skirmishing with Wade Hampton's cavalry, that covered the rear of Hardee's retreating arm, which, as usual, had crossed Cape Fear River, burning the bridge. During the march from the Pedee,

General Kilpatrick had kept his cavalry well on the left and exposed flank. During the night of the 9th of March his three brigades were divided to picket the roads. General Hampton detecting this, rushed in at daylight and gained possession of the camp of Colonel Spencer's brigade, and the house in which General Kilpatrick and Colonel Spencer had their quarters. The surprise was complete, but General Kilpatrick quickly succeeded in rallying his men, on foot, in a swamp near by, and by a prompt attack, well followed up, regained his artillery, horses, camp, and everything, save some prisoners, whom the enemy carried off, leaving their dead on the ground.

The 12th, 13th and 14th were passed at Fayetteville, destroying absolutely the United States arsenal and the vast amount of machinery which had formerly belonged to the old Harper's Ferry United States arsenal. Every building was knocked down and burned, and every piece of machinery utterly broken up and ruined, by the 1st regiment Michigan engineers, under the immediate supervision of Colonel O. M. Poe, Chief Engineer. Much valuable property, of great use to the enemy, was here destroyed or cast into the river.

Up to this period I had perfectly succeeded in interposing my superior army between the scattered parts of the enemy. But I was then aware that the fragments that had left Columbia under Beauregard had been reënforced by Cheatham's corps from the West, and the garrison of Augusta, and that ample time had been given to move them to my front and flank about Raleigh. Hardee had also succeeded in getting across Cape Fear River ahead of me, and could, therefore, complete the junction with the armies of Johnston and Hoke in North Carolina. And the whole, under the command of the skilful and experienced Joe Johnston, made up an army superior to me in cavalry, and formidable enough in artillery and infantry to justify me in extreme caution in making the last step necessary to complete the march I had undertaken.

Previous to reaching Fayetteville, I had dispatched to Wilmington, from Laurel Hill Church, two of our best scouts, with intelligence of our position, and my general plans. Both of these messengers reached Wilmington, and on the morning of the 12th of March, the army tug, Davidson, Captain Ainsworth, reached Fayetteville from Wilmington, bringing me full intelligence of the outside world. On the same day this tug carried back to General Terry, at Wilmington, and General Schofield, at Newbern, my dispatches to the effect that, on Wednesday, the 15th, we would move for Goldsboro, feigning on Raleigh, and ordering them to march straight for Goldsboro, which I expected to reach about the 20th. The same day the gunboat Eolus, Captain Young, United States navy, also reached Fayetteville, and through her I continued to have communication with Wilmington until the day of our actual departure. While the work of destruction was going on at Fayetteville, two pontoon bridges were laid across Cape Fear River, one opposite the town and the other three miles below.

General Kilpatrick was ordered to move up the plank road, to and beyond Averysboro. He was to be followed by four divisions of the left wing, with as few wagons as possible; the rest of the train, under escort of the two remaining divisions of that wing, to take a shorter and more direct road to Goldsboro. In like manner, General Howard was ordered to send his trains, under good escort, well to the right, towards Paison's Dêpôt and Goldsboro', and to hold four divisions light, ready to go to the aid of the left wing if attacked while in motion. The weather continued very bad, and the roads had become mere quagmire. Almost every foot of it had to be corduroyed to admit the passage of wheels. Still, time was so important, that punctually, according to order, the columns moved out from Cape Fear river, on Wednesday, the 16th of March. I accompanied General Slocum, who, preceded by Kilpatrick's cavalry, moved up the river, or plank road, that day, to Kyle's Landing, Kilpatrick skirmishing heavily with the enemy's rear guard, about three miles beyond Taylor's Hole Creek. At General Kilpatrick's request, General Slocum sent forward a brigade of infantry to hold a line of barricades.

Next morning the column advanced in the same order, and developed the enemy, with artillery, infantry and cavalry, in an intrenched position in front of the point where the road branches off towards Goldsboro through Bentonville. On an inspection of the map it was manifest that Hardee, in retreating from Fayetteville, had halted in the narrow, swampy neck between Cape Fear and South Rivers in hopes to hold me to save time for concentration of Johnston's armies at some point to his rear, namely, Raleigh, Smithfield or Goldsboro. Hardee's forces were estimated at twenty thousand men. It was necessary to dislodge him that we might have the use of the Goldsboro road, as also to keep the feint on Raleigh as long as possible. General Slocum was, therefore, ordered to press and carry the position, only difficult by reason of the nature of the ground, which was so soft that horses would sink everywhere, and even men could hardly make their way over the common pine barren.

The Twentieth Corps, General Williams, had the lead, and Ward's division the advance. This was deployed, and the skirmish line developed the position of a brigade of Charleston heavy artillery, armed as infantry (Rhett's,) posted across the road behind a light parapet, with a battery of guns enfilading the approach across a cleared field. General Williams sent a brigade (Casey's) by a circuit to the left and turned this line, and, by a quick charge, broke the brigade which rapidly retreated back to a second line, better built, and more strongly held. A battery of artillery (Winninger's) well posted, under the immediate direction of Major Reynolds, chief of artillery of the Twentieth Corps, did good execution on the retreating brigade, and, on advancing Ward's division over the ground, General Williams captured three guns and two hundred and seventeen prisoners, of which sixty-eight were wounded, and left in a house near by with a rebel officer, four men, and five days' rations. One hundred and eight rebel dead were buried by us. As Ward's division advanced he developed a second and stronger line, when Jackson's division was deployed forward on the right of Ward, and two divisions of Jeff. C. Davis', (Fourteenth) Corps on the left, well towards Cape Fear. At the same time, Kilpatrick, who was acting in concert with General Williams, was ordered to draw back his cavalry and mass it on the extreme right, and in concert with Jackson's right, to feel forward for the Goldsboro Road. He got a brigade on the road, but it was attacked by McLaws' rebel division furiously, and, though it fought well and hard, the brigade drew back to the flank of the infantry. The whole line advanced late in the afternoon, drove the enemy well within his intrenched line, and pressed him so hard that next morning he was gone, having retreated in a miserable, stormy night over the worst of roads. Ward's division of infantry followed to, and through Averysboro, developing the fact that Hardee had retreated, not on Raleigh, but on Smithfield. I had, the night before, directed Kilpatrick to cross South River at a milldam to our right rear, and move up on the east side towards Elevation. General Slocum reports his aggregate loss in the affair known as that of Averysboro, at twelve officers and sixty-five men killed, and four hundred and seventy-seven wounded. We lost no prisoners. The enemy's loss can be inferred from his dead (one hundred and eight,) left for us to bury. Leaving Ward's division to keep up a show of pursuit, Slocum's column was turned to the right, built a bridge across the swollen South River, and took the Goldsboro Road, Kilpatrick crossing to the north, in the direction of Elevation, with orders to move eastward, watching that flank. In the meantime the wagon trains and guards, as also Howard's column, were wallowing along the miry roads towards Bentonville and Goldsboro. The enemy's infantry, as before stated, had retreated across our front in the same direction, burning the bridges across Mill Creek. I continued with the head of Slocum's column, and encamped the night of the 18th with him on the Goldsboro Road, twenty-seven miles from Goldsboro, about five miles from Bentonville, and where the road from Clinton to Smithfield crosses the Goldsboro Road. Howard was at Lee's store, only two miles south, and both columns had pickets three miles forward to where the two roads came together, and became common to Goldsboro.

All the signs induced me to believe that the enemy would make no further opposition to our progress, and would not attempt to strike us in flank while in motion. I, therefore, directed Howard to move his right wing by the new Goldsboro Road, which goes by way of Falling Creek Church. I also left Slocum, and joined Howard's column, with a view to open communication with General Schofield, coming up from Newbern and Terry, from Wilmington. I found General Howard's column well strung out, owing to the very bad roads, and did not overtake him in person until he had reached Falling Creek Church, with one regiment forward to the cross-roads, near Cox's Bridge, across the Neuse. I had gone from General Slocum about six miles, when I heard artillery in his direction, but was soon made easy by one of his staff officers overtaking me, explaining that his leading division (Carlin's) had encountered a division of rebel cavalry (Dibbrell's), which he was driving easily But soon other staff officers came up, reporting that he had developed near Bentonville the whole of the rebel army under General Johnston himself. I sent him orders to call up the two divisions guarding his wagon trains, and Hazen's division of the Fifteenth Corps, still back near Lee's store, to fight defensively until I could draw up Blair's Corps, then near Mount Olive Station, and, with the remaining three divisions of the corps, come up on Johnston's left rear from the direction of Cox's Bridge. In the meantime, while on the road, I received couriers from both Generals Schofield and Terry. The former reported himself in possession of Kinston, delayed somewhat by want of provisions, but able to march so as to make Goldsboro on the 21st; and Terry was at or near Faison's Depôt.

Orders were at once dispatched to Schofield to push for Goldsboro, and to make dispositions to cross Little River in the direction of Smithfield as far as Millard; to General Terry to move to Cox's Bridge, lay a pontoon bridge, and establish a crossing; and to Blair to make a night march to Falling Creek Church; and at daylight the right wing, General Howard, less the necessary wagon guards, was put in rapid motion on Bentonville. By subsequent reports I learned that General Slocum's head of column had advanced from its camp of March 18th, and first encountered Dibbrell's cavalry, but soon found his progress impeded by infantry and artillery. The enemy attacked his head of column, gaining temporary advantage, and took three guns and caissons of General Carlin's division, driving the two leading brigades back on the main body. As soon as General Slocum realized that he had in his front the whole Confederate army, he promptly deployed the two divisions of the Twentieth Corps, General Williams. These he arranged on the defensive, and hastily prepared a line of barricades. General Kilpatrick also came up at the sound of artillery, and massed on the left. In this position, the left received six distinct assaults, by the combined forces of Hoke, Hardee and Cheatham, under the immediate command of General Johnston himself, without giving an inch of ground, and did good execution on the enemy's ranks, especially with our artillery, the enemy having little or none.

Johnston had moved by night from Smithfield with great rapidity, and without unnecessary wheels, intending to overwhelm my left flank before it could be relieved by its coöperating columns. But he "reckoned without his host." I had expected just such a movement all the way from Fayetteville, and was prepared for it. During the night of the 19th General Slocum got up his wagon train, with its guard of two divisions, and Hazen's division of the Fifteenth Corps, which reënforcement enabled him to make his position impregnable. The right wing found rebel cavalry watching its approach, but unable to offer any serious opposition, until our head of column encountered a considerable body behind a barricade at the forks of the road near Bentonville, about three miles east of the battle-field of the day before. On moving forward the Fifteenth Corps, General Logan found that the enemy had thrown back his left flank, and had constructed a line of parapet connecting with that toward General Slocum, in the form of a bastion, its salient on the main Goldsboro Road, interposing between General Slocum on the west, and General Howard on the east, while the flanks rested on Mill Creek, covering the road back to Smithfield. General Howard was instructed to proceed with due caution until he had made strong connection on his left with General Slocum. This he soon accomplished, and at four o'clock on the afternoon of the 29th a complete and strong line of battle confronted the enemy in his intrenched position, and General Johnston, instead of catching us in detail, was on the defensive, with Mill Creek and a single bridge to his rear. Nevertheless, we had no object to accomplish by a battle, unless at an advantage, and therefore my general instructions were to press steadily with skirmishers alone, to use artillery pretty freely on the wooded space held by the enemy, and to feel pretty strongly the flanks of his position, which were, as usual, covered with the endless swamps of this region of country. I also ordered all empty wagons to be sent at once to Kinston for supplies, and other impediments to be grouped near the Neuse, south of Goldsboro, holding the real army in close contact with the enemy, ready to fight him if he ventured outside his parapets and swampy obstructions. Thus matters stood about Bentonville on the 21st of March. On the same day General Schofield entered Goldsboro with little or no opposition, and General Terry had got possession of the Neuse River at Cox's Bridge, ten miles above, with a pontoon bridge laid and brigade across, so that the three armies were in actual connection, and the great object of the campaign was accomplished.

On the 21st a steady rain prevailed, during which General Mower's division of the Seventeenth Corps, on the extreme right, had worked well to the right around the enemy's flank, and had nearly reached the bridge across Mill Creek, the only line of retreat open to the enemy. Of course there was extreme danger that the enemy would turn on him all his reserves, and it might be, let go his parapets to overwhelm Mower. Accordingly, I ordered at once a general attack by our skirmish line, from left to right. Quite a noisy battle ensued, during which General Mower was enabled to regain his connection with his own corps, by moving to his left rear. Still he had developed a weakness in the enemy's position of which advantage might have been taken; but that night the enemy retreated on Smithfield, leaving his pickets to fall into our hands, with many dead unburied, and wounded in his field hospitals. At daybreak on the 22d pursuit was made two miles beyond Mill Creek, but checked by my order. General Johnston had utterly failed in his attempt, and we remained in full possession of the field of battle.

General Slocum reports the losses of the left wing, about Bentonville, at nine officers and one hundred and forty-five men killed, fifty-one officers and eight hundred and sixteen men wounded, and three officers and two hundred and twenty-three missing, taken prisoners by the enemy; total, one thousand two hundred and forty-seven. He buried on the field one hundred and sixty-seven rebel dead, and took three hundred and thirty-eight prisoners. General Howard reports the losses of the right wing as two officers and thirty-five men killed, twelve officers and two hundred and thirty-nine men wounded, and one officer and sixty men missing; total three hundred and ninety-nine. He also buried one hundred rebel dead, and took one thousand two hundred and eighty-seven prisoners. The cavalry of Kilpatrick was held in reserve, and lost but few, if any, of which I have no report as yet. Our aggregate loss at Bentonville was one thousand six hundred and forty-six. I am well satisfied that the enemy lost heavily, especially in his assault on the left wing, during the afternoon of the 19th; but as I have no data save his dead and wounded left in our hands, I prefer to make no comparison. Thus, as I have endeavored to explain, we had completed our march on the 21st, and had full possession of Goldsboro, the real "objective," with its two railroads, back to the seaports of Wilmington and Beaufort, South Carolina. These were being rapidly repaired by strong working parties, directed by Colonel W. W. Wright, of the railroad department. A large number of supplies had already been brought forward to Kinston, to which place our wagons had been sent to receive them. I therefore directed General Howard and the cavalry to remain at Bentonville during the 22d, to bury the dead and remove the wounded, and on the following day all the armies to move to the camps assigned them about Goldsboro, there to rest and receive the clothing and supplies of which they stood in need. In person I went on the 22d to Cox's brigade to meet General Terry, whom I met for the first time, and on the following day rode into Goldsboro, where I found General Schofield and his army. The left wing came in during the same day and next morning, and the cavalry moved to Mount Olive Station, and General Terry back to Faison's. On the 25th the Newbern Railroad was finished, and the first train of cars came in, thus giving us the means of bringing from the dépôt at Morehead City full supplies to the army.

It was all important that I should have an interview with the General-in-Chief, and presuming that he could not at this time leave City Point, I left General Schofield in chief command, and proceeded with all expedition by rail to Morehead City, and thence by steamer to City Point, reaching General Grant's headquarters on the evening of the 27th of March. I had the good fortune to meet General Grant, the President, Generals Meade, Ord, and others, of the Army of the Potomac, and soon learned the general state of the military world, from which I had been, in a great measure, cut off since January. Having completed all necessary business, I reëmbarked on the navy steamer Bat, Captain Barnes, which Admiral Porter placed at my command, and returned *via* Hatteras Inlet and Newbern, reaching my own headquarters, in Goldsboro, during the night of the 30th. During my absence full supplies of clothing and food had been brought to camp, and all things were working well. I have thus rapidly sketched the progress of our columns from Savannah to Goldsboro, but for more minute details must refer to the reports of subordinate commanders and of staff officers, which are not yet ready, but will in due season be forwarded and filed with this report. I cannot, even with any degree of precision, recapitulate the vast amount of injury done to the enemy, or the quantity of guns and materials of war captured and destroyed. In general terms, we have traversed the country from Savannah to Goldsboro, with an average breadth of forty miles, consuming all the forage, cattle, hogs, sheep, poultry, cured meats, corn meal, etc. The public enemy, instead of drawing supplies from that region to feed his armies, will be compelled to send provisions from other quarters to feed the inhabitants. A map herewith prepared by my chief engineer, Colonel Poe, with the routes of the four corps and cavalry, will show, at a glance, the country traversed. Of course, the abandonment to us by the enemy of the whole sea coast, from Savannah to Newbern, N. C., with its forts, dock-yards, gunboats, etc., was a necessary incident to our occupation and destruction of the inland routes of travel and supply. But the real object of this march was to place this army in a position of supply, whence it could take an appropriate part in the spring and summer campaign of 1865. This was completely accomplished on March 21st, by the junction of the three armies and occupation of Goldsboro.

In conclusion, I beg to express, in the most emphatic manner, my entire satisfaction with the tone and temperament of the whole army. Nothing seems to dampen their energy, zeal or cheerfulness. It is impossible to conceive a march involving more labor and exposure; yet I cannot recall an instance of bad temper by the way, or hearing an expression of doubt as to our perfect success in the end. I believe that this cheerfulness and harmony of action reflects upon all concerned quite as much honor and fame as "battles gained" or "cities won," and I therefore commend all, generals, staff officers, and men, for these high qualities, in addition to the more soldierly ones of obedience to orders and the alacrity they have always manifested when danger summoned them "to the front."

The grand march of Sherman's army from Savannah to Goldsboro, North Carolina, secured to us the entire sea coast, as far north as Newbern. The capture of Branchville and Columbia, secured the fall of Charleston, the cradle of secession, and the "hot bed of treason." For long months our naval forces had been thundering away at that strong hold, but without succeeding in its capture. It fell by the strategy of Sherman, without the firing of a single gun.

Early in the evening of February 17th, 1865, Brigadier General Schimmelpfenning, commander of the Northern District of the Department of the South, discovered some indications which led him to believe that the enemy were about to evacuate Charleston and its defenses. He ordered his pickets and picket boats to keep a sharp lookout and report immediately any movement on the part of the enemy. In the night a terrific explosion took place in Charleston, which shook every ship in the harbor and off the bar, and was heard for many miles around. Immediately after the explosion flames broke out in various parts of the city. The first explosion, which was at the railroad depôt, was the means of firing the houses in the vicinity, from whence the flames rapidly spread until the conflagration became general in that part of the city. A large number of women and children were killed by the explosion.

About 6 o'clock on the morning of the 18th, General Schimmelpfenning moved his forces and occupied the city and its defenses. The formidable earthworks on James Island were found abandoned, and the guns spiked.

At 8 o'clock, a detachment was sent to take possession of Fort Sumter, and raise the flag which floated over Sumter when General Anderson surrendered the fort, nearly four years previously. At 9 o'clock the old flag was raised over Sumter, amid deafning cheers.

As fast as our forces could be thrown into the city, they were set to work to put out the fires. Thus, whatever remains of Charleston, was saved from being consumed to ashes by Federal soldiers' Union hands. Thousands of bales of cotton were burned by the enemy.

General Gilmore, in his dispatches to the War Department, states after inspecting the defenses of Charleston, that we had captured *four hundred and* fifty pieces of ordnance, eight locomotives, and a large number of cars, all in good condition.

The Charleston *Courier* gives the following account of the evacuation. This will place the blame of firing the city where it belongs. "Rule or ruin" was still the motto of the conquered enemy. It seemed a righteous act of Providence that that city should be destroyed by the hands of secessionists, its pretended friends:

HORRORS OF THE EVACUATION OF CHARLESTON.

[From the Charleston Courier, Feb. 20.]

The terrible scenes through which this community has passed since our last issue, can only be conceived by those who witnessed the dreadful reality. The saddest part of all is the loss of life which occurred between eight and nine o'clock, Saturday morning, from an accidental explosion of powder and the blowing up of the Northeastern Railroad dëpôt. About one hundred and fifty persons—including men, women, and children—were either instantly killed, or perished in the flames, and about two hundred wounded. Of the immense destruction of property no estimate can be formed, but it will amount to several millions.

Early Saturday morning, before the retirement of General Hardee's troops, every building, warehouse, or shed, stored with cotton, was fired by a guard detailed for that purpose. The engines were brought out, but with the very small force at the disposal of the fire department, very little else could be done than to keep the surrounding buildings from igniting. On the western side of the city the conflagration raged with great fury. On the wharf of the Savannah Railroad depôt, several hundred bales of cotton were awaiting shipment on the blockade runners; also several thousand bushels of rough rice. On Lucas street, leading to the depôt, was a shed containing twelve hundred bales of cotton, which, together with several other sheds and buildings filled with cotton, belonging to private parties, fell a prey to the flames. Lucas' Mill, containing some thirty thousand bushels of rice, and Mr. R. T. Walker's warehouse, at the foot of Broad street, filled with commissary stores, were also destroyed.

Shortly after 8 o'clock the terrible explosion at the Northwestern Railroad occurred. The explosion was tremendous, and shook the whole city. It appears from all accounts that this dreadful catastrophe was caused from the careless handling of powder by some boys, taking handfuls and throwing it into the cotton fire at the depôt. In doing this they unwittingly laid a train to the apartment in which it was stored. The spectacle which followed was horrible. In an instant the whole building was enveloped in smoke and flames. The cries of the wounded, the inability of the spectators to render assistance to those rolling and perishing in the fire, all rendered it a scene of indescribable terror. The fire spread with rapidity, communicating to the adjoining buildings, including the fine large residence of Dr. Seaman Deas, on the northeast corner of Chapel and Alexander streets, all of which were destroyed. The buildings on the opposite side of the street were soon enveloped in flames, and the fire now became unmanageable. All the buildings embraced in the area of four squares on Chapel, Alexander, Washington and Charlotte streets to Calhoun street, with few exceptions, were destroyed. About 10 o'clock fire broke out in the large four-story brick building of Madam Du Ree, at the northeast corner of East Bay and Laurens streets. This, with the adjoining building on the northeast corner of Minority street, was all burned. Another fire broke out about 11 o'clock in a range of buildings on the west side of Meeting street, near to the Court House. Five buildings were burned; the walls only were left standing. The alarm of fire Saturday night, in Ward four, was caused by the burning of the inside of a millinery establishment on King street.

In addition to the above facts, the new bridge from the city to James Island was set on fire, and was still burning on Sunday night.

DESTRUCTION OF THE GUNBOATS.

The burning and blowing-up of the iron-clads Palmetto State, Chicora and Charleston was a magnificent spectacle. The Palmetto State was the first to explode, and was followed by the Chicora, about 9 o'clock, and the Charleston about 11 A. M. The latter, it is stated, had twenty tons of gunpowder on board. Pieces of the iron plates, red hot, fell on the wharves and set them on fire. By the active exertions of Superintendent Thomas Turner, the gas works were saved. The explosions were terrific. Tremendous clouds of smoke went up, forming beautiful wreaths. A full Palmetto tree, with its leaves and stems, was noticed by many observers. As the last wreath of smoke disappeared the full form of the rattlesnake in the centre was remarked by many as it gradually faded away.

INCIDENTS.

When Generals Sherman and Howard rode along the streets of Columbia, the skirmishers who had previously entered the place cheered their much-loved chief. The chorus was taken up by the negroes, who lined the sidewalks, and followed the column, and shouted and danced along the way, and clapped their hands with exclamations of unbounded joy.

"Tank de Almighty God, Mr. Sherman has come at last. We knew it; we prayed for de day, and de Lord Jesus heard our prayers. Mr. Sherman has come with his company."

One fat old woman said to Sherman, while shaking him by the hand, which he always gladly gave to these poor people: " I prayed dis long time for yer, and de blessing ob de Lord is on yer. Yesterday, when yer stopped trowing de shells into de town, and de soldiers run away from de hill ober dar, I thout dat General Burygar' had drive you away, for dey said so; but dey are dun gone, and here yer. Bress de Lord, yer will hab a place in heaben; yer go dare, sure."

The following incidents are related upon the authority and in the words of a well known army correspondent:

CONVERSATIONS WITH PROMINENT CITIZENS.

Constantly improving the many excellent opportunities which I have for conversing with the prominent citizens, I have unquestionable evidence of their desire to end the war by submitting to the national authority. While not disguising their belief in the sovereignty of a state, and illy concealing their hate for the Yankees, they acknowledge their powerlessness to contend against the might of the idea of nationality embodied in **our** armies and navies.

HATRED OF JEFF. DAVIS.

A citizen, whose name may be found in the earliest annals of the State, and which stands forth in high honor in the war of the Revolution, but whose sons are now in high office in the army of treason, said to me to-day:

"Sir, every life that is now lost in this war is murder, *murder*, sir. We have fought you bravely, but our strength is exhausted; we have no resources; we have no more men. The contest was unequal. You have conquered us, and it is best to submit and make wise use of the future. That is not my opinion because the Union flag is flying upon yonder capitol to-day, but it has been my conviction for many months past—a conviction more than confirmed by recent events. We would have peace, sir, were it not for that vain, obstinate, ambitious man, Jeff. Davis. I am not in excitement nor anger, sir, when I assure you that I know that a large majority of our people curse him, not only with their hearts, but their lips. His haughty ambition has been our ruin."

The words of the gentleman which I have thus quoted have been the sentiments of nearly all I see, only they are sometimes expressed with added vehemence and more violent objurgations against Jeff. Davis. Unhappy chief of fallen spirits is he. Failure has brought down upon him hatred and abuse. It would not be cheers, nor friendly greeting, nor welcome that he would receive from the people of South Carolina, were he to visit them now.

GIVING UP THE SLAVES.

There have been many prophecies and theories advanced as to the possible future of the slaves and their owners, but I never thought that the day would ever come to me when South Carolina slaveholders would beg that I should take away their slaves—not because the negroes have been unfaithful, not that they would be unkind when we went away, for a lady bore witness, with tears in her eyes, to their attentions and kindness on the night of the fire; but she said:

"I know they wish to go with your army, and I beg of you to take them, for I have nothing for them to do, and cannot feed them. We have scarcely food for our own mouths, much less theirs."

These requests are not isolated, but general. The motives which prompt them are extended wherever we march; but it is a singular development of the war that South Carolinians should petition us to give freedom to the many slaves to retain whose servitude they have sacrificed so much of the best life-blood of the land.

A NEGRO WOMAN SHOT.

During the skirmishing one of our men who, by the way, was a forager, was slightly wounded. The most serious accident of the day occurred to a negro woman, who was in a house where the rebels had taken cover. When I saw this woman, who would not have been selected as a type of South Carolina female beauty, the blood was streaming over her neck and bosom from a wound in the lobe of her ear, which the bullet had just clipped and passed on.

"What was it that struck you, aunty?" I asked her.

"Lor bress me, massa, I dun know; I jus fell right down."

"Didn't you feel anything, nor hear any sound?"

"Yes, now I 'member, I heerd a s-z-z-z-z-z, and den I jus knock down. I drap on de groun'. I'se so glad I not dead, for if I died den de bad man would git me, cos I dance lately a heap."

REFUGEES AND LOYALISTS.

One of the most significant features of our journey through the South has been the frequent prayer and entreaty of the people that they might be permitted to join our column and march with us to the sea, or wherever we might go, so that they could leave the region of despotism, anywhere out of the South and towards the pure air of freedom again. One is a mechanic, who was born and reared in the old Granite State. He came here four years ago as master mechanic in a railroad machine-shop. He has been able to avoid service in the rebel army, because his services were necessary in the shop. He is taken along for his services and can be made of good use.

Here is a daughter and mother, whose son is in the Federal army. Their little means have long since been exhausted, and they wish to go to Connecticut, where relatives will gladly care for them, and where they can get news of their son and brother. Another is a poor Irish woman, whose husband has been conscripted into the rebel army, and is now a prisoner, sick in a Northern hospital.

At Columbia there were several families of wealth and position, who had always been suspected of loyal proclivities. Upon our occupation of that city it became known to the rebel inhabitants that these people had always assisted our prisoners, and previous to our approach, had secreted a great many at imminent peril. It would be impossible to reject these generous, self-sacrificing friends. The fire had not spared their houses, and they were homeless, but we well knew that to remain after our visit would be certain death. Up to this time the want of means of transportation had necessitated a refusal of these requests. But some of the wagons were now empty; then there were a number of vehicles captured from the enemy; horses and mules we bring in every day, and again, not a few of the families asking our protection, are able to furnish their own transportation.

General Howard was in command of the troops at Columbia, and these unfortunates did not appeal in vain to his generous, sympathetic heart, which never refuses to sympathize with those in distress.

With the approbation of General Sherman, General Howard at once organized an emigrant train, which was placed under guard of the escaped prisoners belonging to other commands. This train has been separated, and apportioned to each division of the Fifteenth and Seventeenth Corps. They are getting along famously. Ladies who have been always accustomed to the refinements of life, seem to enjoy the journey as much as if it were a picnic. In truth it is better than that; for, while they are not exposed to the dangers of war, they participate in its excitements. The column has a singularly *outré* appearance. First, there will be a huge family coach containing ladies, with their personal baggage crowded about them; then an army wagon loaded with men, women and children, comfortably seated upon such articles of household truck as they are allowed to carry. Following this will be a country cart filled with negro women, for the negroes come along also, and hosts of little curly, bullet-headed youngsters, who gaze curiously upon the strange sights which meet their eyes.

General Hazen, whose name can never be mentioned but with inspiring recollections of the assault of Fort McAllister, tells me that the large number who accompany his division, are but little trouble to him, and that they have so quickly learned to forage for themselves that they are no expense to the government. Two of the escaped officers, with a detachment of ten men, have charge of the train, which takes its assigned place in the column; a few tents which are in excess or have been captured are pitched, when the column go into camp, and our little colony, with grateful hearts, go to their night's rest with the glad consciousness that they are step by step approaching a land of civilization and freedom.

In this life, so new and strange to the refugees, numbers of families become separated from each other. Portions of the army, who for days march upon separate roads, will at one time or another come together again, as at this place for example, when three corps, which have been marching upon different roads, unite at Cheraw for the purpose of crossing the river. The troops and trains, although really distinct to the initiated eye, may be mistaken for one another. I have seen the negroes, especially, wandering about as completely lost as if they were in an uninhabited forest.

GENERAL SHERMAN AND THE NEGROES.

I happened to be present to-day (March 3d) at one of those interviews which so often occur between General Sherman and the negroes. The conversation was piquant and interesting, not only as being characteristic of both parties, but it was the more significant because, on the part of the general, I believe it a fair expression of his feelings on the slavery question.

A party of ten or fifteen negroes had just found their way through the lines from Cheraw. Their owners had carried them from the vicinity of Columbia to the other side of the Pedee, with their mules and horses, which they were running away from our army. The negroes had escaped, and were on their way back to find their families. A more ragged set of human beings would not have been found out of the slave states; or perhaps Italy. These negroes were of all ages, and had stopped in front of the general's tent, which was pitched a few feet back from the sidewalk of the main street.

Several officers of the army, and among them General Slocum, were gathered round, interested in the scene. The general asked them:

"Well, men, what can I do for you; where are you from?"

"Wese jus come from Cheraw. Massa took us with him to carry mules and horses away from youins."

"You thought we would get them. Did you wish us to get the mules?"

"Oh, yes, massa! dat's what I wanted. We knowed youins comin, and I wanted you to have dem mules, but no use, dey heard dat youins on de road, and nuthin would stop them. Why, as we cum along, de cavalry run away from the Yanks as if dey fright to def. Dey jumped into de river, and some of them lost dere horses. Dey frightened at de bery name of Sherman."

Some one at this point said: "That is General Sherman who is talking to you."

"God bress me, is you Mr. Sherman?"

"Yes, I am Mr. Sherman."

"Dat's him, su' nuff," said one.

"Is dat de great Mr. Sherman dat we's heard ob so long," said another.

"Why, dey so frightened at your berry name dat dey run right away," shouted a third.

"It is not me they are afraid of," said the general; "the name of another man would have the same effect with them if he had this army. It is these soldiers that they run away from."

"Oh, no," they all exclaimed," its de name ob Sherman, su'; and we hab wanted to see you so long while you trabbel all roun' jis whar you like to go. Dey said dat dey wanted to git you a little furder on, and den dey whip all your soldiers; but God bress me, you keep cumin' and cumin', an' dey allers git out.'

"Dey mighty fraid ob you, sar; dey say you kill de colored men, too," said an old man, who had not heretofore taken part in the conversation.

With much earnestness, General Sherman replied:

"Old man, and all of you, understand me. I desire that bad men should fear me, and the enemies of the Government which we are all fighting for. Now we are your friends; you are now free. ("Tank you, Massa Sherman," was ejaculated by the group.) You can go where you please; you can come with us or go home to your children. Wherever you go you are no longer slaves. You ought to be able to take care of yourselves. (We is; we will.") You must earn your freedom, then you will be entitled to it, sure; you have a right to be all that you can be, but you must be industrious, and earn the right to be men. If you go back to your families, and I tell you again you can go with us if you wish, you must do the best you can. *When you get a chance, go to Beaufort or Charleston, where you will have a little farm to work for yourselves.*"

The poor negroes were filled with gratitude and hope by these kind words, uttered in the kindest manner, and went away with thanks and blessings on their lips.

THE DESOLATION OF WAR — FORAGERS AND FORAGING.

Our foragers spread in irregular and regular parties skirmishing over the country. These enterprising characters were known by the names of "Bummers," "Smoke-house Rangers" and "Do-Boys." A bummer is an individual who by favor of a wagon-master becomes possessed of a broken down mule, or else starts, if needs be, on foot, in either case, of course, armed with his musket. He makes his way into the enemy's country, finds horses in numbers by help of the negroes, hitches a team to a wagon, loads on it all the stores and supplies he can find in the nearest house, mounts his negroes on the rest of the horses, and returns with his spoils. He never objects to gold watches or silver plate "if he can find them in a swamp a mile away from any house." These men were stragglers not in the rear but in front of the army, and they went before it like a cloud, being often twenty or thirty miles in advance of the head of the column. They would fight anything. Three "bummers" together would at any time attack a company of rebel cavalry, and, in favorable circumstances, would disperse them and capture their booty. With the exception of Columbia alone, every town in South Carolina through which the army passed was first entered by the bummers. At Chesterfield they were two days and a half ahead of the army, the whole corps having congregated at this point.

At Robertsville we struck the Savannah and Augusta Railroad, and in obedience to the "file left" order, turned towards Augusta. Half a mile out I noticed the smouldering ruins of Colonel Lawton's fine plantation, the fence and negro shanties alone remaining undisturbed. The plantation hands were all at home, but before the column had disappeared but one or two of Lawton's blacks remained to tell the tale of devastation, when the rebel lord returned to his deserted grounds.

CHAPTER XV.

SHERMAN'S CAMPAIGN IN THE CAROLINAS.

IN THE HEART OF NORTH CAROLINA — RESULTS OF THE CAMPAIGN — THE SENTINEL — DAVIS AND AN ENGLISH PAPER — ADVANCE OF SHERMAN AND RETREAT OF THE ENEMY — EFFECT OF THE CAPTURE OF RICHMOND — FALL OF RICHMOND AND SURRENDER OF LEE'S ARMY — CO-OPERATION OF SHERMAN — MEMORANDUM OR AGREEMENT BETWEEN SHERMAN AND JOHNSTON — SPECIAL ORDER OF SHERMAN — DISAPPROVAL OF THE AGREEMENT BY THE CABINET — GRANT SENT TO NORTH CAROLINA — RESULT OF HIS MISSION — EXPLANATION OF SHERMAN'S COURSE — REMARKS.

In the last chapter we left General Sherman and his splendid army, after their successful march, at Goldsboro, North Carolina.

One thousand miles triumphantly traversed, brought the captors of Atlanta, Milledgeville, Savannah, Charleston, Columbia, Fayettville and Goldsboro, into the very heart of North Carolina.

Some of the results of this campaign were fourteen cities captured, hundreds of miles of railroad destroyed, thousands of bales of cotton burned; 85 cannon, 4,000 prisoners and 25,000 animals captured, and over fifteen thousand white and black refugees were set free. Thousands of stands of small arms were secured at various places on the march, and large quantities of machinery, ammunition and stores.

The Richmond *Sentinel* pronounced the grand march of Sherman, "simply the flight of a bird through the air."

Jefferson Davis admitted, that having conquered the West, Sherman seriously threatened Richmond itself.

"Recent military operations of the enemy," he says, "have been successful in capturing some of our seaports; in interrupting some of our lines of communications and in devastating large districts of our country. These events have had the natural effect of encouraging our foes and dispiriting many of our people."

The *Sentinel*, however, in common with the *Army and Navy Gazette*, the leading military publication of England, persisted in uttering the prediction that Sherman would be "annihilated." "Bonaparte," said this rebel organ, "found at last a Moscow and a Waterloo, and a Swedish madman a Pultona and a Frederickshall. Sherman, though he plays at a less important game, dares a greater danger and shall surely share their fate."

While these extracts show that the papers of the South were false prophets, they indicate plainly that Sherman has accomplished what to them seemed an impossibility.

After Sherman had destroyed the arsenal, machinery and other property that might be of service to the enemy — without resting his army at Fayetteville, as he would have been excused for doing, and as any other commander would have done — marched across the country to Goldsboro! With his habitual but astonishing fearlessness, he moved for the north and rear of Goldsboro for the purpose of flanking it. The move was a perfect success. Bragg and Johnston moved back on Raleigh. The flanking of Goldsboro at once relieved the pressure which kept Schofield at Kinston.

Sherman's army moved forward, and without much serious opposition captured Raleigh, the capital of the State.

The unfailing success of Sherman in driving the rebel army before him, from point to point, until he had reached a position so threatening to Richmond, compelled General R. E. Lee to send reënforcements to Johnston from Richmond. The enemy knew that unless Sherman could be checked both armies would be caged inside the fortifications of Richmond. But to reënforce Johnston was to present a strong temptation to General Grant to attack Richmond. The experiment was tried, "*ex necessitate.*" Grant, with his eagle eye saw the prey, darted down upon it and seized it.

Richmond, the nest of traitors and treason, and Petersburgh fell after a desperate conflict, and great was the fall thereof. On the 3d day of April, 1865, they were occupied by the United States forces.

The retreating army of Lee was rapidly pursued until he was completely surrounded in the vicinity of Appomattox Court House, about twenty-two miles east of Lynchburg and one hundred and three miles west of Richmond. Here it was that General Lee surrendered the army of Northern Virginia to General Grant, April 9th, 1865, on such conditions as were regarded as very lenient, even by Lee himself.

The details of this great event, as given by an eye witness, will be read with interest:

It will be recollected that General Grant's first letter to Lee was dated on the 7th, Friday, the day of the battle of Farmville, and the correspondence was kept up during the following day and up to 11 o'clock on Sunday, as already published. In response to General Grant's last letter, General Lee appeared on the picket line of the Second Corps, Miles' division, with a letter addressed to General Meade, requesting a cessation of hostilities while he considered General Grant's terms of surrender. General Meade replied that he had no authority to accede to the request, but that he would wait two

1*

hours before making an attack. In the meantime General Grant sent word to General Meade that he would be up in half an hour, and the matter was turned over to him. A flag of truce proceeded to Appomattox Court House shortly after noon, and at about 2 o'clock P. M. the two generals met at the house of Mr. Wilmer McLean. General Lee was attended by General Marshal, his adjutant general, and General Grant, by Colonel Parker, one of his chief aides-de-camp. The two generals met and greeted each other with dignified courtesy, and proceeded at once to the business before them. General Lee immediately alluded to the conditions of the surrender, characterized them as exceedingly lenient, and said he would gladly leave all the details to General Grant's own discretion. General Grant stated the terms of parole: that the arms should be stacked, the artillery packed, and the supplies and munitions turned over to him, the officers retaining their side arms, horses and personal effects. General Lee promptly assented to the conditions, and the agreement of surrender was engrossed and signed by General Lee at 3.30 o'clock.

General Lee asked General Grant for an interpretation of the phrase "personal effects," and said that many of his cavalrymen owned their own horses. General Grant said he construed it to mean that the horses must be turned over to the United States Government. General Lee admitted the correctness and justice of the interpretation, when General Grant said he would instruct his officers to allow those men who owned their horses to retain them, as they would need them for the purpose of tilling their farms. General Lee expressed a great sense of gratification for such a generous consideration, and said it would have a very good effect. He subsequently expressed a hope that each soldier might be furnished with a certificate of his parole, as evidence to prevent him from being forced into the army until regularly exchanged. General Grant assented to the suggestion, and the printing presses were soon put to work to print the documents required.

In regard to the strength of his army, General Lee said he had no idea of the number of men that he should be able to deliver up. There had been so many engagements and such heavy losses from desertion and other causes within the past few days, and the retreat so rapid, that no regular morning reports had been made since leaving Petersburg; but it is generally believed by the best informed officers that Lee surrendered eighteen to twenty thousand men. Of the army horses, wagons, &c., there is no official account. General Lee informed

General Grant that his men were short of provisions, whereupon General Grant ordered twenty-five thousand rations to be distributed to them. Thus substantially ended the interview. Both generals were the very impersonation of dignity and courtesy in their bearing. Lee was in fine health, and though apparently impressed with the vital effect and importance of the act he was performing, he was cheerful and pleasant in his demeanor. The house where the stipulations were signed was a fair brick structure, with neat grounds, and quite neatly furnished. The room in which the interview took place was a comfortable parlor, about eighteen by twenty feet, and adorned by the usual furnishing common to the average of Virginia houses.

Both generals were attired in full uniform. Lee wore a very fine sword. Grant had no side arms, having left camp the day previous with the intention of being gone but a few hours, but, on the contrary, being gone all night. When the two generals first met they were attended only by the staff officers already mentioned; but, during the interview, several of our officers entered and were introduced to General Lee, who received them cordially and made no objections to their presence. They were Major Generals Ord and Sheridan, Brevet Major General Ingalls, Brigadier Generals

Williams, Rawlins and Barnard, Lieutenant Colonels Parker, Dent, Badeau, Bowers, A. A. G., Porter and Babcock, and Captain Lincoln. E. B. Washburn, M. C. from Illinois, was the only civilian present.

It should be said that General Grant had anticipated the surrender for several days, and had resolved beforehand not to require the same formalities which are required in a surrender between the forces of two foreign nations or belligerent powers; that they were our own people, and to exact no conditions for the mere purpose of humiliation.

After the interview General Lee returned to his own camp, about half a mile distant, where his leading officers were assembled awaiting his return.

He announced the result and the terms, whereupon they expressed great satisfaction at the leniency of the conditions. They then approached him in order of rank, shook hands, expressing satisfaction at his course and their regret at parting, all shedding tears on the occasion.

The fact of surrender and the liberal terms were then announced to the troops, and when General Lee appeared among them he was loudly cheered. On Monday, between 9 and 10 o'clock A. M., General Grant and staff rode out in the direction of the rebel lines, and on a hill just beyond the court house, where a full view of the rebel army could be obtained, General Lee was met, attended by but one staff officer and orderlies. The generals halted, and, seated on their horses, conversed for nearly an hour upon the prospects of the future, each seeming to realize the mighty influence which the events of the present were to have upon it. General Lee signified very emphatically his desire for a total cessation of hostilities, and indicated his intention to do all in his power to effect that end. The best of good feeling prevailed, and this was the last interview between the two commanders. General Grant returned to McLean's house, and soon after Generals Longstreet, Gordon, Pickett and Heth, with a number of staff officers, arrived, and after recognitions and introductions, an hour of very friendly intercourse took place, during which many scenes and incidents of college days, and days of service together in the regular army, were revived and retold with much good nature.

General Grant gave General Lee and his principal officers passes to proceed whither they wished. The parties then separated, and early on Tuesday morning General Grant and staff left the scene of the great event for their head-quarters at City Point, arriving at 4.30 A. M. General Meade was left in command to superintend the details of the surrender, which would occupy several days, the work of providing each man and officer with an individual parole being a slow and tedious one; part of them are written and part printed by the little printing presses which accompany the head-quarters.

Thus in exactly two weeks, to almost an hour, from the time General Grant and staff broke up their head-quarters at City Point for the spring campaign, they return with the spring campaign not only complete, but the entire opposing army destroyed, and the war substantially closed. The complete character of the destruction of Lee's army thus accomplished, forcibly appears from these facts, viz: That when the operations began two weeks ago, his army numbered not less than 65,000 men; that we have captured from him 25,000 prisoners; that his killed and wounded are not less than 14,000; and that the balance of the army deserted on the retreat, or fell into our hands at the surrender.

The congratulations at head-quarters were very hearty.

All honor to General Grant and his heroic soldiers, for the utter overthrow of the army of Northern Virginia. But let it never be forgotten that they could not have accomplished that great result without the coöperation of Sherman and his noble army. The long and successful march of Sherman through Georgia and the Carolinas, made that event possible. Every effort hitherto to capture Richmond had failed.

After the surrender of Lee's army it was the general expression that Johnston would also surrender to Sherman without another battle. Day after day rumors were afloat of the expected surrender. At length a bearer of dispatches from General Sherman arrived at Washington City on the evening of April 21st, with the following agreement between Sherman and Johnston, to be submitted to the War Department for *approval or disapproval:*

MEMORANDUM OR BASIS OF AGREEMENT

Made this 18th day of April, A. D., 1865, near Durham's Station, in the State of North Carolina, by and between Gen. Jos. Johnston, commanding Confederate Army, and Major-General W. T. Sherman, commanding the Army of the United States in North Carolina:

1. The contending armies now in the field to maintain their *statu quo* until notice is given by the commanding general of either one to its opponents, and a reasonable time, say forty-eight hours, allowed.

2. The Confederate armies now in existence to be disbanded and conducted to their several State capitals, there to deposit their arms and public property in the State arsenals, and each of five men to execute and file an agreement to cease from acts of war and abide the action of both State and Federal authority. The number of arms and munitions of war to be reported to the Chief of Ordnance at Washington City, subject to the future action of

the Congress of the United States, and in the meantime to be used solely to maintain peace and order within the borders of the States respectively.

3. The recognition by the executive of the United States of the several State governments and their officers and Legislatures, and taking the oath prescribed by the Constitution of the United States, and where conflicting State governments have resulted from war, the legitimacy of all shall be submitted to the Supreme Court of the United States.

4. The reëstablishment of all the Federal Courts in the several States, with powers as delegated by the Constitution and laws of Congress.

5. People and inhabitants of all the States to be guaranteed, so far as the executive can, their political rights and franchises, as well as their rights of persons and property, as defined by the Constitution of the United States, and of States respectively.

6. The executive authority of the Government of the United States not to disturb any of the people by reason of the late war, so long as they live in peace and quiet, abstain from acts of armed hostilities, and obey the laws in existence, in any place of their residence.

7. The general terms we leave to a general amnesty, so far as the executive power of the United States can convey, or on condition of disbandment of the Confederate armies, and the distribution of arms and resumption of peaceable pursuits by officers and men, as hitherto composing the said armies, not being fully empowered by our respective principals to fulfil these terms. We individually and officially pledge ourselves to promptly obtain the necessary authority, and to carry out the above programme.

W. T. SHERMAN,
Commander Army United States in North Carolina.

J. E. JOHNSTON,
General Commanding Confederate Army, North Carolina.

The next day, April 19th, 1865, General Sherman issued the following order:

"HEADQUARTERS MILITARY DIVISION OF THE
"MISSISSIPPI, IN THE FIELD,
"RALEIGH, N. C., April 19, 1865.

"SPECIAL FIELD ORDER, No. 58.

"The general commanding announces to the army a suspension of hostilities and an agreement with General Johnston, and high officials, which when formally ratified, will make peace from the Potomac to the Rio Grande. Until absolute peace is arranged, a line passing through Tyrell's Mount, Chapel Hill, University, Durham's Station and West Point, on the Neuse River, wil separate the armies. Each army commander will group his camp entirely with a view to comfort, health and good discipline. All details of military discipline must still be maintained. The general hopes and believes that in a very few days it will be his good fortune to conduct you all to your homes.

"The fame of this army for courage, industry and discipline is admitted all over the world. Then let each officer and man see that it is not stained by any act of vulgarity, rowdyism and petty crime.

"Cavalry will patrol the front of the line; General Howard will take charge of the district from Raleigh up to the cavalry; General Slocum to the left of Raleigh; and General Schofield in Raleigh, its right and rear. The quartermaster and commissaries will keep their supplies up to a light load for the wagons, and the railroad superintendent will arrange a dépôt for the convenience of each separate army.

"By order of Major-General W. T. SHERMAN.
"L. M. DAYTON, *A. A. G.*"

The Cabinet held a meeting promptly after the reception of the dispatches from Sherman, and disapproved of the agreement, for the following reasons:

1. It was an exercise of authority not vested in General Sherman; and its face shows that both he and Johnston knew that he (General Sherman) had no authority to enter into any such arrangements.

2. It was a practical acknowledgment of the Rebel Government.

3. It undertook to reëstablish the rebel State governments, that had been overthrown at the sacrifice of many thousand loyal lives and an immense treasure, and placed arms and ammunition in the hands of rebels at their respective capitals, which might be used as soon as the armies of the United States were disbanded, and used to conquer and subdue the loyal States.

4. By the restoration of the rebel authorities in their respective States, they would be enabled to reëstablish slavery.

5. It might furnish a ground of responsibility by the Federal Government to pay the rebel debt, and would certainly subject loyal citizens of the rebel States to the debt incurred by rebels in the name of the State.

6. It puts in dispute the existence of loyal State governments, and the new State of West Virginia, which had been recognized by every department of the United States Government.

7. It practically abolished the confiscation laws, and relieved rebels of every degree, who had slaughtered our people, from all pains and penalties for their crimes.

8. It gave terms that had been deliberately, repeatedly and solemnly rejected by President Lincoln, and better terms than the rebels had ever asked in their most prosperous condition.

9. It forms no basis of true and lasting peace, but relieved the rebels from the pressure of our victories, and left them in a condition to renew their efforts to overthrow the United States Government and subdue the loyal States whenever their strength was recruited and an opportunity should offer.

General Grant was sent to North Carolina to inform General Sherman of the conclusions of the Cabinet in regard to his agreement with Johnston, and to take such steps as might be necessary to secure the surrender of Johnston's army on the same terms of Lee's surrender.

The following correspondence announces the result of General Grant's mission to Sherman:

NEW YORK, May 1.

The *Herald's* Washington special says: "General Grant has returned in the most excellent spirits. He expresses much gratification at the prompt execution of the orders of the Government in reference to the agreement between General Sherman and Joe Johnston. General Sherman met the lieutenant general twenty miles from the front. He received the order of disapproval with most commendable good grace. There was no hesitation, no murmuring, nor any expression of dissatisfaction at the disapproval of the terms entered into between him and the rebel general, but without any delay or argument in defense of the course previously pursued, General Sherman and his generals, with a true soldierly spirit, set to work with alacrity to carry out the views of the Government communicated by General Grant. Within five minutes a dispatch was sent to Johnston terminating the armistice. Upon the receipt of the notification by the rebel pickets, orders were given for our troops in the rear to move up to the front. In a few hours General Frank Blair, with his corps, was in motion. General Sherman had informed Johnston that the Government would not sanction the terms proposed, and that he should immediately resume hostilities. Immediately upon receipt of this notice, Johnston sent back a flag of truce, asking an interview with Sherman to arrange other terms of surrender, which was promptly made upon the basis of the terms given to General Lee."

The New York *Tribune's* Washington special says: "General Grant is reported to have said that when he informed General

Sherman of the terms he had forwarded to Washington, the latter frankly admitted that he had made a mistake in not having it put in writing that slavery was dead, but that was the understanding between them. As to permitting the rebel legislatures to assemble, he agreed to that because he had just learned that the Virginia Legislature was permitted to assemble by the authority of the President, and in the absence of official instructions, he interpreted the President's desire to be that the rebel civil governments should be retained for the preservation of order, and to avoid maintaining a military force in those States, as well as to do away with the irritation likely to grow out of military government. As to the amnesty, it was only to cover officers and soldiers. When his attention was called to the wording, he replied, with much spirit, 'That doesn't express the understanding between us.'"

It cannot be denied that the agreement between Sherman and Johnston was received by the country with astonishment and universal regret. Various explanations have been given of the course of the general in this matter.

It has been said that Sherman signed, and forwarded to Washington, the agreement, simply for the consideration and action of the proper authorities. That, so far as he was concerned, he neither approved nor disapproved the terms of agreement. The promptness with which he carried out the will of the Government, when made known to him by the lieutenant general, certainly gives some plausibility to this opinion.

It has also been stated that the magnanimity of our great and good President, who had fallen by the hand of the cowardly assassin, and the magnanimity of General Grant to Lee and his army, had impressed Sherman with the idea that magnanimity was the order of the day, and that he, therefore, determined to outflank them all in this respect.

Whatever may have been Sherman's reasons for his course in this matter, let it not be forgotten that if he was not equal to Johnston and his counselors in diplomacy, he was more than a match for them in the field and with the sword.

This mistake, or blunder, if it may be so called, did not have its origin in any special love for slavery, or desire to preserve that wretched and fallen institution, or from any shadow of feeling that might be characterized disloyal.

The following extracts from letters written by Sherman to subordinate commanders, and other parties, during the war, together with other documents in previous chapters of this volume, will give to the reader very clear views of his opinions on several questions that were necessarily connected with the prosecution of the war. The war and its relation to the Government, subjects which in both cases have led to much speculation among politicians and writers, are discussed by the general from a military stand-point, which probably will prove the best and most successful in the end. He says:

"The war which prevails in our land is essentially a war of races. The Southern people entered into a clear compact of government, but still maintained a species of separate interests, history and prejudices. These latter became stronger and stronger, till they have led to a war, which has developed fruits of the bitterest kind.

"We of the North are, beyond all question, right in our lawful cause, but we are not bound to ignore the fact that the South have prejudices which form part of their nature, and which they cannot throw off without an effort of reason or the slower process of natural change. Now the question arises, should we treat as absolute enemies all in the South who differ from us in opinion or prejudices—kill or disable them? Or, should we give them time to think, and gradually change their conduct so as to conform to the new order of things which is slowly and gradually creeping into their country?

"When men take arms to resist our rightful authority, we are compelled to use force, because all reason and argument cease when arms are resorted to. When the provisions, forage, horses, mules, wagons, etc., are used by our enemy, it is clearly our duty and right to take them, because otherwise they may be used against us.

"In like manner, all houses left vacant by an inimical people are clearly our right, or such as are needed as store-houses, hospitals and quarters."

In another place:

"For my part, I believe that this war is the result of false political doctrine, for which we are all as a people responsible, viz.: that any and every people have a right to self-government; and I would give all chances to reflect, and when in error to recant.

"In this belief, while I assert for our Government the highest military prerogatives, I am willing to bear in patience that political nonsense of slave-rights, State rights, freedom of conscience, freedom of press, and such other trash as have deluded the Southern people into war, anarchy, bloodshed and the foulest crimes that have disgraced any time or any people.

"I know slave owners, finding themselves in possession of a species of property in opposition to the growing sentiment of the whole civilized world, conceived their property in danger, and foolishly appealed to war; and by skilful political handling involved with them the whole South in the doctrine of error and prejudice. I believe that some of the rich and slaveholding are prejudiced to an extent that nothing but death and ruin will extinguish; but hope that as the poorer and industrial classes of the South realize their relative weakness, and their dependence upon the fruits of the earth, and the good-will of their fellow-men, they will not only discover the error of their ways, and repent of their hasty action, but bless those who persistently maintained a Constitutional Government, strong enough to sustain itself, protect its citizens, and promise peaceful homes to millions yet unborn."

His opinions in regard to the rights of the Government, and the inevitable consequences of a much longer continuance of the war, are still more apt, forcible and logical. He writes:

"The Government of the United States has in North Alabama any and all rights which they choose to enforce in war—to take their lives, their homes, their every thing, because they cannot deny that war does exist there, and war is simply power unrestrained by constitution or compact. If they want eternal warfare, well and good; we will accept the issue and dispossess them, and put our friends in possession. I know thousands and millions of good people, who, at simple notice, would come to

North Alabama and accept the elegant houses and plantations there.

"If the people of Huntsville think differently, let them persist in war three years longer, and then they will not be consulted. Three years ago, by a little reflection and prudence they could have had a hundred years of peace and prosperity, but they preferred war. Very well; last year they could have saved their slaves, but now, it is too late—all the powers of earth cannot restore to them their slaves any more than their grandfathers. Next year their lands will be taken, for in war we can take them, and rightfully, too, and another year they may beg in vain for their lives. A people who will persevere in war beyond a certain limit ought to know the consequences. Many, many people, with less pertinacity than the South, have been wiped out of national existence."

On the question of guerrillas, perhaps the most difficult of all the problems of the war, the general has shown his soundness of policy. We recommend his views to the particular attention of all officers. In a letter written from Kenesaw Mountain, Georgia, to General Burbridge, commanding in Kentucky during the raid of Morgan in the summer of '64, the general spoke upon the subject of the raid freely, the substance of his letter being summed up by himself as follows:

"1st. You may order all your post and district commanders that guerillas are not soldiers, but wild beasts, unknown to the usages of war. To be recognized as soldiers, they must be enlisted, enrolled, officered, uniformed, armed and equipped, by recognized belligerent power, and must, if detailed from a main army, be of sufficient strength, with written orders from some army commander, to do some military thing. Of course we have recognized the Confederate Government as a belligerent power, but deny their right to our lands, territories, rivers, coasts, and nationality—admitting the right to rebel and move to some other country, where laws and customs are more in accordance with their own ideas and prejudices.

"2d. The civil power being insufficient to protect life and property, *ex necessitate rei*, to prevent anarchy, 'which nature abhors,' the military steps in, and is rightful, constitutional, and lawful. Under this law everybody can be made to 'stay at home and mind his and her own business,' and if they won't do that, can be sent away where they cannot keep their honest neighbors in fear of danger, robbery and insult.

"3d. Your military commanders, provost marshals and other agents may arrest all males and females who have encouraged or harbored guerillas and robbers, and you may cause them to be collected in Louisville, and when you have enough—say three or four hundred—I will cause them to be sent down the Mississippi, through their guerilla gauntlet, and by a sailing ship send them to a land where they may take negroes and make a colony, with laws and a future of their own. If they won't live in peace in such a garden as Kentucky, why, we will send them to another, if not a better, land, and surely this would be a kindness to them, and a God's blessing to Kentucky."

One of the greatest embarrassments experienced by our armies arose out of the hostility of the non-combatants of the South. Upon this point the general also speaks. He says:

"But a question also arises as to dwellings used by women, children and non-combatants. So long as non-combatants remain in their houses, and keep to their accustomed business, their opinions and prejudices can in nowise influence the war, and, therefore, should not be noticed. But if any one comes out into the public streets, and creates disorder, he or she should be punished, restrained or banished, either to the front or rear, as the officer in command adjudges. If the people, or any of them, keep up a correspondence with the parties in hostility, they are spies, and can be punished with death or minor punishment.

"To those who submit to the rightful law and authority, all gentleness and forbearance; but to the petulant and persistent secessionists, why, death is mercy, and the quicker he or she is disposed of the better. Satan and the rebellious saints of heaven were allowed a continuance of existence in hell merely to swell their just punishment. To such as would rebel against a government so mild and just as ours was in peace, a punishment equal would not be unjust."

HEADQUARTERS MILITARY DIVISION OF THE MISSISSIPPI, }
IN THE FIELD, NEAR MARIETTA, GA., June 30, 1864. }

MRS. ANNA GILMAN BOWEN,
   Baltimore, Md.—

DEAR MADAM: Your welcome letter of June 18th came to me here amid the sound of battle, and, as you say, little did I dream, when I knew you, playing as a school girl on Sullivan's Island beach, that I should control a vast army, pointing, like the swarm of Alaric toward the plains of the South. Why, oh, why is this? If I know my own heart, it beats as warmly as ever toward those kind and generous families that greeted us with such warm hospitality in days long past but still present in memory; and to-day were Frank and Mrs. Porcher, and Eliza Gilman, and Mary Lamb, and Margaret Blake, the Barksdales, the Quashis, the Priors, indeed any and all of our cherished circle, their children, or even their children's children, to come to me as of old, the stern feeling of duty and conviction would melt as snow before the genial sun, and I believe I would strip my own children that they might be sheltered; and yet they call me barbarian, vandal, and monster, and all the epithets that language can invent that are significant of malignity and hate. All I pretend to say is, on earth as in heaven man must submit to some arbiter. He must not throw off his allegiance to his government or his God without just reason and cause. The South had no cause — not even a pretext. Indeed, by her unjustifiable course, she has thrown away the proud history of the past, and laid open her fair country to the tread of devastating war. She bantered and bullied us to the conflict. Had we declined battle, America would have sunk back, coward and craven, meriting the contempt of all mankind. As a nation, we were forced to accept battle, and that once begun, it has gone on till the war has assumed proportions at which even we, in the hurly-burly, sometimes stand aghast. I would not subjugate the South in the sense so offensively assumed, but I would make every citizen of the land obey the common law, submit to the same that we do — no worse, no better — our equals, and not our superiors. I know, and you know that there were young men in our day, now no longer young — but who control their fellows — who assumed to the gentlemen of the South, a superiority of courage and manhood, and boastingly defied us of Northern birth to arms. God knows how reluctantly we accepted the issue, but once the issue joined, like in other ages, the Northern race, though slow to anger, once aroused, are more terrible than the more inflammable of the South. Even yet my heart bleeds when I see the carnage of battle, the desolation of homes, the bitter anguish of families, but the very moment the men of the South say that instead of appealing to war they should have appealed to reason, to our Congress, to our courts, to religion, and to the experience of history, then will I say Peace — Peace; go back to your point of error, and resume your places as American citizens, with all their proud heritages. Whether I shall live to see this period is problematical, but you may, and may tell your mother and sisters that I never forgot one kind look or greeting, or ever wished to efface its remembrance; but in putting on the armor of war I did it that our common country should not perish in infamy and dishonor. I am married, I have a wife and six children living in Lancaster, Ohio. My course has been an eventful one, but I hope when the clouds of anger and passion are dispersed and truth emerges bright and clear, you and all who knew me in early years will not blush that we were once dear friends. Tell Eliza for me that I hope she may live to realize that the doctrine of "secession" is as monstrous in our civil code as disobedience was in the Divine law. And should the fortunes of war ever bring you or your sisters, or any of our old clique under the shelter of my authority, I do not believe they will have cause to regret it.

Give my love to your children, and the assurance of my respects to your honored husband.

Truly,
W. T. SHERMAN.

The reader should consider, without prejudice, the contents of this chapter.

Remember the gallant bearing of Sherman at the battle of Bull Run; his efficiency in Kentucky while confronting a powerful Confederate army with a handful of men; his heroic bearing on the bloody field of Shiloh, and how he saved the day and the army from destruction; his march to and the siege and capture of Corinth; his soldierly and fearless bearing in the campaigns against Vicksburg; his long and perilous march from Memphis to Chattanooga; see him on the formidable heights of Lookout Mountain and Missionary Ridge, thundering away at the enemy above the clouds; follow him in his rapid march to the relief of Knoxville before the blood and sweat of battle had been wiped from his face; then go with him through the expedition of central Mississippi; follow him back to Chattanooga, and from thence through the most wonderful campaign the world ever witnessed; a campaign which ended with the *surrender of Johnston's army to Sherman on the 26th day of April, 1865, and which gave the finishing blow to the Rebellion;* remember and consider all these facts, and then tell me, do you not see in Major-General W. T. Sherman a patriot, soldier and hero? Under God, does not our country owe to this man a debt of gratitude?

CHAPTER XVI.

SHERMAN'S OFFICIAL REPORT AND FAREWELL ADDRESS

THE MARCH BY WAY OF RICHMOND TO WASHINGTON — THE GRAND MILITARY REVIEW — OFFICIAL REPORT AND FAREWELL ADDRESS.

Since the previous chapter was written, the grand army of Gen. Sherman marched to Washington City by way of Richmond, Va., where it took part in the most magnificent military review that the world has ever witnessed, and since that time Sherman has issued his official report and farewell address to his army. With these important documents we close this volume, leaving the reader free to draw his own conclusions from the statements of General Sherman.

GENERAL SHERMAN'S OFFICIAL REPORT.

[Published under Authority of the Committee of Congress on the Conduct of the War.]

WASHINGTON, May 22, 1865.

Major-General *William T. Sherman* sworn and examined.
By the Chairman —
Q. What is your rank in the army?
A. I am a Major-General in the regular army.

Q. As your negotiations with the rebel General Johnston, in relation to his surrender, has been the subject of much public comment, the committee desire you to state all the facts and circumstances in regard to it that you deem of public interest, or which you wish the public to know.

A. On the 15th day of April last I was at Raleigh, in command of an army composed of three armies; the Army of the Ohio, the Army of the Cumberland, and the Army of Tennessee. My enemy was General Joseph E. Johnston, of the Confederate army, who commanded about 50,000 men, retreating along the railroad from Raleigh to Hillsboro, Greensboro, Salisbury and Charlotte. I commenced pursuit by crossing the curve of that road in the direction of Ashboro and Charlotte. After the head of my column had crossed the Cape Fear River, at Aven's Ferry, I received a communication from General Johnston, and answered it; copies of which I sent promptly to the War Department, with a letter addressed to the Secretary of War, as follows:

HEADQUARTERS MILITARY DIVISION OF THE MISSISSIPPI,
IN THE FIELD, RALEIGH, N. C., April 15, 1865.

GENERAL U. S. GRANT, AND SECRETARY OF WAR:

I send copies of a correspondence begun with General Johnston, which I think will be followed by terms of capitulation. I will grant the same terms as General Grant gave General Lee, and be careful not to complicate any points of civil policy. If any cavalry has started towards me, caution them that they must be prepared to find our work done. It is now raining in torrents, and I shall await General Johnston's reply here, and will prepare to meet him in person at Chapel Hill.

I have invited Governor Vance to return to Raleigh with the civil officers of his State. I have met ex-Governor Graham, Messrs. Badger, Moore, Holden and others, all of whom agree that the war is over, and that the States of the South must resume their allegiance, subject to the Constitution and laws of

Congress, and must submit to the national arms. This great fact once admitted, all the details are easy of arrangement.

(Signed,) W. T. SHERMAN,
Major General.

I met General Johnston in person, at a house five miles from Durham Station, under a flag of truce. After a few preliminary remarks, he said to me, that since Lee had surrendered his army at Appomattox Court House, of which he had just been advised, he looked upon further opposition by him as the greatest possible of crimes; that he wanted to know whether I would make him any general concessions; anything by which he could maintain his hold and control of his army, and prevent its scattering; anything to satisfy the great yearning of their people; if so, he thought we could arrange terms satisfactory to both parties. He wanted to embrace the condition and fate of all the armies of the Southern Confederacy, to the Rio Grande, "to make one job of it," as he termed it.

I asked him where his powers were, whether he could command and control the fate of all the armies to the Rio Grande. He answered, that he thought he could obtain the power, but he did not possess it at that moment. He did not know where Mr. Davis was, but he thought if I would give him time he could find Mr. Breckinridge, whose orders would be obeyed everywhere, and he could pledge to me his personal faith, that whatever he undertook to do would be done.

I had had frequent correspondence with the late President of the United States, with the Secretary of War, with General Halleck and with General Grant. And the general impression left upon my mind was, that if a settlement could be made, consistent with the Constitution of the United States, the laws of Congress, and the Proclamation of the President, they would be not only willing, but pleased, thus to terminate the war by one single stroke of the pen.

I needed time to finish the railroad from the Neuse Bridge up to Raleigh, and thought I could put in four or five days' good time in making repairs to my road, even if I had to send the propositions to Washington. I therefore consented to delay twenty-four hours, to enable General Johnston to procure what would satisfy me as to his authority and ability as a military man, to do what he undertook to do. I therefore consented to meet him the next day, the 17th, at 12 o'clock noon, at the same place.

We did meet again. After a general interchange of courtesies, he remarked that he was there prepared to satisfy me that he could fulfil the terms of our conversation of the day before. He then asked me what I was willing to do. I told him, in the first place, that I could not deal with anybody except men recognized by us as belligerents, because no military man could go beyond that fact. The Attorney General has since so decided, and every man of common sense so understood it before; there was no difference of opinion on that point. As to the men and officers composing the Confederate armies, I told him that the President of the United States, by a published proclamation, had enabled every man of the Southern Confederate army, of the rank of colonel and under, to procure and obtain amnesty, by simply taking the oath of allegiance to the United States, and agreeing to go to his house and live in peace. The terms of General Grant to General Lee extended the same principles to officers of the rank of brigadier general and upward, including the highest officer in the Confederate army, viz., General Lee, the commander-in-chief. I was therefore willing to proceed with him upon the same principles.

Then a conversation arose as to what form of government they were to have in the South. Were the States there to be dissevered? And were the people to be denied representation in Congress? Were the people there to be, in the common language of the people of the South, the slaves of the people of the North?

Of course, I said, "No; we desire that you shall regain your positions as citizens of the United States, free, and equal to us in all respects, and with representation upon the condition of submission to the lawful authority of the United States, as defined by the Constitution, the United States Courts, and the authorities of the United States, supported by these courts."

He then remarked to me that General Breckinridge, a major general in the Confederate army, was near by, and, if I had no objection, he would like to have him present. I recalled his attention to the fact that I had, on the day before, explained to him that any negotiations between us must be confined to belligerents. He replied that he understood that perfectly. "But," said he, "Breckinridge, whom you do not know, save by public rumor as the Secretary of War, is, in fact, a major general." I replied, "I have no objection to any military officer you desire being present, as a part of your personal staff." I myself had my own officers near me at call.

Breckinridge came, a stranger to me, to whom I had never spoken in my life, and he joined in the conversation. While that conversation was being carried on, a courier arrived and handed to General Johnston a package of papers. He and Breckinridge sat down and looked over them for some time, and put them away in their pockets. What they were I know not. But one was a slip of paper, written, as General Johnston told me, by Mr. Regan, Postmaster General of the Southern Confederacy. They seemed to talk about it, *sotto voce*, and finally handed it to me. I glanced over it. It was preceded by a preamble and closed with a few general terms. I rejected it at once. We then discussed matters; talked about slavery — talked about everything. There was a universal assent that slavery was as dead as anything could be; that it was one of the issues of the war, long since determined. And even General Johnston laughed at the folly of the Confederate Government in raising negro soldiers, whereby they gave us all the points of the case. I told them that slavery had been treated by us as a dead institution, first by one class of men from the initiation of the war; and then from the date of the Emancipation Proclamation of President Lincoln by another, and finally by the assent of all parties.

As to reconstruction, I told them I did not know what the views of the Administration were. Mr. Lincoln had, up to that time, in letters and by telegrams to me, encouraged me by all the words that could be used in general terms, to believe in, not only his willingness, but his desire, that I should make terms with civil authorities, governors and legislators; even as far back as 1863. It then occurred to me that I might write off some general propositions, meaning little or meaning much, according to the construction of parties; what I would term "glittering generalities," and send them to Washington, which I could do in four days. That would enable the new President to give me a cue to his policy in the important juncture which was then upon us. For the war was over. The highest military authorities of the Southern Confederacy so confessed to me, openly, unconcealedly and repeatedly.

I therefore drew up the memorandum (which has been published to the world,) for the purpose of referring it to the proper authority of the United States, and enabling him to define to me what I might promise, simply to cover the pride of the Southern men, who thereby became subordinate to the laws of the United States, civil and military. I made no concessions to General Johnston's army, of the troops under his direction and immediate control. And if any concessions were made in those general terms, they were made because I then believed, and I now believe, they would have delivered into the hands of the United States the absolute control of every Confederate officer and soldier, all their muster-rolls and all their arms. It would save us all the incidental expenses resulting from the military occupation of that country by provost marshals, provost guards, military governors and all the machinery by which alone military power can reach the people of a civilized country. It would have surrendered to us the armies of Dick Taylor and Kirby Smith, both of them capable of doing infinite mischief to us by exhausting the resources of the whole country upon which we were to depend for the future extinguishment of our debt, forced upon us by their wrongful and rebellious conduct.

I never designed to shelter any human being from any liability incurred, in consequence of past acts, to the civil tribunals of our country; and I do not believe a fair and manly interpretation of my terms can so construe them, for the words "United States Courts," "United States authorities," "limitations of Executive power," occur in every paragraph.

And if they seemingly yield terms better than the public would desire to be given to the Southern people, if studied clearly and well, it will be found that there is an abundant submission on their part to the Government of the United States, either through its executive, legislative or judicial authorities. Every step in the progress of these negotiations was reported punctually, clearly and fully by the most rapid means of communication that I had. And yet I neglected not one single precaution to reap the full benefits of my position, in case the Government amended, altered or absolutely annulled these terms.

As these matters are necessarily mingled with the military history of the period, I would like, at this point, to submit to the committee my official report, which has been in the hands of the proper officer, viz: General Rawlings, Chief of Staff of the Army of the United States, since about the 12th instant. It was made by me at Manchester, Va., after I had returned from Savannah, whither I went to open up the Savannah River and reap the fruits of my negotiations with General Johnston, and to give General Wilson, far in the interior, a safe and sure base from which he could draw the necessary supply of clothing and food for his command.

It was only after I had fulfilled all this that I learned, for the first time, through the public press, that my conduct had been animadverted upon, not only by the Secretary of War, but by General Halleck and the press of the country at large. I did feel hurt and wronged that Mr. Stanton coupled with the terms of my memorandum confided to him, a copy of a telegram to General Grant which he had never sent to me. He knew, on the contrary, that when he was at Savannah I had negotiations with civil parties there, for he was present in my room when those parties were conferring with me, and I wrote him a letter setting forth many points of it, in which I said I aimed to make a split in Jeff. Davis' dominions, segregating Georgia from their cause. Those were civil negotiations, and far from being discouraged from making them, I was encouraged by Secretary Stanton himself to make them.

By coupling the note to General Grant with my memorandum, he gave the world fairly and clearly to infer that I was in possession of it. Now, I was not in possession of it, and have reason to know that Mr. Stanton knew I was not in possession of it.

Next met me, General Halleck's telegram, indorsed by Mr. Stanton, in which they publicly avowed an act of perfidy, viz: the violation of my truce, which I had a right to make, and which, by the laws of war, and by the laws of Congress, is punishable by death, and no other punishment.

Next they ordered an army to pursue my enemy, who was known to be surrendering to me, in the presence of General Grant himself, their superior officer, and finally they sent orders to General Wilson and to General Thomas, my subordinates, acting under me on a plan of the most magnificent scale, admirably executed, to defeat my orders and to thwart the interests of the Government of the United States.

I did feel indignant; I do feel indignant. As to my own honor, I can protect it. In my letter of the 15th of April, I used this language: "I have invited Governor Vance to return to Raleigh with the civil officers of his State." I did so because President Lincoln had himself encouraged me to a similar course with the Governor of Georgia, when I was in Atlanta. And here was the opportunity which the Secretary of War should have taken to put me on my guard against negotiations with civil authorities, if such were the settled policy of our Government. Had President Lincoln lived, I know he would have sustained me.

The following is my report, which I desire to have incorporated into and made a part of my testimony:

REPORT.

HEAD-QUARTERS MILITARY DIVISION OF THE MISSISSIPPI, IN THE FIELD, CITY POINT, Va., May 9, 1865.

General JOHN A. RAWLINGS, Chief of Staff, Washington, D. C.:

GENERAL—My last official report brought the history of events, as connected with the armies in the field, subject to my immediate command, down to the 1st of April, when the Army of the Ohio, Major General J. M. Schofield commanding, lay at Goldsboro, with detachments distributed so as to secure and cover our routes of communication and supply, back to the sea at Wilmington and Morehead City; Major General A. H. Terry, with the Tenth Corps, being at Faxon's Depôt. The Army of the Tennessee, Major General O. O. Howard commanding, was encamped to the front and right of Goldsboro, and the Army of the Georgia, Major General H. W. Slocum commanding, to its left and front. The cavalry, Brevet Major General Kilpatrick commanding, at Mount Olive. All were busy in repairing the wear and tear of our then recent hard march from Savannah, and in replenishing clothing and stores necessary for a further progress. I had previously, by letter and in person, notified the lieutenant general commanding the armies of the United States, that the 10th of April would be the earliest possible moment at which I could hope to have all things in readiness, and we were compelled to use our railroads to the very highest possible limit, in order to fulfil that promise.

Owing to a mistake in the railroad department in sending locomotives and cars of the five foot gauge, we were limited to the use of the few locomotives and cars of the four feet eight and a half inch guage, already in North Carolina, with such of the old stock as was captured by Major General Terry at Wilmington and on his way up to Goldsboro. Yet such a judicious use was made of them, and such industry displayed in the railroad management by Generals Easton and Beckwith, and Colonel Wright and Mr. Van Dyne, that by the 10th of April our men were all reclad, the wagons reloaded, and a fair amount of forage accumulated ahead. In the meantime, Major General George Stoneman, in command of a division of cavalry, operating from East Tennessee, in connection with Major General George H. Thomas, in pursuance of my orders, had reached the railroad at Greensboro, N. C., and had made sad havoc with it; and had pushed along it to Salisbury, destroying *en route* bridges, culverts, dépôts, and all kinds of rebel supplies, and had extended the breach in the railroad down to the Catawba Bridge. This was fatal to the hostile armies of Lee and Johnston, who depended on that road for supplies, and as their ultimate line of retreat. Brevet Major General Wilson, also in command of the cavalry corps, organized by himself, under special field orders No. — of —, in 1864, at Gaylesville, Alabama, had started from the neighborhood of Decatur and Florence, Alabama, and moved straight into the heart of Alabama, on a route prescribed for General Thomas, after he had defeated Hood at Nashville, Tennessee. But the roads being too heavy for infantry, General Thomas had devolved the duty on that most energetic young cavalry officer, General Wilson, who, imbued with the proper spirit, has struck one of the best blows of the war at the waning strength of the Confederacy. His route was one never before touched by our troops, and afforded him abundant supplies as long as he was in motion, viz.: by Tuscaloosa, Selma, Montgomery, Columbus and Macon. Though in communication with him, I have not been able to receive as yet his full and detailed reports, which will in due time be published and appreciated.

Lieutenant General Grant, also in immediate command of the armies about Richmond, had taken the initiative in that magnificent campaign which, in less than ten days, compelled the evacuation of Richmond, and resulted in the destruction and surrender of the entire rebel Army of Virginia, under command of General Lee. The news of the battles about Petersburg reached me at Goldsboro on the 6th of April. Up to that time my purpose was to move rapidly northward, feigning on Raleigh, and striking straight for Burkesville, thereby interposing between Johnston and Lee. But the auspicious events in Virginia had changed the whole military problem, and in the expressive language of Lieutenant General Grant, the "Confederate armies of Lee and Johnston" became the "stragetic points." General Grant was fully able to take care of the former, and my task was to destroy or capture the latter.

Johnston, at the time, April 6, had his army well in hand about Smithfield, interposing between me and Raleigh. I estimated his infantry and artillery at thirty-five thousand (35,000), and his cavalry at from six to ten thousand (6,000 to 10,000). He was superior to me in cavalry, so that I held General Kilpatrick in reserve at Mount Olive, with orders to recruit his horses, and be ready to make a sudden and rapid march on the 10th of April.

At daybreak on the day appointed, all the heads of columns were in motion straight against the enemy; Major General Slocum taking the two direct roads for Smithfield, Major General O. O. Howard making a circuit by the right and feigning up the Weldon Road to disconcert the enemy's cavalry; Generals Terry and Kilpatrick moving on the west side of the Neuse River, and to reach the rear of the enemy, between Smithfield and Raleigh. General Schofield followed General Slocum in person. All the columns met, within six miles of Goldsboro, more or less cavalry, with the usual rail barricades, which were swept before us as chaff. And by ten o'clock on the morning of the 11th, the Fourteenth Corps entered Smithfield, the Twentieth Corps close at hand. Johnston had rapidly retreated across the Neuse River, and, having his railroad to lighten up his trains, could retreat faster than we could pursue. The rains had also set in, making the resort to corduroy absolutely necessary, to pass even ambulances. The enemy had burned the bridge at Smithfield, and, as soon as possible, Major General Slocum got up his pontoons, and crossed over a division of the Fourteenth Corps.

We there heard of the surrender of Lee's army, at Appomattox Court House, Virginia, which was announced to the armies in orders, and created universal joy. Not an officer or soldier of my armies but expressed a satisfaction that it had fallen to the lot of the Armies of the Potomac and James so gloriously to overwhelm and capture the entire army that had held them in check so long; and their success gave a new impulse to finish up our task.

Without a moment's hesitation, we dropped our trains, and marched rapidly in pursuit to and through Raleigh, reaching that place at half-past seven in the morning, on the 13th, in a heavy rain. The next day the cavalry passed on through the rain to Durham's Station, the Fifteenth Corps following as far as Morrisville Station, and the Seventeenth to Jones' Station. On the supposition that Johnston was tied to his railroad, as a line of retreat by Hillsboro, Greensboro, Salisbury and Charlotte, I had turned the other columns across the head of that road toward Ashboro (see special field orders, No. 55). The cavalry, Brevet Major General J. Kilpatrick commanding, was ordered to keep up a show of pursuit toward the "Company's Shops," in Alamancer county; Major General O. O. Howard to turn the left by Hackney's Cross Roads, Pittsboro, St. Lawrence and Ashboro; Major General H.W. Slocum to cross Cape Fear River at Aven's Ferry, and move rapidly by Carthage, Caledonia and Cox's Mills; Major General J. W. Schofield was to hold Raleigh and the road back, and with his spare force to follow an intermediate route.

By the 15th, though the rains were incessant, and the roads almost impracticable, Major General Slocum had the Fourteenth Corps, Brevet Major General Davis commanding, near Martha's Vineyard, with a pontoon bridge laid across Cape Fear River at Aven's Ferry, with the Twentieth Corps, Major General Mower commanding, in support; and Major General Howard had the Fifteenth and Seventeenth Corps stretched out on the roads toward Pittsboro, while General Kilpatrick held Durham Station and Chapel Hill University. Johnston's army was retreating rapidly on the roads from Hillsboro to Greensboro, he himself at Greensboro.

Although out of place, as to time, I here invite all military critics who study the problems of war, to take their maps and compare the position of my army, on the 15th and 16th of April, with that of General Halleck, about Burkesville and Petersburg, Virginia, on the 26th of April, when, according to his telegram to Secretary Stanton, he offered to relieve me of the task of cutting off Johnston's retreat. Major General Stoneman, at the time, was at Statesville, and Johnston's only line of retreat was by Salisbury and Charlotte. It may be that General Halleck's troops can out-march mine, but there is nothing in their past history to show it. Or, it may be that General Halleck can inspire his troops with more energy of action. I doubt that, also, save and except in this single instance, when he knew the enemy was ready to surrender or "disperse," as advised by letter of April 18, addressed to him when chief of staff, at Washington City, and delivered into his hands by Major Hitchcock, of my army.

Thus matters stood at the time I received General Johnston's first letter and made my answer of April 14th, copies of which were sent, with all expedition, to Lieutenant General Grant and the Secretary of War, with my letter of April 15th. I agreed to meet General Johnston, in person, at a point intermediate between our pickets, on the 17th, at noon, provided the position of the troops remained *statu quo*. I was both willing and anxious thus to consume a few days, as it would enable Colonel Wright to finish our railroad to Raleigh. Two bridges had to be built and twelve miles of new road made. We had no iron, except by taking up that on the march from Goldsboro to Weldon. Instead of losing time, I gained in every way; for every hour of delay possible was required to reconstruct the railroad to our rear and improve the condition of our wagon roads to the front, so desirable in case the negotiations failed, and we be forced to make the race of near two hundred miles to head off or catch Johnston, then retreating toward Charlotte.

At noon of the day appointed, I met General Johnston for the first time in my life, although we had been exchanging shots constantly since May, 1863. Our interview was frank and soldier-like, and he gave me to understand that further war on the part of the Confederate troops was folly, that "the cause" was lost, and that every life sacrificed after the surrender of Lee's army was the highest possible crime. He admitted that the terms conceded to General Lee were magnanimous, and all he could ask; but he did want some general concessions, that would enable him to allay the natural fears and anxieties of his followers, and enable him to maintain his control over them until they could be got back to the neighborhood of their homes, thereby saving the State of North Carolina the devastation inevitably to result from turning his men loose and impoverished on the spot; and our pursuit across the State. He also wanted to embrace in the same general proposition the fate of all the Confederate armies that remained in existence. I never made any concession as to his own army, or assumed to deal finally and authoritatively in regard to any other. But it did seem to me that there was presented a chance for peace that might be deemed valuable to the Government of the United States, and was at least worthy the few days that would be consumed in reference. To push an army, whose commander had so frankly and honestly confessed his inability to cope with me, were cowardly and unworthy the brave men I led.

Inasmuch as General Johnston did not feel authorized to pledge his power over the armies in Texas, we adjourned to meet the next day at noon. I returned to Raleigh, and conferred freely with my general officers, *every one* of whom urged me to concede terms that might accomplish so complete and desirable an end. All dreaded the weary and laborious march after the fugitive and disbanding army back toward Georgia, over the very country where we had toiled so long. There was but one opinion expressed, and if contrary ones were entertained, they were withheld, or indulged in only by that class who shun the fight and the march, but are loudest, bravest, and fiercest, when danger is past.

I again met General Johnston on the 18th, and we renewed the conversation. He satisfied me then of his power to disband the rebel armies in Alabama, Mississippi, Louisiana and Texas, as well as those in his immediate command, viz: North Carolina, South Carolina, Georgia and Florida. The points on which he expressed especial solicitude were lest their States should be dismembered and denied representation in Congress, or any separate political existence whatever; and the absolute disarming of his men would leave the South powerless, and exposed to depredations by wicked bands of assassins and robbers.

The President's (Lincoln's) Message of 1864; his Amnesty Proclamation; General Grant's terms to General Lee, substantially extending the benefit of that proclamation to all officers above the rank of a colonel; the invitation to the Virginia Legislature to reässemble in Richmond, by General Weitzel, with the supposed approval of Mr. Lincoln and General Grant, then on the spot; a firm belief that I had been fighting to reëstablish the Constitution of the United States, and last, but not least, the general and universal desire to close a war any longer without organized resistance, were the leading facts that induced me to pen the "memorandum" of April 18th, signed by myself and General Johnston. It was designed to be, and so expressed on its face,

L*

as a mere "basis" for reference to the President of the United States and constitutional commander-in-chief, to enable him, if he chose, at one blow to dissipate the military power of the Confederacy, which had threatened the national safety for years. It admitted of modification, alteration and change. It had no appearance of an ultimatum, and by no false reasoning can it be construed into an usurpation of power on my part. I have my opinion on the questions involved, "and will stand by the memorandum;" but this forms no part of a military report.

Immediately on my return to Raleigh, I dispatched one of my staff, Major Hitchcock, to Washington, enjoining him to be most prudent, and careful to avoid the spies and informers that would be sure to invest him by the way, and to say nothing to anybody until the President could make known to me his feelings and wishes in the matter.

The news of President Lincoln's assassination (wrongly reported to me, by telegraph, as having occurred on the 11th,) reached me on the 17th, and was announced to my command on the same day, in field orders No. 56. I was duly impressed with its horrible atrocity and probable effect on the country. But when the property and interests of millions still living were involved, I saw no good reason why to change my course, but thought rather to manifest real respect for his memory by following, after his death, that policy which, if living, I felt certain he would have approved, or at least not rejected with disdain.

Up to that hour I had never received one word of instruction, advice or counsel, as to the plan or policy of the Government, looking to a restoration of peace on the part of the rebel States of the South. Whenever asked for an opinion on the points involved, I had always evaded the subject. My letter to the Mayor of Atlanta has been published to the world, and I was not relieved by the War Department for it. My letter to Mr. ———, of Savannah, was shown by me to Mr. Stanton, before its publication, and all that my memory retains of his answer is, that he said, like my letters generally, it was sufficiently "emphatic, and could not be misunderstood." Both of these letters asserted my belief that, according to Mr. Lincoln's proclamations and messages, when the people of the South had laid down their arms, and submitted to the lawful power of the United States, *ipso facto* the war was over as to them; and furthermore, that if any State in rebellion would conform to the Constitution of the United States, "cease war," elect senators and representatives to Congress, if admitted, (of which each House of Congress alone is the judge,) that State becomes instanter as much in the Union as New York or Ohio. Nor was I rebuked for these expressions, though it was universally known and commented on at the time. And, again, Mr. Stanton in person, at Savannah, speaking of the terrific expense of the war, and difficulty of realizing the money for the daily wants of Government, impressed me most forcibly with the necessity of bringing the war to a close as soon as possible, for *financial reasons*.

On the evening of April 23d, Major Hitchcock reported his return to Morehead City with dispatches, of which fact General Johnston, at Hillsboro, was notified, so as to be ready in the morning for an answer. At six o'clock on the morning of the 24th, Major Hitchcock arrived, accompanied by General Grant and members of his staff, who had not telegraphed the fact of his coming over our exposed roads, for prudential reasons. I soon learned that the memorandum was disapproved, without reasons assigned, and I was ordered to give the forty-eight hours' notice, and resume hostilities at the close of that time; governing myself by the substance of a dispatch, then inclosed, dated March 3d, twelve o'clock noon, at Washington, D. C , from Secretary Stanton to General Grant, at City Point, but not accompanied by any part of the voluminous matter so liberally lavished on the public inthe New York journals of the 24th of April. That was the *first* and *only* time I ever saw that telegram, or had one word of instructions on the important matters involved in it. And it does seem strange to me that every bar-room loafer in New York can read in the morning journals "official" matter that is withheld from a general whose command extends from Kentucky to North Carolina.

Within an hour a courier was riding from Durham Station toward Hillsboro, with notice to General Johnston of the suspension of the truce, and renewing my demand for the surrender of the command, (see two dispatches of April 24th, six o'clock in the morning,) and at twelve at noon I had the receipt of his picket officer. I therefore published my orders, No. 62, to the troops, terminating my truce at twelve at noon, on the 26th, and ordered all to be in readiness to march at that hour, on the routes prescribed in special field orders No. 55, of April 14th, from the positions held April 18th. General Grant had orders from the President to direct military movements, and I explained to him the exact position of the troops, and he approved of it most emphatically; but he did not relieve me or express a wish to assume command.

All things were in readiness, when on the evening of the 25th, I received another letter from General Johnston, asking another interview to renew negotiations. General Grant not only approved, but urged me to accept, and I appointed a meeting at our former place, at noon of the 26th, the very hour fixed for the renewal of hostilities. General Johnston was delayed by an accident to his train, but at two o'clock in the afternoon arrived.

We then consulted, concluded and signed, the final terms of capitulation. These were taken by me back to Raleigh, submitted to General Grant, and met his immediate approval and signature. General Johnston was not even aware of the presence of General Grant at Raleigh at the time. There was surrendered to us the second great army of the so-called Confederacy; and, though undue importance has been given the so-called "negotiations" which preceded it, and a rebuke and public disfavor cast upon me entirely unwarranted by the facts, I rejoice in saying that it was accomplished without further ruin and devastation to the country—without the loss of a single life to those gallant men who had followed me from the Mississippi to the Atlantic; and without subjecting brave men to the ungracious task of pursuing a fleeing foe that did not want to fight. As for myself, I know my motives, and challenge the instance during the past four years, when an armed and defiant foe stood before me that I did not go in for a fight. And I would blush for shame if I had ever insulted or struck a fallen foe. The instant the terms of surrender were approved by General Grant I made my orders No. 56, assigning to each of my subordinate commanders his share of the work, and with General Grant's approval, made special field orders No. 66, putting in motion my old army, no longer required in Carolina, northward for Richmond.

General Grant left Raleigh at nine o'clock on the morning of the 27th, and I glory in the fact that during his three days' stay with me, I did not detect in his language or manner one particle of abatement of the confidence, respect and affection that have existed between us throughout all the various events of the past war; and though we have honestly differed in other cases as well as this, still we respect each other's honest convictions. I still adhere to my then opinions, that by a few general concessions— "glittering generalities"—all of which in the end *must* and will be conceded to the organized States of the South, this day there would not be an armed battalion opposed to us within the broad area of the dominions of the United States. Robbers and assassins must, in any event, result from the disbandment of large armies, but even these would be, and can be, taken care of by the local civil authorities, without being made a charge upon the national treasury.

On the morning of the 28th, having concluded all business requiring my personal attention at Raleigh, and having conferred with every army commander, and delegated to him the authority necessary for his future action, I dispatched my headquarters wagons by land along with the Seventeenth Corps, the office in charge of General Webster, to Alexandria, Va., and in person, accompanied only by my personal staff, hastened to Savannah, to direct matters in the interior of Georgia and South Carolina.

I had received across the rebel telegraph wires, cypher dispatches from General Wilson to the effect that he was in receipt of my order, No. 35, and would send General Upton's division to Augusta, and General McCook's division to Tallahassee, to receive the surrender of those garrisons, take charge of the public property, and execute the paroles required by the terms of surrender. He reported a sufficiency of forage for his horses in Southwest Georgia, but asked me to send him a supply of clothing, sugar, coffee, etc., by way of Augusta, Georgia, where he could get it by rail. I therefore went rapidly to Goldsboro and Wilmington, reaching the latter city at ten in the morning of the 29th, and the same day embarked for Hilton Head on the blockade runner Russie, Captain A. H. Smith.

I found General Q. A. Gillmore, commanding Department of the South, at Hilton Head, on the evening of April 30th, and ordered him to send to Augusta at once, what clothing and small stores he could spare, for General Wilson, and to open up a line of certain communication and supply with him at Macon. Within an hour, the captured steamboats Jeff. Davis and Amazon, well adapted to the shallow and crooked navigation of the Savannah River, were being loaded; the one at Savannah and the other at Hilton Head. The former started up the river on the 1st of May, in charge of a very intelligent officer, (whose name I cannot recall,) and forty-eight men, (all the boat could carry,) with orders to occupy temporarily, the United States Arsenal at Augusta, and open up communication with General Wilson at Macon, in the event that General Upton's division of cavalry was not already there. The Amazon followed the next day, and General Gillmore had made the necessary orders for a brigade of infantry to be commanded by General Molyneaux, to follow by a land march to Augusta, as its permanent garrison. Another brigade of infantry was ordered to occupy Orangeburg, South Carolina, the point furthest in the interior that can at present be reached by rail from the sea coast (Charleston).

On the 1st of May I went to Savannah, where General Gilmore also joined me, and the arrangements ordered for the occupation of Augusta were consummated. At Savannah I found the city in the most admirable police, under direction of Brevet Major General Grover, and the citizens manifested the most unqualified joy to hear that so far as they were concerned, the war was over. All classes, Union men as well as former rebels, did not conceal however, the apprehensions naturally arising from a total ignorance of the political conditions to be attached to their future state. Anything at all would be preferable to this dread uncertainty.

On the evening of the 2d of May I returned to Hilton Head, and there for the first time, received the New York papers of April 28th, containing Secretary Stanton's dispatch of nine in the forenoon of the 27th of April, to General Dix, including General Halleck's, from Richmond, of nine in the evening the night before, which seems to have been rushed with extreme haste before an excited public, viz: on the morning of the 28th. You will observe from the dates, that these dispatches were running back and forth from Richmond and Washington to New York, and there published, while General Grant and I were in Raleigh, North Carolina, adjusting to the best of our ability, the terms of surrender of the only remaining formidable rebel army in existence at the time east of the Mississippi River. Not one word of intimation had been sent to me of the displeasure of the Government with my official conduct, but only the naked disapproval of a skeleton memorandum, sent properly for the action of the President of the United States. The most objectionable features of my memorandum had already (April 24th) been published to the world, in violation of official usage; and the contents of my accompanying letters to General Halleck, General Grant, and

Secretary Stanton, of even date, though at hand, were suppressed. In all these letters I stated clearly and distinctly that Johnston's army would *not* fight, but if pushed, would "disband" and scatter into small and dangerous guerilla parties, as injurious to the interests of the United States as to the people themselves; that all parties admitted that the rebel cause of the South was abandoned; that the negroes were free, and that the temper of all was most favorable to a lasting peace. I say all these opinions of mine were withheld from the public with a seeming purpose; and I do contend that my official experience and former services, as well as my past life and familiarity with the people and geography of the South, entitled my opinions to at least a decent respect.

Although this dispatch (Mr. Stanton's, of April 27th,) was printed "official," it had come to me only in the questionable shape of a newspaper paragraph, headed "Sherman's truce disregarded." I had already done what General Wilson wanted me to do, viz: Had sent him supplies of clothing and food, with clear and distinct orders and instructions how to carry out in Western Georgia the terms for the surrender of arms, and paroling the prisoners made by General Johnston's capitulation of April 26th, and had properly and most opportunely ordered General Gillmore to occupy Orangeburg and Augusta, stragetic points of great value at all times, in peace and war. But as the Secretary had taken upon himself to order my subordinate generals to disobey my "orders," I explained to General Gillmore that I would no longer confuse him or General Wilson with "orders" that might conflict with the Secretary, which as reported, were sent, not through me, but in open disregard of me and of my lawful authority.

It now becomes my duty to paint, in justly severe character, the still more offensive and dangerous matter of General Halleck's dispatch of April 26th, to the Secretary of War, embodied in his to General Dix, of April 27th. General Halleck had been chief-of-staff of the army at Washington, in which capacity he received my official letter of April 18th, wherein I wrote clearly that if Johnston's army, about Greensboro, was pushed, it would "disperse," an event I wished to prevent. About that time he seems to have been sent from Washington to Richmond to command the new military Division of the James; in assuming charge of which on the 22d, he defines the limits of his authority to be "the Department of Virginia, the Army of the Potomac, and such part of North Carolina as may not be occupied by the command of Major General Sherman." [See his General Orders, No. 1.] Four days later, April 26th, he reports to the Secretary that he had ordered Generals Meade, Sheridan and Wright, to invade that part of North Carolina which *was* occupied by my command, and "pay no regard to any truce or orders of mine." They were ordered to "push forward, regardless of any orders, save those of Lieutenant General Grant, and cut off Johnston's retreat." He knew at the time he penned this dispatch that Johnston was not retreating, but was halted under a forty-eight hours truce with me, and was laboring to surrender his command and prevent it dispersing into guerilla bands; that I had on the spot a magnificent army at my command, amply sufficient for all purposes required by the occasion. The plan of cutting off a retreat from the direction of Burkesville and Danville is hardly worthy of one of his military education and genius.

When he contemplated an act so questionable as the violation of a truce made by a competent authority, he should have gone himself, and not have sent subordinates; for he knew I was bound in *honor* to *defend and maintain* my *own* truce and pledge of faith, even at the cost of many lives. When an officer pledges the faith of his Government, he is bound to defend it; and he is no soldier who would violate it knowingly.

As to Davis and his stolen treasure, did General Halleck, as chief of staff, or commanding officer of the neighboring military division, notify me of the facts contained in his dispatch to the Secretary? No; he did not. If the Secretary of War wanted

Davis caught, why not order it, instead of, by publishing in the newspapers, putting him on his guard to hide away and escape? No orders or intimation to arrest Davis or his stolen treasure ever came to me, but, on the contrary, I was led to believe that the Secretary of War rather preferred he should escape from the country, if it was made unknown to him.

But, even on this point, I inclose a copy of my letter to Admiral Dahlgren, at Charleston, sent him by a fleet steamer from Wilmington, on the 25th of April, two days before the bankers of Richmond had imparted to General Halleck the important secret of Davis' movements, designed, doubtless, to stimulate his troops to march their legs off to catch *their* treasure for *their* own use. I know that Admiral Dahlgren did receive my letter on the 26th, and had acted on it *before* General Halleck had even thought of the matter. But I don't believe a word of the treasure story; it is absurd on its face, and General Halleck, or anybody, has my full permission to chase Jeff. Davis and cabinet, with their stolen treasure, through any part of the country occupied by my command.

The last and most obnoxious feature of General Halleck's dispatch is where he goes out of his way, and advises that my subordinates, Generals Thomas, Stoneman and Wilson, should be "instructed not to obey Sherman's commands." This is too much, and I turn from the subject with feelings too strong for words, and merely record my belief that so much mischief was never before embraced in so small a space as the newspaper paragraph headed, "Sherman's truce disregarded," authenticated as "official" by Mr. Secretary Stanton, and published in the newspapers of April 28th.

During the night of May 2d, at Hilton Head, having concluded my business in the Department of the South, I began my return to meet my troops, then marching toward Richmond, from Raleigh. On the morning of May 3d, we ran into Charleston Harbor, where I had the pleasure to meet Admiral Dahlgren, who had, in all my previous operations from Savannah northward, aided me with a courtesy and manliness that commanded my entire respect and deep affection. Also, General Hatch, who, from our first interview at the Tullifinny camp, had caught the spirit of the move from Pocataligo northward, and had largely contributed to our joint success in taking Charleston and the Carolina coast. Any one who is not satisfied with the war, should go and see Charleston, and he will pray louder and deeper than ever that the country may, in the long future, be spared any more war. Charleston and secession being synonymous terms, the city should be left as a sample, so that centuries will pass away before that false doctrine is preached again in our Union.

We left Charleston the evening of the 3d of May, and hastened with all possible speed back to Morehead City, which we reached at night of the 4th. I immediately communicated by telegraph to General Schofield, at Raleigh, and learned from him the pleasing fact that the lieutenant general, commanding the armies of the United States, had reached the Chesapeake in time to countermand General Halleck's order, and prevent his violating my truce, invading the area of my command, and driving Johnston's surrendering army into fragments. General Johnston had fulfilled his agreement to the very best of his ability, and the officers charged with issuing the paroles, at Greensboro, reported about 30,000 already made, and that the greater part of the North Carolina troops had gone home without waiting for their papers; but that all of them would doubtless come in to some of the miltary posts, the commanders of which were authorized to grant them.

About eight hundred of the rebel cavalry had gone South, refusing to abide the terms of the surrender, and it was supposed they would make for Mexico. I would sincerely advise that they be urged to go and stay. They would be a nuisance to any civilized government, whether loose or in prison.

With the exception of some plundering on the part of Lee's and Johnston's disbanded men, all else was quiet. When, to the number of men surrendered at Greensboro, are added those at Tallahassee, Augusta and Macon, with the scattered squads who will come in at other military posts, I have no doubt full fifty thousand armed men will be disarmed and restored to civil pursuits, by the application made near Durham Station, North Carolina, on the 26th of April, 1865, and that, too, without the loss of a single life to us.

On the 5th of May, I received and here subjoin a further dispatch from General Schofield, which contains inquiries I have been unable to satisfy, similar to those made by nearly every officer in my command, whose duty brings him into contact with citizens. I leave you to do what is expedient to provide the military remedy.

[By telegraph from Raleigh, North Carolina.]

"RALEIGH, N. C., May 5, 1865.

"To Major General W. T. SHERMAN, Morehead City:

"When General Grant was here, as you doubtless recollect, he said the lines had been extended to embrace this and other States South. The order, it seems, has been modified to include only Virginia and Tennessee. I think it would be an act of wisdom to open this State to trade at once. I hope the Government will make known its policy as to organizing State government without delay. Affairs must necessarily be in a very unsettled state until this is done. The people now are in a mood to accept almost anything which promises a definite settlement. What is to be done with the freedmen is the question of all, and it is the all-important question. It requires prompt and wise action to prevent the negro from becoming a huge elephant on our hands. If I am to govern this State, it is important for me to know it at once. If another is to be sent here, it cannot be done too soon, for he will probably undo the most that I shall have done. I shall be glad to hear from you fully, when you shall have time to write. I will send your message to General Wilson at once.

(Signed) "J. M. SCHOFIELD, *Major General.*"

I give this dispatch entire, to demonstrate how intermingled have become such matters with the military, and how almost impossible it has become for an officer in authority to act a purely military part. There are no longer armed enemies in North Carolina, and a soldier can deal with no other sort. The marshal and sheriff, with their *posses* (of which the military may become a part), are the only proper officers to deal with civil criminals and marauders. But I will not be drawn out into a discussion of this subject, but instance this case to show how difficult the task has become to military officers, when men of the rank, education, experience, nerve and good sense of General Schofield feel embarrassed by them.

General Schofield, at Raleigh, has a well-appointed and well-disciplined command; is in telegraphic communication with the controlling posts in his department, and remoter ones in the direction of Georgia, as well as with Washington, and has military possession of all strategic points. In like manner, General Gillmore is well situated in all respects, except as to communication with the seat of the General Government. I leave him, also, with every man he ever asked for, and in full and quiet possession of every strategic point in his department. And General Wilson has, in the very heart of Georgia, the strongest, best-appointed and best-equipped cavalry corps that ever fell under my command; and he has now, by my recent action, opened to him a source and route of supply, by way of the Savannah River, that simplifies his military problem. So that I think I may, with a clear conscience, leave them, and turn my attention once more to my special command, the army with which I have been associated through some of the most eventful scenes of this or any war.

I hope, and believe, none of these commanders will ever have reason to reproach me for any "orders" they may have received from me. And the President of the United States may be assured that all of them are now in position ready and willing to execute, to the letter, and in spirit, any orders he may give. I shall, henceforth, cease to give them any orders at all, for the occasion that made them subordinate to me is passed, and I shall confine my attention to the army composed of the Fifteenth and Seventeenth, the Fourteenth and Twentieth Corps, unless the commanding general of the armies of the United States orders otherwise.

At four o'clock in the afternoon of May 9th I reached Manchester, on the James River, opposite Richmond, and found all the four corps had arrived from Raleigh, and were engaged in replenishing their wagons for the resumption of the march toward Alexandria.

I have the honor to be your obedient servant,
(Signed) W. T. SHERMAN,
Major General Commanding.

GENERAL SHERMAN'S EXAMINATION CONTINUED.

Question. Did you have, near Fortress Monroe, a conference with President Lincoln, and, if so, about what time?

Answer. I met General Grant and Mr. Lincoln on board a steamboat lying at the wharf at City Point, during the evening of the 27th of March. I renewed my visit to the President, on board the same steamer, anchored in the stream, on the following day, General Grant being present on both occasions.

Q. In those conferences, was any arrangement made with you and General Grant, or either of you, in regard to the manner of arranging business with the Confederacy, or in regard to terms of peace?

A. Nothing definite; it was simply a matter of general conversation; nothing specific and definite.

Q. At what time did you learn that President Lincoln had assented to the assembling of the Virginia rebel legislature?

A. I knew of it on the 18th of April, I think; but I procured a paper with the specific order of General Weitzel; also, a copy of the Amnesty Proclamation on the 20th of April.

Q. You did not know, at that time, that the arrangement had been rescinded by the President?

A. No, sir; I did not know of that until afterward; the moment I heard of that, I notified General Johnston of it.

Q. Then at the time you entered into this arrangement with General Johnston, you knew that General Weitzel had approved of the calling together of the rebel Legislature of Virginia, by assent of the President?

A. I knew of it by some source unofficially, and succeeded in getting a copy of the paper containing General Weitzel's order on the 20th or 21st of April.

Q. But at the time of your arrangement you did not know that the order had been rescinded?

A. No sir; I learned that several days afterward, and at once sent word to General Johnston.

Q. At the time of your arrangement, you also knew of the surrender of Lee's army, and the terms of that surrender?

A. I had that officially from General Grant; I got that at Smithfield on the 12th of April.

Q. I have here what purports to be a letter from you to Johnston, which seems to imply that you intended to make the arrangement on the terms of Lee's surrender. The letter is as follows:

[Here follows General Sherman's published letter to General Johnston, in reply to that general's first letter proposing a surrender.]

A. Those were the terms as to his own army; but the concessions I made him were for the purpose of embracing other armies.

Q. And the writings you signed were to include other armies?

A. The armies of Kirby Smith and Dick Taylor, so that afterward no man within the limits of the Southern Confederacy could claim to belong to any Confederate army in existence.

Q. The President addressed a note to General Grant, perhaps not to you, to the effect of forbidding officers of the army from entering into anything but strictly military arrangements, leaving civil matters entirely to him?

A. I never saw such a paper, signed by President Lincoln. Mr. Stanton made such a paper, and says it was by President Lincoln's dictation. He made it to General Grant, but never to me. On the contrary, while I was in Georgia, Mr. Lincoln telegraphed to me, encouraging me to discuss terms with Gov. Brown and Mr. Stephens.

Q. Then you had no notice of that order of General Grant?

A. I had no knowledge of it, official or otherwise.

Q. In the published report of your agreement, there is nothing said about slavery, I believe?

A. There was nothing said about slavery, because it did not fall within the category of military questions, and we could not make it so. It was a legal question, which the President had disposed of, overriding all our action. We had to treat the slave as free, because our President, the commander-in-chief, said he was free. For me to have renewed the question, when that agreement was made, would have involved the absurdity of an inferior undertaking to qualify the work of his superior.

Q. That was the reason why it was not mentioned?

A. Yes, sir. Subsequently I wrote a note to Johnston, stating that I thought it would be well to mention it for political effect, when we undertook to draw up the final terms with precision. It was written pending the time my memorandum was going to Washington, and before an answer had been returned.

Q. At the time you entered into these negotiations, was Johnston in a condition to offer any effectual resistance to your army?

A. He could not have resisted my army an hour, if I could have got hold of him. But he could have escaped from me by breaking up into small parties and taking the country roads, traveling faster than any army could have pursued.

Q. Then your object in negotiating was to keep his army from scattering into guerilla bands?

A. That was my chief object. I so officially notified the War Department.

Q. And not because there was any doubt about the result of a battle?

A. There was no question as to the result, and I knew it; every soldier knew it; every man in North Carolina knew it. Johnston said, in the first five minutes of our conversation, that any further persistance on his part would be an act of folly, and all he wanted was to keep his army from dispersing.

By MR. LOAN, —

Q. In your examination by the Chairman, you stated that you were acting in pursuance of instructions from Mr. Lincoln, derived from his letters and telegrams at various times?

A. Yes sir.

Q. Have you any of these letters and telegraphs which you can furnish to the committee?

A. I can furnish you a copy of a dispatch to General Halleck, from Atlanta, in which I stated that I had invited Governor Brown and Vice President Stephens to meet me, and I can give you a copy of Mr. Lincoln's answer, for my dispatch was referred to him, in which he said he felt much interested in my dispatch, and encouraged me to allow their visit. But the letter to which I refer specifically was a longer letter which I wrote to General Halleck from my camp on Big Black, Mississippi, at General Halleck's instigation, in September, 1863, which was received in Washington, and submitted to Mr. Lincoln, who desired to have it published, to which I would not consent. In that letter I gave my opinions, fully and frankly, not only on the military situation, but also the civil policy necessary. Mr. Lincoln expressed himself highly pleased with my views, and desired to make them public, but I preferred not to do so.

Q. And by subsequent acts he induced you to believe he approved of those views?

A. I know he approved of them, and always encouraged me to carry out those views.

By the CHAIRMAN,—

Q. The following is a letter published in the newspapers, purporting to have been addressed to you by Johnston, dated April 21, 1865:

[Here follows the published letter of General Sherman, dated Raleigh, April 21, 1865.]

Q. That is the letter in which you say that it would be well to declare publicly that slavery is dead?

A. Yes sir; that is the letter.

By MR. LOAN,—

Q. Will you furnish the committee a copy of the letters written by you to Mr. Stanton, in January last, from Savannah?

A. I will do so.

The CHAIRMAN,—

And when the manuscript of your testimony is prepared, it will be submitted to you for revision, and you can add to it any statement or papers that you may desire, or consider necessary.

I have revised the above, and now subjoin copies of letters from my letter-book, in the order of their bearing, on the questions raised by this inquiry.

HEAD-QUARTERS MILITARY DIVISION OF THE MISSISSIPPI,
IN THE FIELD, RALEIGH,
NORTH CAROLINA, April 18, 1865.

Lieutenant General U. S. GRANT, or Major General HALLECK, Washington, D. C.:

GENERAL—I inclose herewith a copy of an agreement made this day between General Joseph E. Johnston and myself, which, if approved by the President of the United States, will produce peace from the Potomac to the Rio Grande. Mr. Breckinridge was present at our conference in the capacity of Major General, and satisfied me of the ability of General Johnston to carry out, to the full extent the terms of this agreement, and if you will get the President to simply indorse the copy and commission me to carry out the terms, I will follow them to the conclusion.

You will observe that it is an absolute submission of the enemy to the lawful authority of the United States, and disperses his armies absolutely; and the point to which I attach most importance is, that the dispersion and disbandment of these armies is done in such a manner as to prevent their breaking up into guerilla bands On the other hand, we can retain just as much of our army as we please. I agreed to the mode and manner of the surrender of arms set forth, as it gives the States the means of suppressing guerillas, which we could not expect them to do if we stripped them of all arms.

Both Generals Johnston and Breckinridge admitted that slavery was dead, and I could not insist on embracing it in such a paper, because it can be made with the States in detail. I know that all men of substance South sincerely want peace, and I do not believe they will resort to war again during this century.

I have no doubt but that they will, in the future, be perfectly submissive to the laws of the United States. The moment my action in this matter is approved, I can spare five (5) corps, and will ask for orders to leave General Schofield here with the Tenth Corps, and to march myself with the Fourteenth, Fifteenth, Seventeenth, Twentieth and Twenty-third Corps, *via* Burkesville and Gordonsville to Frederick or Hagerstown, and there be paid and mustered out.

The question of finance is now the chief one, and every soldier and officer not needed should be got home at work. I would like to begin the march North by May 1st.

I urge, on the part of the President, speedy action, as it is important to get the Confederate armies to their homes, as well as our own.

    I am, with great respect, your obedient servant,
 (Signed,)   W. T. SHERMAN,
            Major General Commanding.

HEAD-QUARTERS MILITARY DIVISION OF THE MISSISSIPPI, }
IN THE FIELD, RALEIGH, N. C., April 18, 1865. }

General H. W. HALLECK, Chief of Staff, Washington, D. C.:

GENERAL—I received your dispatch describing the man, Clark, detailed to assassinate me. He had better be in a hurry, or he will be too late.

The news of Mr. Lincoln's death produced a most intense effect on our troops. At first, I feared it would lead to excesses, but now it has softened down, and can easily be guided. None evinced more feeling than General Johnston, who admitted that the act was calculated to stain his cause with a dark hue, and he contended that the loss was most serious to the South, who had begun to realize that Mr. Lincoln was the best friend the South had.

I cannot believe that even Mr. Davis was privy to the diabolical plot, but think it the emanation of a set of young men at the South, who are very devils. I want to throw upon the South the care of this class of men, who will soon be as obnoxious to their industrial classes as to us.

Had I pushed Johnston's army to an extremity, it would have dispersed and done infinite mischief. Johnston informed me that General Stoneman had been at Salisbury, and was now about Statesville. I have sent him orders to come to me. General Johnston also informed me that General Wilson was at Columbus, Georgia, and he wanted me to arrest his progress. I leave that to you.

Indeed, if the President sanctions my agreement with Johnston, our interest is to cease all destruction.

Please give all orders necessary, according to the views the Executive may take, and influence him, if possible, not to vary the terms at all, for I have considered everything, and believe that, the Confederate armies once dispersed, we can adjust all else fairly and well. I am yours, etc.,

(Signed) W. T. SHERMAN,
Major General Commanding.

Lest confusion should result to the mind of the committee, by the latter part of the above letter, I state it was addressed to General Halleck, as chief of staff, when he was the proper "maker of orders" to the commander-in-chief. The whole case changed when, on the 26th of April, he became the commander of the separate Division of the James.

As stated in my testimony, General Grant reached Raleigh on the 24th. On the 25th, on the supposition that I would start next day to chase Johnston's army, I wrote him the following letter, delivered in person:

> HEAD-QUARTERS DIVISION OF THE MISSISSIPPI,
> IN THE FIELD,
> RALEIGH, N. C., April 25, 1865.

Lieutenant General U. S. GRANT, Present:

GENERAL—I had the honor to receive your letter of April 21st, with inclosures, yesterday, and was well pleased that you came along, as you must have observed that I held the military control so as to adapt it to any phase the case might assume.

It is but just I should record the fact that I made my terms with General Johnston under the influence of the liberal terms you extended to the army of General Lee, at Appomattox Court House, on the 9th, and the seeming policy of our Government, as evinced by the call of the Virginia Legislature and Governor back to Richmond, under yours and President Lincoln's very eyes. It now appears the last act was done without any consultation with you, or any knowledge of Mr. Lincoln, but rather in opposition to a previous policy, well conducted.

I have not the least desire to interfere in the civil policy of our Government, but would shun it as something not to my liking; but occasions do arise when a prompt seizure of results is forced on military commanders not in immediate communication with the proper authority. It is probable that the terms signed by General Johnston and myself were not clear enough on the point well understood between us, that our negotiations did not apply to any parties outside the officers and men of the Confederate armies—which could easily have been remedied.

No surrender of any army, not actually at the mercy of an antagonist, was ever made without "terms," and these always define the military *status* of the surrendered. Thus, you stipulated that the officers and men of Lee's army should not be molested at their homes, so long as they obeyed the laws at the place of their residence. I do not wish to discuss those points involved in our recognition of the State government in actual existence, but will merely state my conclusions, to await the solution of the future.

Such action, on our part, in no manner recognizes for a moment the so-called Confederate Government, or makes us liable for its debts or acts.

The laws and acts done by the several States, during the period of rebellion, are *void*, because done without the oath prescribed by our Constitution of the United States, which is a "condition precedent."

We have a right to use any sort of machinery to produce military results, and it is the commonest thing for military commanders to use the civil governments, *in actual existence*, as a means to an end. I do believe we could and can use the present State governments lawfully, constitutionally, and as the very best possible means to produce the object desired, viz: entire and complete submission to the lawful authorities of the United States.

As to punishment for past crimes, that is for the judiciary, and can in no manner or way be disturbed by our acts; and, so far as I can, I will use my influence, that rebels shall suffer all the personal punishment prescribed by law, as also civil liabilities arising from their past acts.

What we now want is the mere form of law, by which common men may regain the positions of industry so long disturbed by the war.

I now apprehend that the rebel armies will disperse, and instead of dealing with six or seven States, will have to deal with numberless bands of desperadoes, headed by such men as Mosby, Forrest, Red Jackson, and others, who know not, and care not for danger and its consequences.

I am, with great respect, your obedient servant,
(Signed) W. T. SHERMAN,
Major General.

On the same day I wrote and mailed to the Secretary of War the following:

HEAD-QUARTERS MILITARY DIVISION OF THE MISSISSIPPI, }
IN THE FIELD, RALEIGH, N. C., April 27, 1865. }

Hon. E. M. STANTON, Secretary of War, Washington:

SIR—I have been furnished a copy of your letter of April 21st, to General Grant, signifying your disapproval of the terms in which General Johnston proposed to disarm and disperse the insurgents, on condition of amnesty, etc. I admit my folly in embracing in a military convention any civil matters, but, unfortunately, such is the nature of our situation, that they seem inexplicably united, and I understood from you at Savannah that the financial state of the country demanded military success, and would warrant a little heeding to policy.

When I had my conference with General Johnston, I had the public examples before me of General Grant's terms to Lee's army and of General Weitzel's invitation to the Virginia Legislature to assemble.

I still believe the General Government of the United States made a mistake; but that is none of my business. Mine is a different task, and I had flattered myself that by four years of patient, unremitting and successful labor, I deserved no reminder such as is contained in the last paragraph of your letter to General Grant. You may assure the President that I heed his suggestion. I am, truly, etc.,
(Signed) W. T. SHERMAN,
Major General Commanding.

The last sentence refers to the fact that General Grant had been sent to Raleigh to direct military movements. That was the first time in my life I had ever had a word of reproof from the Government of the United States, and I was naturally sensitive. But all I said to any one was to General Meigs, who came with General Grant, that it was not kind on the part of Mr. Secretary Stanton. The fact, however, did not qualify my military conduct. The final interview with General Johnston followed, and the terms of capitulation were agreed on and signed, and General Grant started for Washington, bearing the news, when, on the 28th of April, I received in the New York *Times* the most extraordinary budget of Mr. Stanton, which, for the first time, startled me, and I wrote to General Grant this letter:

HEAD-QUARTERS MILITARY DIVISION OF THE MISSISSIPPI, }
IN THE FIELD, April 28, 1865. }

Lieutenant General U. S. GRANT, General-in-Chief, Washington, D. C.:

GENERAL—Since you left me yesterday, I have seen the New York *Times* of the 24th instant, containing a budget of military news, authorized by the signature of the Secretary of War, which is grouped in such a way as to give very erroneous impressions. It embraces a copy of the basis of agreement between myself and General Johnston, of April 18th, with commentaries which it will be time enough to discuss two or three years hence, after the Government has experienced a little more in the machinery by which power reaches the scattered people of the vast country known as the South. But, in the mean time, I do think that my rank (if not my past services) entitled me, at least, to the respect of keeping secret what was known to none but the Cabinet, until further inquiry could be made, instead of giving publicity to documents I never saw, and drawing inferences wide of the truth.

I never saw or had furnished to me a copy of Mr. Stanton's dispatch to you, of the 3d of March, nor did Mr. Stanton or any human being ever convey to me its substance, or anything like it; but, on the contrary, I had seen General Weitzel's invitation to the Virginia Legislature, made in Mr. Lincoln's very presence, and I had failed to discover any other official hint, or any ideas calculated to allay the fears of the people of the South, after the destruction of their armies and civil authorities would leave them without any civil government at all. We should not drive a people into anarchy, and it is simply impossible for our military power to reach all the masses of their unhappy country.

I confess I did not want to drive General Johnston's army into bands of armed men, going about without purpose, and capable only of infinite mischief. But you saw, on your arrival at Raleigh, that I had my armies so disposed that his escape was only possible in a disorganized shape; and as you did not choose to direct military operations in this quarter, I infer that you were satisfied with the military situation. At all events, as soon as I learned, what was proper enough, the disapproval of the President, I acted in such a manner as to compel the surrender of General Johnston's whole army on the same terms as you had prescribed to General Lee's army, when you had it surrounded and in your absolute power.

Mr. Stanton, in stating that my orders to General Stoneman would likely result in the escape of "Mr. Davis to Mexico or Europe," is in deep error. General Stoneman was not at Salisbury then, but had gone back to Statesville. Davis was supposed to be between us, and Stoneman was beyond him. By turning toward me he was approaching Davis, and had he joined me, as ordered, I then would have had a mounted force, needed for that and other purposes. But even now, I don't know that Mr. Stanton wants Davis caught; and as my official papers, deemed sacred, are hastily published to the world, it will be imprudent for me to state what has been done in that respect.

As the editor of the *Times* has (it may be) logically and fairly drawn the inference from this singular document that I am insubordinate, I can only deny the intention. I have never in my

N*

life questioned or disobeyed an order, though many and many a time have I risked my life, my health and reputation in obeying orders, or even hints, to execute plans and purposes not to my liking. It is not fair to withhold from me plans and policy (if any there be), and expect me to guess at them, for facts and events appear quite different from different stand points. For four years I have been in camp, dealing with soldiers, and I can assure you that the conclusions at which the Cabinet arrived with such singular unanimity, differ from mine. I conferred freely with the best officers in this army as to points involved in this controversy, and, strange to say, they were singularly unanimous in the other conclusion, and they will learn with pain and sorrow that I am deemed insubordinate and wanting in common sense. I, who have labored day and night, winter and summer, for four years, and have brought an army of 70,000 men, in magnificent condition, across a country deemed impassable, and placed it just where it was wanted, almost on the day appointed, have brought discredit on the Government.

I do not wish to boast of this, but I do say that it entitled me to the courtesy of being consulted before publishing to the world a proposition rightfully submitted to higher authority for adjudication, and then accompanied by statements which invited the press to be let loose upon me.

It is true that non-combatants—men who sleep in comfort and security while we watch on the distant lines—are better able to judge than we poor soldiers, who rarely see a newspaper, hardly can hear from our families, or stop long enough to get our pay. I envy not the task of reconstruction, and am delighted that the Secretary has relieved me of it. .

As you did not undertake to assume the management of the affairs of this army, I infer that, on personal inspection, your mind arrived at a different conclusion from that of Mr. Secretary Stanton. I will, therefore, go on and execute your orders to the conclusion, and when done, will, with intense satisfaction, leave to the civil authorities the execution of the task of which they seem to be so jealous; but, as an honest man and soldier, I invite them to follow my path, for they may see some things there — some things that may disturb their philosophy.

With sincere respect,

(Signed)   W. T. SHERMAN,
Major General Commanding.

P. S. As Mr. Stanton's singular paper has been published, I demand that this also be made public, though I am in no manner responsible to the press, but to the law and my proper superiors.

W. T. SHERMAN,
Major General Commanding.

Since my arrival at Washington I have learned from General Grant that this letter was received, but he preferred to withhold it until my arrival, as he knew I was marching towards Washington with my army. Upon my arrival, I did not insist on its publication till it was drawn out by this inquiry. I also append here the copy of a letter from Colonel T. S. Bowers, Assistant Adjutant General, asking me to modify my report as to the point of perfidy in violating my truce, with my answer:

"HEAD-QUARTERS, ARMIES OF THE UNITED STATES,
WASHINGTON, May 25, 1865.

"Major General W. T. SHERMAN, Commanding Military Division of the Mississippi:

"General Grant directs me to call your attention to the part of your report in which the necessity of maintaining your truce at the expense of many lives is spoken of. The general thinks that, in making a truce, the commander of an army can control only his own army, and that the hostile general must make his own arrangements with other armies acting against him.

"While independent generals, acting against a common foe, would naturally act in concert, the general deems that each must be the judge of his own duty and responsible for its execution.

"If you should wish, the report will be returned, for any change you may deem best.

"Very respectfully your obedient servant,
(Signed) "T. S. BOWERS,
"*Assistant Adjutant General.*"

HEAD-QUARTERS MILITARY DIVISION OF THE MISSISSIPPI,
WASHINGTON, May 26, 1865.

Col. T. S. BOWERS, Assistant Adjutant General, Washington, D. C.:

COLONEL—I had the honor to receive your letter of March 25th, last evening, and I hasten to answer. I wish to precede it by renewing the assurance of my entire confidence and respect for the President and Lieutenant General Grant, and that in all matters I will be most willing to shape my official and private conduct to suit their wishes. The past is beyond my control, and the matters embraced in the official report, to which you refer, are finished. It is but just that the reasons that actuated me, right or wrong, should stand on record, but in all future cases, should any arise, I will respect the decision of General Grant, though I think it wrong.

Supposing a guard has prisoners in charge, and officers of another command should aim to rescue or kill them, is it not clear the guard must defend the prisoners? Same of a safeguard. So jealous is the military law to protect and maintain *good faith* when pledged, that the law adjudges death, and no alternative punishment, to one who violates a safe-guard in foreign ports. [See Article of War, No. 55.] For murder, arson, treason and the highest military crimes, the punishment prescribed by law is death, or some minor punishment, but for the violation of a safe-guard, death, and death alone, is the prescribed penalty. I instance this to illustrate how, in military stipulations to an enemy, our Government commands and enforces good faith. In discussing this matter, I would like to refer to many writers on military law, but am willing to take Halleck as the test. [See his chapter 27.] In the very first article he states that *good faith* should always be observed between enemies in war, because, when our faith has been pledged to him, so far as our promise extends, he ceases to be our enemy. He then defines the meaning of *compacts* and *conventions*, and says they are made sometimes for a general or a partial suspension of hostilities, "for the surrender of an army," etc. They may be *special*, limited to particular places or particular forces, but, of course, can only bind the armies subject to the general who makes the truce, and coëxtensive only with the extent of his command. This is all I have claimed, and clearly covers the whole case. All of North Carolina was in my immediate command, with General Schofield, its department commander, and his army present with me. I never asked the truce to have effect beyond my own *territorial* command. General Halleck himself, in his order No. 1, defines his own limits clearly enough, viz: "Such part of North Carolina as was *not* occupied by the command of Major General Sherman." He could not pursue and cut off Johnston's retreat towards Salisbury and Charlotte without invading my command, and so potent was his purpose to *defy* and violate my truce, that Mr. Stanton's publication of the fact, not even yet recalled, modified, or explained, was headed "Sherman's truce disregarded," that the whole world drew but one inference. It admits of no other. I never claimed that that truce bound Generals Halleck or Canby within the sphere of *their* respective commands, as defined by themselves.

It was a *partial truce*, of very short duration, clearly within my limits and right, justified by events; and, as in the case of prisoners in my custody, or the violation of a safe-guard given by me in my own territorial limits, I was bound to maintain *good faith*.

I prefer not to change my report; but again repeat, that in all future cases, I am willing to be governed by the interpretation of General Grant, although I again invite his attention to the limits of my command and those of General Halleck at the time, and the pointed phraseology of General Halleck's dispatch to Mr. Stanton, wherein he reports that he had ordered his generals to pay no heed to *my orders* within the clearly-defined area of my command. I am, etc.,

(Signed,) W. T. SHERMAN,
Major General U. S. A., Commanding.

I now add the dispatch from Atlanta, mentioned in the body of my testimony, with Mr. Lincoln's answer:

HEAD-QUARTERS MILITARY DIVISION OF THE MISSISSIPPI,
IN THE FIELD,
ATLANTA, Ga., September 15, 1864.

General HALLECK, Washington, D. C.:

My report is done, and will be forwarded as soon as I get a few more of the subordinate reports. I am awaiting a courier from General Grant. All well, and troops in fine, healthy camps, and supplies coming forward finely.

Governor Brown has disbanded his militia, to gather the corn and sorghum of the State. I have reason to believe that he and Stephens want to visit me, and I have sent them a hearty invitation.

I will exchange 2,000 prisoners with Hood, but no more.

(Signed,) W. T. SHERMAN,
Major General Commanding.

"WASHINGTON, D. C., 10 A. M.,
September 17, 1864.

"Major General SHERMAN:

"I feel great interest in the subjects of your dispatch, mentioning corn and sorghum, and contemplate a visit to you.

(Signed,) "A. LINCOLN,
"*President United States.*"

I have not possession here of all my official records, most of which are out West, and I have selected the above from my more recent letter-books, and offer them to show how prompt and full have been my official reports, and how unnecessary was all the clamor made touching my actions and opinions, at the time the basis of agreement, of April 18th, was submitted to the President.

All of which is most respectfully submitted.

W. T. SHERMAN,
Major General United States Army.

SHERMAN'S FAREWELL TO HIS ARMY.

HEAD-QUARTERS MILITARY DIVISION OF THE MISSISSIPPI,
IN THE FIELD, WASHINGTON, May 30, 1865.

SPECIAL FIELD ORDERS No. 76.

The general commanding announces to the Armies of the Tennessee and Georgia that the time has come for us to part. Our work is done, and armed enemies no longer defy us. Some of you will be retained in the service until further orders, and now that we are about to separate, to mingle with the civil world, it becomes a pleasing duty to recall to mind the situation of national affairs, when but little more than a year ago we were gathered about the towering cliffs of Lookout Mountain, and all the future was wrapped in doubt and uncertainty; three armies had come together from different fields, with separate histories, bound together by one common cause—the union of our country and the government of our inheritance. There is no need to recall to your memories Tunnel Hill, with its rocky-faced mountain, and Buzzard Roost Gap, with the ugly forts of Dalton behind. We were in earnest, and paused not for danger and difficulty, but dashed through Snake Creek Gap and fell on Resaca; then on to Dallas, Kenesaw, and the heats of summer found us on the banks of the Chattahoochee, far from home and dependent on a single line for supplies. Again, we were not to be held back by any obstacle, and crossed over and fought four heavy battles for the possession of the citadel of Atlanta.

That was the crisis of our history. A doubt still clouded our future, but we solved the problem, and destroyed Atlanta, struck boldly across the State of Georgia, severed all the main arteries of life to our enemy, and Christmas found us at Savannah Waiting there only long enough to fill our wagons, we again began a march which, for peril, labor and results, will compare with any ever made by an organized army. The floods of the Savannah, the swamps of the Combahee and Edisto; the high hills and rocks of the Santee; the flat quagmires of the Pedee and Cape Fear Rivers were all passed in midwinter, with its floods and rains, in the face of an accumulating enemy, and after the battles of Averysboro and Bentonville, we once more came out of the wilderness to meet our friends at Goldsboro. Even there we paused only long enough to get new clothing, to reload our wagons, and again pushed on to Raleigh and beyond, until we met the enemy, sueing for peace instead of war, and offering to submit to the injured laws of his and our country.

As long as that enemy was defiant, not rivers, nor mountains, nor swamps, nor hunger, nor cold had checked us, but when he who had fought us hard and persistently offered submission, your general thought it wrong to pursue him further, and negotiations followed, which resulted, as you know, in his surrender. How far the operations of the army have contributed to the overthrow of the Confederacy and the peace which now dawns on us, must be judged by others, not by us, but that you have done all that men could do, has been admitted by those in authority, and we have a right to join in the universal joy that fills our land, because the war is over, and our Government stands vindicated before the world by the joint action of the volunteer armies of the United States.

To such as remain in the military service, your general need only remind you that the successes in the past are due to hard work and discipline, and that the same work and discipline are equally important in the future. To such as go home, he will only say that our favored country is so grand, so extensive, so diversified in climate, soil and productions, that every man can find a home and occupation suited to his tastes, and none should yield to the natural impotence sure to result from our past life of excitement and adventure. You will be invited to seek new adventures abroad; but do not yield to the temptation, for it will lead only to death and disappointment.

Your general now bids you all farewell, with the full belief that, as in war you have been good soldiers, so in peace you will make good citizens; and if, unfortunately, a new war should arise in our country, Sherman's army will be the first to buckle on the old armor and come forth to defend and maintain the Government of our inheritance and choice.

By order of Major General W. T. SHERMAN.

(Signed) M. DAYTON,
Assistant Adjutant General.

HENRY M. SHERWOOD,

MANUFACTURER AND DEALER IN

School Furniture,

And General School Merchandise,

Office, No. 21 Lombard Block, { First door West of the Post Office, } Chicago, Ill.

SCHOOL DESKS AND SEATS,

OF ALL SIZES, IN EVERY DESIRABLE STYLE.

The above cut represents the best *Cheap Desk and Seat* made. It is neat, convenient, strong and durable. It accommodates two pupils, and is of five different heights, suitable for scholars of all sizes. ☞*CASTINGS for this Desk* sold seprately if desired.

LIQUID SLATING, for Black Boards.

This, like every Good Article, has its imitations. Every Can ordered directly of me will be warranted.

SCHOOL APPARATUS,

Adapted to the wants of Common Schools; Numerical Frames Object Teaching Forms, Cube Root Blocks, Solids, Orreries, Tellurians, &c. &c.

GLOBES, of all Sizes and Styles; Outline Maps, Charts, &c.

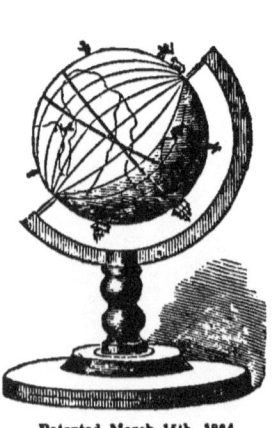

Patented March 15th, 1864,
By ELBERT PECK.

No. 1 — Primary Basket Arm Chair.

No. 18 — Grammar Double Desk.

No. 26 — Teacher's Desk, with Two Drawers and Deep Tray.

No. 29 — Teacher's Desk, with Eight Drawers.

G. & H. M. SHERWOOD'S
PATENT INK WELL FOR SCHOOLS.

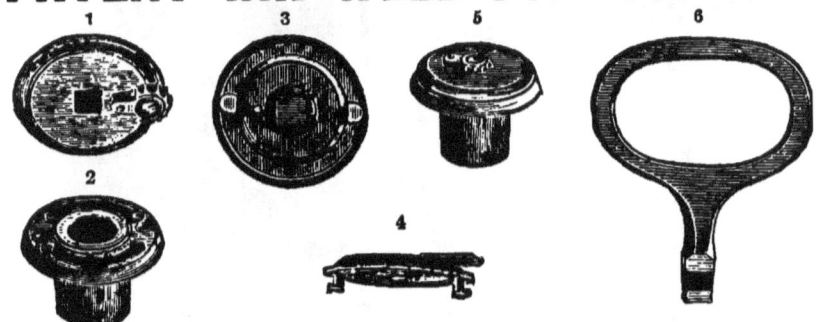

Explanation.—Fig. 1 represents a top view of the cover. Fig. 2, a top view of the well without the cover. Fig. 3, a bottom view of the cover. Fig. 4, an edge view of the cover. Fig. 5, a view of the well complete. Fig. 6, a key to screw on and unscrew cover.

The above cuts represent the best school ink well in use. It is neat, convenient, cheap and durable.

The iron well, (Fig. 2,) when fastened to the desk by two common screws, never has to be removed. Into this is set a glass well to hold the ink. This glass *only* has to be taken out to clean the well.

The cover, (Fig. 4,) is easily fastened to the well by a single turn of the key, and when fastened can only be removed with the key, which should be kept by the teacher or janitor. (It will not be necessary to remove the cover oftener than the well needs cleaning.)

The pen hole is covered by a small cap, turning horizontally, as seen in Fig. 5.

By this simple arrangement, we have a well that cannot get out of order. It will not corrode. It cannot upset. It cannot be made noisy by turning on or off the cap. It cannot burst and spill the ink; nor can it be removed and lost by the pupils.

It can be used in the holes made for other wells.

It is economical, as the expenditure for each pupil, (where double desks are used,) is less than fifteen cents for his whole school-going time.

Price of Ink Wells — per dozen, $3.50; necessary keys furnished gratis.
Address

HENRY M. SHERWOOD,
No. 21 Lombard Block, { First door West of the Post Office } CHICAGO, ILL.

www.ingramcontent.com/pod-product-compliance
Lightning Source LLC
Chambersburg PA
CBHW051849300426
44117CB00006B/328